GAA GRASSROOTS

Volume 2

THE SECOND HALF

*This book is dedicated to the memory of two of the finest
GAA club members it has been my privilege to know –
Mick Sheridan and John Buckley of Clara GAA club in Co. Offaly*

GRASSROOTS
Volume 2

THE SECOND HALF

Stories From The Heart Of The GAA

Compiled by PJ Cunningham

Ballpoint Press

Published in 2022 by Ballpoint Press
4 Wyndham Park, Bray,
Co Wicklow, Republic of Ireland.

Telephone: 00353 86 821 7631
Email: pj@gaastories.ie
Web: www.ballpointpress.ie

ISBN 978-1-9160863-9-5

Book design and production by Joe Coyle Media&Design,
joecoyledesign@gmail.com

Front cover map by Ryan McGuinness at gaapitchfinder.com

Printed in Ireland by Sprint Print, Hume Avenue, Dublin 12
www.sprintprint.ie

Contents

CONTENTS

CONTENTS

POEMS AND SONGS

Acknowledgements

PJ Cunningham

As many of you already know, this is the second volume of Grassroots Stories which is subtitled, 'The Second Half'.

Sometimes people expect that the first volume would have the better stories but I can honestly say having edited and compiled both editions, it is a case of first among equals.

In some ways, what is contained in the second volume is more traditional and I think the reason for that is because contributors saw the type of story we wanted in the first book and were clearer as a result in penning their contributions for this edition.

Between photos and stories, if we had to lump all the information into one book, we would have had close to 1,000 pages so in conjunction with the GAA's Director of Communications, Alan Milton, we took a decision early on in the process to publish across two volumes.

Despite Covid's attempt to play spoilsport, the reality is we got the opportunity to meet, phone or write to hundreds of people who were eager to have their stories recorded. That for me meant hundreds of hours of talking to GAA lovers across the length and breadth of the country, and in some memorable occasions beyond to the UK, USA, Europe and the Antipodes.

I wish to remember here the late Noel Hughes, who attended last November's launch, but sadly passed away four days later. According to his son Darren, there was great solace for the family in the fact that Noel had one of his most enjoyable evenings by being part of a big Croke Park launch as a contributor.

Similarly, it was with great sadness that I learned of the death of John Dowling from Laois at the end of June. We spoke regularly and in its own way, his story is a bequest to the Grassroots stories series. It was a particular nugget for it told the story of how his uncle, Tommy Dowling was dropped by his own team just before a Laois final and was promptly invited to play with the opposition – The Heath. Tommy then duly helped his new teammates beat his own club.

I would like to thank the GAA for their continued backing in this project and to Alan and President Larry McCarthy in particular. Having the launches in Croke Park is something I know has meant a lot, particularly to the contributors.

Joe Coyle's design of our books has made them different and special and the use of Ryan McGuinness's artwork (*gaapitchfinder.com*) again for the front cover is much appreciated. Each dot on the map on the front cover represents a GAA club.

A sincere thank you to Ray McManus and Sportsfile for the use of his exhaustive photographic libraries.

Without the support of my family, this would have been a chore rather than the delightful experience it turned out to be and my sincere thanks to Rosemary and our five adult children for their support.

Finally, to you the GAA fans and readers, this book is both by you and for you and hopefully the content in these pages will live on for generations to come.

PJ Cunningham
Editor

Réamhrá Uachtarán Chumann Lúthchleas Gael

Cuirim fáilte roimh an dara cuid den bhailiúchán seo agus saibhreas Chumann Lúthchleas Gael le feiceáil tríd an leabhar arís – díreach mar a bhí sa chéad eagrán.

It gives me great pleasure to welcome the publication of the second instalment of 'Grassroots – Volume 2 – The Second Half' (Stories from the Heart of the GAA) following on from the success of the first edition released in November 2021.

Editor PJ Cunningham was a firm believer that there were many local stories out there, unrecorded, that deserved a wider audience, and his assertion has been realised.

Such was the response from our request for stories first time around, it became apparent quite quickly that there would be a need for a second volume and that too has no come to fruition.

I would like to thank all who engaged to make this publication possible and also acknowledge PJ, whose enthusiasm and energy for the project has ensured that some of these highly entertaining and amusing tales have been preserved for the enjoyment of current and future generations.

Bainigí sult as na scéalta.

Labhrás Mac Carthaigh
Uachtarán Chúmann Lúthchleas Gael

Foreword

Message from the GAA's Director of Communications

Is cúis mhór áthais dom fáilte a chur roimh fhoilsiú an leabhair iontaigh seo – an dara heagrán den bhailiúchán speisialta seo do Chumann Lúthchleas Gael.

Gaelic games and our clubs and members are firmly rooted in community and by extension in the oral tradition and the success of this project has been to transfer some great stories to paper to ensure that they are not lost to the generations to come.

The first edition of 'Grassroots – Stories from the Heart of the GAA' – lifted a lid on the treasure trove of stories and tales that we all knew existed across the GAA family but had rarely been collected and published in one space.

It touched upon many different areas of the GAA and captured a variety of stories that represent the lifeblood of our clubs and the characters that make them what they are.

Thanks to all who have contributed to either book and best of luck to PJ Cunningham with the latest instalment of the project.

I hope great satisfaction is derived from the collection.

Beirigí bua.

Alan Mac Maoldúin (Milton)
Stiúrthóir Cumarsáide (Director of Communications)
Cumann Lúthchleas Gael

When Monaghan And Cavan Enmity Almost Created A Fifth Province

Malachy Clerkin

For as long as there has been football, there have been Monaghan teams and Cavan teams pulling and dragging out of each other because of it. When Maghera (Cavan) beat Inniskeen (Monaghan) in the first Ulster final in 1888, it took three games to find a winner. The first of them was scoreless. Look, nobody ever claimed it to have been a particularly sexy rivalry.

Here's how thick they are with each other, in fact. Cavan v Monaghan holds the record for draws in a championship fixture – they've ended with the scores tied 13 times in 58 games. For context, Kerry v Cork is next on the list, with 12 draws in 122 games. Galway and Mayo have only ever drawn six times in championship. Cavan and Monaghan had that many racked up by 1923.

Though the GAA in Ulster first took root in Cavan, it was a pair of Monaghan administrators – Eoin O'Duffy and JP Whelan – that modernised the Ulster Council in the 1910s. O'Duffy would become a hugely controversial figure in later life as a Fine Gael TD, a self-promoting fascist and ally of General Franco, not to mention the man who invited a Nazi to the 1940 All-Ireland final.

In Cavan though, they'd regard all that as minor stuff. Far more pertinent was the stroke he pulled – or tried to pull – after the replayed 1915 Ulster final. It was such an egregious piece of chicanery that it almost brought about a rupture of the very foundations on which the GAA is built.

Here's how it went. The first game took place in Belturbet and ended in a draw, Cavan 2-5 Monaghan 3-2. The replay came a fortnight later, on September 5th in Clones. The Irish Independent reported that, "The number present was greatly in excess of any seen at previous events in Ulster." They made their presence felt.

The record books say that Cavan beat Monaghan by a point, 0-4 to 0-3. But the record books hide a multitude. They make no mention of the fact that a Monaghan goal was disallowed by Cavan umpires. Or that a Cavan point was first called wide but eventually awarded after a pitch invasion by Cavan supporters. The game was held up for a long period before full-time as the referee – a Mr A Rogers from Dundalk, tried and generally failed to clear the field. In the end, the point stood, the game was blown up and Cavan were Ulster champions.

Except, that wasn't the end. Far, far from it. O'Duffy was the Monaghan delegate at the next meeting of the Ulster Council and at it he demanded nothing less than that the result be overturned.

He read out a long rap sheet against his Cavan neighbours. The crowd had been on the pitch for the final 10 minutes of the game. The goalposts were broken, rendering it impossible for them to score. The umpire saved a certain Monaghan goal three minutes from the end. Cavan's star player, Felix McGovern, had played for Leitrim.

Even for O'Duffy, this was all a bit of a stretch. Crowds going on the pitch was hardly unprecedented, for one thing. If the posts were broken – and there wasn't much corroboration to be found – but even if they were, it was no grounds to strip a game from a team. And going after umpires was the oldest one in the book. Even the McGovern claim was sketchy and basically unproveable.

But two things went against Cavan on the night. One, they didn't send any delegates to argue their case. They stayed out of it in protest, knowing full well that O'Duffy was highly likely to turn it into a circus. And two, the president of the Ulster Council at the time was none other than O'Duffy's Monaghan compatriot, JP Whelan.

With a brazenness that takes breath away over a century later, Whelan overturned the result and ordered a replay for October 10th in Belfast. Gilding the lily even further, Monaghan were nominated as the Ulster representatives in the following year's All-Ireland semi-finals. All in all, it was a pretty outrageous piece of political hocus-pocus.

They might have gotten away with it too, had the association's top brass not intervened. In those days, it generally wasn't the done thing for Central Council to get involved with squabbles within provinces. But the sheer effrontery shown by O'Duffy and Whelan here in awarding their own county an Ulster title they hadn't won on the field prompted action from above. The two men were officially rebuked, the title was Cavan's and they went forward to the All-Ireland semi-final, where they lost to Wexford.

In the two years that followed, the bad blood between the counties only got thicker and the row got so bitter that it very nearly had far-reaching consequences. Cavan wanted the two Monaghan men kicked out of the Ulster Council on account of their rank and obvious bias but O'Duffy and Whelan dug in and kept their posts.

So enraged were Cavan by this that they tried to break away and set up a fifth GAA province. They invited Meath, Louth, Westmeath and Longford to join them and proposed to call it Tara. They took a motion to Congress in 1918 and everything. It didn't fly in the end but it's as close as the GAA has come to genuine structural change in all of its 138 years.

All because Cavan and Monaghan couldn't play nice.

Malachy Clerkin is a native of Monaghan and works as a sports journalist in 'The Irish Times'. Married to Olivia, they have one daughter Cara and now live in Dublin. Malachy writes for his newspaper across a wide variety of sports and is a former Sports Journalist Of The Year.

Beware Of The Unattended Dog On The Sideline

Peter Sobolewski

Parochial GAA matches on a Sunday afternoon have always been a source of excitement for the local dogs. Most of us remember with mirth, matches coming to a sudden halt when a nosey canine wandered onto the pitch to compete for the ball. The junior hurling team at Kilmacud Crokes were not exempt from such intrusions.

One old-timer remembers: "My recollection is that there was a Kerryman, a sub on the team this particular day. He was togged out on the sideline and wearing a duffel coat to keep warm. At half-time, as the team huddled together to get instructions (and keep warm) he and the other subs, were pucking the ball about. He took off his duffel coat, folded it and left it on the sideline.

"When play resumed, our friend came on early in the second half, his duffel coat still in position on the sideline. The ball was played down the centre of the field, he snatched it and broke through the defence. He had a straight run towards goal with only the goalkeeper to beat. The undefended goalie tried to look as if he had the situation under control...and indeed he had.

As the Crokes man advanced on goal, he became aware of action on the sideline. From the corner of his eye, he spotted a dog lifting his leg and using his neatly folded coat for target practice!

A quick decision was required. The ball was smashed with extra vigour, but not at the goal. And it had the desired result...

Peter Sobolewski is a New Yorker but says his home parish is Kiltimagh, Mayo where he was a teacher for most of his life. He served as chairperson of the Ladies football section in Kilmacud Crokes and the Kilmacud Stillorgan Local History Society. He is the author of 'A History of Kilmacud Crokes'.

'I Will Not Cry This Year
– I Will Not Cry'

Joe Kearney

'You can never step into the same river twice," according to the Greek Philosopher Heraclites. If the water into which you step is continually changing, it can never be considered the same river.

However, sometimes a thing happens, a thing unexpected, and it completely debunks theories you have previously relied upon. This is one such incident.

We must have seemed an odd pairing on that Sunday afternoon. Myself, the fledgling hippy and the man in the blue suit huddled against a telephone pole in Dollis Hill Park, North London. I had drifted into the tired acres of beaten grass and gaunt shrubbery with a melancholic indifference that can only be induced by empty pockets, nothing to do and nowhere to go. The park was cheating autumn on that September day in 1967 by delivering a display of hot sunny defiance.

I observed the man in the blue suit, saw him press a small transistor radio against the telephone pole and would have sauntered past him had my ears not been arrested by a familiar voice; the unmistakable singsong-chant ebbing and flowing from the tinny speaker. The man in the blue suit was using the pole as a conduit to enhance his radio reception. Its own aerial, even fully extended, was as useless as a broken tine on a hayfork.

The voice on the radio was the voice of my childhood Sundays, from a place I thought I'd lost and a self I thought had vanished.

I gestured to the man in the blue suit. Was it OK if I joined him to listen? He responded with an indifferent shrug and a grunted "Suit yourself."

I watched him, under the screen of his tobacco smoke, appraise my appearance. Saw him take in the tie-dyed, bearded, longhaired creature that was as opposite to his white drip-dry nylon conservative-self as one could imagine.

The national anthem followed the county anthems. Emotion building in incremental steps. The hair standing on my arms and on the back of my neck. The water level building behind the fragility of the dam behind my eyes. I defied the overspill with sheer willpower and self-control for as long as I could.

That was until Michael O'Hehir extended a welcome to all those listening in Boston, New York, Chicago…London. The Croke Park roar reached us in waves like the phantom seas in a shell held to the ear of memory. It was then that the tears found the line of least resistance and coursed down my embarrassed cheeks.

The man in the blue suit observed all.

"It's times like this that you'd miss the auld place," he said, offering me a cigarette from the fresh packet of Major.

The softness of his lilt hinted his origins.

"You're from Cork?" I asked.

His eyes crinkled with mischief. He trotted out his icebreaker, his party-piece:

"Cork me hole!" he spluttered. "I'm from Mallow."

Seeing my reaction, he crumpled under the power of his own wit and was overtaken by a spasm that was part laughter, part cough until the tears that sprung to his own eyes matched mine.

"What county man are you, yourself?" he enquired. I hesitated before replying, for I had grown up in a divided household where the waspish black-and-amber jostled with the banner of the red and white blooded-bandage. I could assume either allegiance. However on this afternoon county loyalty was unimportant.

What was important was the reawakening of memories of previous All-Ireland Sundays and all that they meant; the end of summer and the return to school. Pencils in their wooden-case, pointed and sharp, schoolbooks that would leak knowledge from the wallpapered protection of their covers. Copybooks with pictures of round-towers also pointed and sharp; as sharp as the attention we promised to pay to our teachers, as sharp as the bittersweet blackberries of the hedgerow. As sharp as the crack of tar bubbles when they burst beneath bicycle-tyres in potholed country lanes, as sharp as the memories flowing down the tarred pole and out of the radio.

When finally the "Hip, hips" were counted out, we shook hands and parted. Back home, soda-bread was being cut for tea. Ash plants were being picked up, Wellingtons pulled on and cows collected for milking.

Win, lose or draw, the patient cows were indifferent to the results when they were milked once more in the velvet batwings of twilight.

The head that leaned a cheek against the warm flank of a cud-chewing cow heard the milk cascade into the galvanised bucket and it became the echo of that crowd-roar lingering on in evocative memory.

We left Dollis Hill Park, the man and I and returned not to the small fields of our origins but to the bed-sits of Cricklewood and Kilburn, but not before I insisted that he join me in a demi-verse of the Rose of Mooncoin. A victors reward after all.

'Where the thrush and the robin their sweet notes entwine
On the banks of the Shure that flows down by Mooncoin.'

Heraclites was wrong, it is possible to walk in the same river twice but you have to be patient and wait for one of those unscripted, unexpected moments in your life.

I often recall the man in the blue suit and particularly so on All-Ireland Sundays. It is then I renew my vow, when the commentator welcomes those listening in Sydney, New York, Brazil... London and the roar goes up, "I will not cry; this year I swear I will not cry."

Dr Joe Kearney is a native of Callan, Co Kilkenny. A retired oil industry executive, he is an award-winning documentary maker for RTÉ and has written a number of published collections, including his latest book, 'The Beekeeper And The River', which was published this year. He is married and now lives in Co Wicklow.

Mystery Of Stolen Fahey Cup Solved

Tommie Kenoy

The Fahey Cup story, which was published in Grassroots Volume 1 in 2021, has taken a new and very welcome twist since first appearing in that book.

Michael Fahey, a son of J.J. Fahey, after whom the cup is named, got in touch with me and told me this amazing tale. In 2019, a couple of trophies that had been presented in 2018 hadn't been returned. So the Roscommon Co Committee issued a plea to all clubs to return any trophies in their possession including old cups/shields that had gone out of use. A room was used in the Co Committee offices to store any such trophies that came in.

Michael Fahey was in the offices one day – he was Co Chairman between 2011-2015 and went in to have a look at the trophies when lo and behold, there in the middle of the collection was the missing Fahey Cup.

He brought it home but forgot to tell his old friends in Kilmore GAA. Then he read the story and rang me up.

None of the staff have any idea who left it in. Presumably the person in question surreptitiously dropped it into the above mentioned room without anyone noticing. Clearly they didn't want to be identified.

So the good news is that the cup has been found. Unfortunately the base, which contained the names of all winners pre-1983, was not returned. Kilmore are considering buying one, inscribing the names and giving it to the Faheys.

In any event thank you Grassroots GAA, first volume, for the role played in solving the story of the missing Fahey Cup.

Tommie Kenoy was born in New York but has lived in Kilmore, Co Roscommon since 1957. Married to Teresa, before retiring he served as a member of An Garda Síochána and is also a former chairman of Roscommon Co Board.

My GAA Stories From Outside Looking In

Ollie Campbell

Although my father played for Louth minors, I only ever managed to play one game of Gaelic football in my entire life and that was for the Jimmy Magee All-Stars. I lined out at full-forward but unfortunately my opposite number was the enormous Martin Quinn of Meath, who sadly passed away just last year. It was like being marked by Cuchulainn!

Yet Croke Park, the GAA's citadel on Jones's Road, has been omnipresent in my life having passed it twice a day almost every day of my life since I first attended Belvedere College as an eight-year-old. At that time I was introduced to the game of rugby at the school ground which was literally in the shadow of the old Cusack Stand.

Years later I was fascinated to discover that Michael Cusack had actually founded a rugby club in Dublin called Cusack's Academy before he founded the GAA and these days I can see Croke Park from my apartment in Clontarf where I have lived for the past 30 years or so.

The first match I attended there was the 1974 All Ireland final between Dublin and Galway thanks to my great school friend Michael Hickey, brother of David Hickey, who was playing that day.

This was the start of 'Heffo's Army' and such was the colour and atmosphere as I sat down beside Mick in the Cusack Stand, it was like I had landed on a different planet. It was a defining day of my life and I have been a Dubs and GAA fan ever since and I owe a big 'thank you' to Mick for introducing me to this rich dimension of Irish sport and life. Interestingly, as far as I am aware, he is the only Dubliner to have won a Leinster Schools Senior Cup rugby medal [with Belvedere in 1972] and an All-Ireland football medal, so he has a unique place in Dublin's sporting history.

David played a leading role in helping Dublin win their first

All-Ireland for 11 years that day, would go on to win further All Ireland's in '76 and '77 and become a two-time All-Star.

He also played rugby for a few seasons with Clontarf and ultimately also with La Rochelle in France in the early '80s – as neither Mick nor myself were available! He had such an impact there on and off the field that he was made a Freeman of the City and could easily have played for Ireland.

Years later, Mick and myself were sitting beside each other again in Croke Park for the 2011 All Ireland between Dublin and Kerry, this time in the comfort of the Hogan Stand. This was the day Stephen Cluxton landed that free kick to win the match by a point with virtually the last kick of the game. The kick was taken right in front of where we both had sat in the Cusack Stand back in '74.

Speaking of Kerry, back in the halcyon days of the Micko era, I was in Killarney one early summer's evening and heard the Kerry team would be training that night at Fitzgerald Stadium, so naturally I went along to observe the session.

What followed frightened me. I had never seen a training session like it. They ran and they ran and they ran seemingly non-stop for nearly two hours, sometimes with the ball, sometimes without one. I was in very good shape myself at the time but would not have survived this Micko session and left before the end feeling quite disillusioned.

Years later I was at the annual Renault Irish Youth Foundation Sports Awards in the Burlington Hotel in Dublin as were that great Kerry team, including their iconic manager Mick O'Dwyer.

At the drinks reception beforehand Mikey Sheehy invited me over to join them and introduced me to Micko and the team. Rather teasingly Mikey asked me: "Ollie, do you remember attending a training session of ours in Killarney in the early eighties?".

"Of course I do, I'll never forget it as long as I live," I replied.

"Do you know what happened that night?" he said with a glint in his eye.

"No idea," I said honestly.

"Well, Micko spotted you in the stand before the session began and enthusiastically addressed us in a huddle saying: 'Lads, let's show him what a Kerry football training session is really like'."

Everyone laughed heartily on being reminded of this, particularly Micko himself as I did too, before Mikey went on to say: "Ollie, none of us shared Micko's enthusiasm that night, so for the sake of every future Kerry Gaelic football team if you are ever in Killarney again on an evening when a Kerry team are training, will you please find something else to do?"

I laughed at discovering the twist in this story for the rest of the night – and have done so many times since!

PS. Nelson Mandela once said: "Sport has the power to change the world." How right he was! I was privileged to be in Croke Park on the day that sport changed Ireland when we beat England 43-13 in 2007 after the GAA made the ground-breaking decision to allow Ireland's rugby and soccer teams play there while Lansdowne Road was being redeveloped. The wheel had come full circle for me that day as I went from playing rugby in the shadow of the Cusack Stand to watching a game of rugby from it.

Dubliner Ollie Campbell is a former British and Irish Lions outhalf who won 22 caps for Ireland in a career severely shortened by persistent hamstring problems. He was instrumental in leading Ireland to its first Triple Crown in 33 years with his performances in the then Five Nations Championship of 1982. Considered by many to be the country's most complete No 10 since the legendary Jack Kyle, he retired prematurely in 1984 at just 29.

GAA's Generous 'Donation' Of All Star Hurleys To Vancouver

Pearse Walsh

I was one of the founders and first captain of the newly formed Irish and Sporting Social Club (ISSC) Gaelic Football team in Vancouver, British Columbia. We decided to make a trip to San Francisco in 1975 to coincide with the Carrolls All Star festivities.

We played a curtain-raiser to the All Star games. Our main reason for going, aside from enjoying meeting all the top players from home, was to see if we could get a meeting with Seán Ó Síocháin, General Secretary of the GAA, to see what support the GAA might be able to give us exiles in our efforts to spread the game.

I can reveal we had absolutely no success with our hearing. However, at the banquet, we were recognised as exiles keeping the traditions of football and hurling alive and consequently were invited to say a few words.

Never one to look a gift horse in the mouth, I got up and was fulsome in my thanks to Secretary General Ó Síocháin for "donating the extra hurling sticks they had brought with them to San Francisco to our Vancouver club. Well what could he do but smile and I must say I got immense satisfaction as I loaded the sticks into my car.

In truth, it was how hurling got started in Vancouver and today the JP Ryan Hurling Club, which is an offshoot of the ISSC, has three teams playing the game!

Pearse Walsh is a retired professional engineer living in Kelowna, British Columbia. He was born in Foxford, Co Mayo and played his club football with Knockmore and UCD and played minor football with Mayo in 1967. He emigrated to Canada in late 1971 and played football with the Clann Na Gael club in Toronto for three years, before he relocated to Vancouver, just as the Irish Sporting and Social Club was being formed.

The 'Waiting Game' I Played
With Lone Soldier On
Dark Country Road

Sambo McNaughton

In these parts, I marvel at how times have changed for hurlers in the past two decades. It's as different as night and day when I was 16 in the early eighties to the 16 and 17-year-olds I now coach in Cushendall.

And thanks God for that.

During the summer I was having the banter with these lads about new films and they were all raving about the 'Elvis' movie. When they asked me my favourite tv programme, I mentioned 'Sopranos." None of them had heard of it but then life goes on. I'm sure most of them wouldn't know what UDR stands for at this remove but our generation knew exactly what they stood for.

Every one of us remembers our first date. Mine was particularly memorable for two reasons. That was the night I met my future wife, Ursula, in Ballymena where she's from. Coming out of the disco in the town, it was the night my four finest hurls were smashed up as a bit of fun by UDR members.

They recognised me as I approached the car – how could they not, as one of soldiers was a lad who grew up 100 yards from my home. He, like his brothers, had joined the UDR and moved away from the village.

That night he was there laughing with the rest of them as they searched me, opened the boot of the car, took out the four hurls and broke them into smithereens, all the while joking among them-selves and obviously enjoying our discomfort.

By then I was used to that sort of hassle. We got it going to and from matches every other week. Sometimes half our back line would be deliberately delayed and the game would have to be put back half an hour or an hour so they could play when they were finally allowed to pass on.

Those experiences were bad but were nothing like the worst night I ever encountered during the years of the 'Troubles'. It's an encounter I have never mentioned before, not even in the 'Laochra Gael' programme …but it is a night I will never forget.

I was picked on the GAA All-Star hurling team of 1991 and given that there weren't too many hurling All-Stars in these parts – my fellow county men Ciaran Barr and Olcan McFettridge had been honoured in the 80s. As a consequence, I was invited to every dinner dance and medal presentation across Ulster in the aftermath of the team's announcement.

Just as the award itself was a great honour, I was similarly delighted to accept these invitations as a way of giving something back to the GAA.

On the night I'm referring to, I went to Omagh to attend their dinner dance and had a very enjoyable evening. I decided to head for the long journey back sometime after midnight. I took to the by-roads and back roads over the mountains around Cookstown. There wasn't a sinner about on these country roads until I noticed a red light some distance ahead of me. I slowed down as I approached the light and figured out that there was a person flagging me down. By now it was after one o'clock in the morning and here I was on my own in the car, with the only other living person this silhouette between my car headlights and the pitch darkness of the night behind him.

When the guy walked over to me, I wound down my window and saw that he had his face painted in black as camouflage.

He made no effort to communicate other than with a one-word demand: "Licence!"

I gave him my driver's licence and immediately he walked to the back of the car where I could no longer see him as it was pitch black. I didn't know what he was doing but, in such situations, I knew I had to sit tight.

Five minutes passed.

Ten minutes passed.

Half-an-hour went by.

I could neither hear nor see what this soldier was at. You don't sit there in such a situation for long without your mind starting to play games with you.

The fact that there were no other cars coming or going meant it was just me and him. A strange fear built up inside me.

I was there sitting in the driver's seat for almost two hours, trying to stay calm but sweating and imagining all sorts of scenarios.

I knew if I attempted to drive on, he would shoot me or even if he didn't, it could be a case that there was a road block mounted further up the road and they'd get me as I approached.

It took everything I had inside me not to give way to the rising panic that got worse with each slow passing minute which seemed more like a lifetime.

Around three o'clock, just shy of two hours after he stopped me, he came back out of the night, stuck his hand into the car and said: "There's your licence."

There was still no clear instruction for me to go, so as I'm driving away, I'm wondering will I hear the crack of a bullet any moment now?

As a potential defence, I start to move my head away from the centre of the seat, thinking if he is taking aim behind me now, at least I'll make it difficult for him. I drove and flipped my head over and back for about half-a-mile up the road. I knew then I was clear but I also knew I was totally shattered.

I had another hour and a half on the road and by the time I got home, I decided there would be no more rounds of dinner dances for me.

As I said, times were different then and even going to work, you had to alternate your routes. I remember going to work in Guinness one morning at seven o'clock and I heard this bang which I knew was a gun shot and looked around to see what was happening.

The Mother's Pride bakery yard next to where I worked had only a steel partition between us. The killing had taken place about 20 yards from where I was and the victim was a bread delivery man.

Even family life was affected quite regularly. You couldn't go to Ballymena then with an Antrim jersey on. My eldest son was only three or four when we went to visit my wife's family. There was a band marching by who began spitting at him because he had the GAA gear on.

When I was growing up, you could never carry hurls. A priest used to come around on a Friday night and gather them up as he didn't want to make us targets coming from training or matches.

The country has changed so much for the good, it's unreal. Our new generation, fortunately, is oblivious to all of those dark times but the one constant they have with us is the same love of the game. Hurling will always win out in these parts.

The love of the game is still with me the same as ever; I look forward to going to training sessions and coaching the young lads. And I think I know where it originated. In 1981 we won our first senior hurling title and I was only 16 and still at school. It was my first year. That win caused so much rejoicing in our village that the team bus couldn't get in on the main road. People were gathered everywhere so we had to come in a back road.

John Delargy was one of the elder statesmen of the team and the two of us were standing at the corner of Cushendall taking it all in. The 'bandwagon brigade' as I called them, the fair-weather supporters, kept coming up shaking his hand and ignoring me, as they didn't realise that I had played every minute of the drawn game and the replay. I was a regular on the seniors by then but they didn't think I was old enough to be playing at that level.

John got annoyed at this and said: "C'mon, we'll go up to the pub." He took me into the pub – which incidentally is the one that I now own – and bought me a Coca-Cola and directed me down to the corner where there were six men sitting together. These were real supporters and they were crying, and I mean crying, with the emotion and the delight of what our village had just achieved for the first time.

That taught me, maybe not straight away but subconsciously it was the first seed planted in my mind about how much a club means to people. To these great men and thousands like them, it's more than just a game. Your mates on the county team are the ones you invite to your stag and wedding but it's your club mates who will carry you to your grave. They will be there at the start and they will be there at the end.

The truth is that ever since that year in 1981 when we won our first senior title at 16, the GAA has given me a purpose and is still a massive part of my life at 58 years of age. In the interim I've either been playing or coaching or managing teams right up to the present.

I stand on the line of a Sunday and maybe our team is getting beat but at least I'm there and feel alive. Going home from such a match, I often drive by and see people not involved in the GAA cutting their grass or washing their cars of a Sunday and I say: "Feck me, am I not glad I have the GAA?"

Terence 'Sambo' McNaughton is a native of Cushendall and is a former Antrim hurling star who was named Ulster GAA Personality of the Year in 1989 after helping Antrim reach the All-Ireland final which they lost to Tipperary. Two years later, he had the rare honour for an Ulster man when chosen on the hurling All-Stars team. A publican in his native village, he is married to Ursula and they have three children, two boys and a girl. Aside from his passion with hurling and GAA, 'Sambo' loves all kinds of music and walking and says he got great satisfaction from completing the Camino walk.

'*The toughest match I ever attended was between Inniskeen and Donaghmoyne. The exchanges from the beginning were fierce with players being felled all over the place. It was 10 minutes before anyone noticed the referee had not thrown the ball in...*'

Monaghan poet and sometimes GAA goalkeeper, Patrick Kavanagh

Junior Referees –
A Daring Breed of Men

John B Keane

There is a daring breed of men whose exploits have never made the front pages of newspapers, whose heroics forever remain unsung, whose visages will never be seen on our television screens and about whom no songs are made.

Be that as it may, what matters is this breed of man is common to every generation and no matter what abuses and tortures the breed suffered in previous generations, it will always bob to the surface in the present one. It will show itself to be unsullied and untainted by previous wrong, and it will carry on with the job regardless.

I refer, of course, as if you didn't know, to the dauntless band of gentlemen, none others than those heroes who referee junior football matches.

Now, don't get me wrong. There are few of us who loved the game who did not at one time or another find ourselves with a whistle in the hand when the appointed referee failed to turn up. This is all very well but while we may have acted the part once, nothing on this earth could induce us to do so again. We did it and then we wrote it down to experience. We were grateful to escape without injury, and those who suffered physically were even more resolved never to be caught again with a whistle in the hand.

The hero to whom I refer is the one who comes out Sunday after Sunday to do the needful in the matter of refereeing. Often, his task is easy and pleasant, but only where one team is so much better than another that a referee is not needed at all.

His life is in danger however when there is nothing between the teams. Then, in the eyes of the partisans, his every decision is riddled with prejudice, and no matter which way he points in the picture he is greeted with a storm of catcalls and booing. To these he is impervious and takes them for granted. It is when he makes the genuine mistake that he is in serious trouble. Nothing will convince the injured party but that it was deliberate. First the ball is flung at the referee. Then, he is abused with a wide range of choice epithets.

At this stage, experienced referee goes to where the ball is, sit on it, and wait until the whole thing blows over. The worst he is likely to suffer if he chooses this course is a belt of a cadhrawn or a scraw.

However, if he attempts to hand the whistle to one of his tormentors, it is felt by one and all that he is stepping outside the part, and is no longer, as it were, in sanctuary.

Acts like this are regarded as impertinence. Once he ignores his enemies, he is more or less ignored himself, but once he takes them seriously, he is asking for trouble.

After the game is over is the worst time. There is no police protection and it is quite true to add that the game may have been contested in a village where there never were police.

His best bet here is to pick out the biggest man in the vicinity and to open a conversation with him. Those who are out for his blood can never be sure if it's his brother or maybe his uncle he is talking to.

A referee who togs out in white is taken far more seriously than a ref who does not tog out at all. Like a singer who appears on stage wearing a dress suit, he has a head-start over those who treat the occasion lightly. The referee who merely stuffs his trousers inside his socks and hands his coat to his girlfriend is asking for trouble.

Whatever way one looks at it, it is a hazardous occupation. Referees are, for the most part, even-tempered men who do not court trouble. This, however, is not protection and the good referee must know a few tricks if he is to survive. Before I close, I would like to recall one of those tricks as I saw it. The match was a junior football semi-final. All went well and our friend staggered around without falling. What saved him was the fact that he did not blow the whistle. Then following a long bout of booing, he blew the whistle but could not remember why. The pitch was invaded but completely in command, our friend raised his hand and announced that he had blown the whistle in order that two minutes might be observed. Nobody asked who was dead. It wouldn't do to exhibit such ignorance.

This article first appeared in a Munster Football final programme and was reprinted in a New York GAA programme as part of the home team's Connacht SF championship game against Sligo in 2002. The programme was given to us by Billy and the late Nanto Reynolds and the piece is published thanks to the generosity of the Keane family of Listowel. This year marks the 20th anniversary of the death of Ireland's most loved playwright John B.

Clerical Student Out Of Bounds

John Kenny

During this era, and indeed for some years afterwards, a number of clerical students played Gaelic football for various counties under assumed names. This arose because the church authorities forbade clerical students and priests from active participation on the field of play.

Mayo was no exception.

The late Fr. Martin Hannon played for Mayo in the 1936 provincial championship under an assumed name but, as he had returned to Maynooth, was not available for the All-Ireland final.

As radio was out of bounds to the students, an arrangement was made that the result would be communicated to him verbally after the match. It was agreed that two Mayo players would get a taxi on O'Connell Street and travel to Maynooth College to convey the result.

It was believed that my father, Henry Kenny and Paddy Moclair, got that taxi and arrived in Maynooth at the appointed time. As the college gates were closed, it was arranged that Martin Hannon would walk down the avenue to the gates reading his breviary. He was not allowed to talk but it is not known whether this restriction was observed.

It was reported later that he walked back up the avenue "smiling".

John and Henry Kenny are sons of the late Henry and brother of former Taoiseach, Enda Kenny. John has the unusual distinction of winning a minor league medal with Mayo in 1965 which was finally presented to him in 2005, 40 years later.

A Summer Like No Other For Meath Fans

Gráinne Daly

It may have been Kevin Foley's late goal or 'Jinksy' Beggy's point that ruined what was left of my childhood. After 14 halves of football, decades upon decades of the rosary and an unhealthy amount of excitement, by any human standards, the saga of the summer was settled on the fourth time of asking, when Dublin met Meath in Croke Park on July 6, 1991.

The preliminary round of the Leinster football championship had been a draw, the replay a further draw, the replay of the replayed game was to have the same fate: a draw after extra time, so it's not surprising that by the fourth game, the battle had the attention of every man, woman and child in the land.

My brother and I were two of those children, I was 10 and he five. We had grown up in Kingscourt, Co. Cavan but by some kink of 'feckituppery' our dad had gone and blown the marriage so we had been hauled to Tallaght to live with our Nanny – our house sold to clear the debts and with nothing more than two redhaired kids and a silver Datsun Cherry she'd bought for a few bob that she borrowed off her sister, it was back home to Dublin for Mam and us.

The car was her first one to own. It had an orange stripe running along the side and crumbled to scabs of rust in your hands, but it was Mam's car and we loved it.

The first game came around and seeing as I had grown up close to the Cavan-Meath border, I knew the Meath team inside out. On my bedroom wall I had a centrefold of a match programme of the Meath team as well as Dublin. Not because I liked the Royals might I add, but what's that they say about keeping your friends close?

When Meath won the All Ireland in '88, the Sam Maguire, full of sweets, was brought into our school PE hall in Kingscourt by Brian Stafford, who you could almost call a local man. He was from just out the road in Kilmainhamwood, and was one of the very rare breed of Meath players I can say I ever liked. My mam used to cut his hair so maybe I was biased.

I remember the morning well, the hall was filled with eager Cavan kids being shown the cup by a Meath man; a strange state of affairs for most of the assembly, with the exception of the few who lived the dark side of the Meath border. 'Up Cyaaaaavan' roared one of the McKennas after he had taken a fist full of sweets from the cup, 'up the Riyls' replied the Meath crew.

On June 2, there was the usual fever pitch you used to get whenever the pair would meet. Back then Meath were good, and since Dublin hadn't been in winning mode since the 80s, there was added hunger. My mam had to work that day; she had returned to a job she'd had in her teens in the Macari take-away in Tallaght village.

Sometimes she would do a few nights in Borza's too. It paid the bills although there wasn't enough for me to ask her for a Dublin jersey. Arnotts had taken over the sponsorship and jerseys were just becoming a thing, taking over from the rosettes and the soft cardboard caps. Everyone had them, my cousins left Tallaght that morning to head to the match in their new blue Arnotts jerseys. I would have loved one but there was simply no money.

By that stage we had been in Dublin a year and Dad had recently got back in touch with Mam and I knew he'd be watching that game. I guess I wished I could be watching it with him, like old times. Things were looking good for Dublin until Colm Coyle ruined any chances of a Dublin victory. Mam brought home leftover Southern Fried Chicken and we ate it in the kitchen after midnight. She told me that Dublin would do it the next day. I believed her.

By the time the next day came, which was June 9, the weather had changed into a soft and dirty old day in Dublin, Dad had been in touch again and talks of the pair reconciling had progressed. Of course, aside from wanting a Dublin jersey, I wanted a normal family, all my cousins' mothers and fathers were together, none of them were poor, I didn't want to be an anomaly. To tell the truth, I had been praying for them to get back together ever since he had walked out. I prayed and I prayed and I prayed. That I wanted Dublin to win was unquestionable, but wanting Dad back was the sum total of everything.

Mam decided to meet up with him and we would go for a drive on the Sunday. Of course, we would have the match on in the car. So, in the pouring rain on a slate grey Sunday we found ourselves up on the Military Road pulled in by Lemass's Cross. Barney Rock was in blistering form and was bringing the game to Meath. My least favourite player, Mick Lyons, saw red. A draw meant it went to extra time. Dad was sitting in the passenger seat, both him and Mam in good form, my brother beside me chewing sweets, smiling every time Dublin scored, pinching me when Meath did. As days go, it was turning out to be a good one. Sheet rain poured across the windscreen; a mountain breeze shook the Datsun Cherry and the four of us in it; Tommy Howard got a cramp in Croke Park but got seen to and continued to referee what seemed to be Dublin's game.

Dad stretched across and held Mam's hand, she smiled and said something that sounded like "typical trucking Meath you can never rule them out." It was nearing the end of the game and my brother was out of sweets so he decided to pinch no matter who scored: I sat there, hands in full-on prayer mode, imploring God in the month of the Sacred Heart to help Dublin win. David Beggy put Meath ahead, Jack Sheedy equalised, Tommy Howard found the whistle.

Whatever it is they say about third time being lucky I don't buy. The third game (second replay) took place on June 23, Mam was again in work, so I watched it with my Nanny. I can't remember where my brother was for the day, gone off fishing with my uncle probably, but I recall that Mam had left me a pound if I wanted to go to the shops to get some 'foocies' for the game. What I wanted was to be at the game, preferably in a jersey of my own, with Dad by my side.

Nanny had never been a cursing woman, even a few years before when she had watched her own son, my uncle, play for Dublin; but that day was an exception. The inspiration for her language was Bernard Flynn's extra time goal that choked Dublin's lead. She was also ticked off with Brian Stafford's points that sealed the deal and drew it level for the Royals. Suffice to say, there were a few rounds of the Angelus said in Nanny's cottage in Old Court that evening. I knew what Dad would say "oh well, that's sport", which I was grateful I didn't have to hear in the aftermath of another nail-biter, but I still prayed that night that maybe by the next game my parents would be back together.

The sun came out in all its splendour for the fourth game on Saturday, July 6. Lo and behold, Dad had been in touch with Mam and decided we would watch the match together, only there isn't really anywhere to watch a match given he was living in a shoe box bedsit in Terenure with a portable black and white telly, and Nanny didn't allow us have any visitors (and by that stage, hated Dad anyway).

The GAA club was too local and would only fuel rumours of a 'they're back together' nature, which I would have been more than proud with, Mam's family less so. It being a Saturday, and the first time the GAA were to televise a Saturday game, Mam thought that the pubs would be too busy. Truth is, she hadn't a washer to her name and didn't want to let him know that. The decision was made to listen to it in the car on another drive up the mountains. We went out towards the Glencree Centre, ironically now a centre for reconciliation, then up to Kippure only to discover that the radio in the car wouldn't tune in properly that far up, so back towards Glencree we came. Reception clear as day. A purple blush of heather stretched up the shoulder of the hill beside us. The valley before us ablaze with furze. My brother chewed through a penny mix. There was no pinching this time as the four of us sat in relative silence save for the odd breakout of 'come on the Dubs'.

There was no handholding in the front. Keith Barr missed a penalty for Dublin and I kicked the back of the seat only to get an earful from Mam. Then, in a case of excruciating familiarity, it ended a draw after full time. Exhausted sighs, shakes of heads, Dad lit another cigarette, my brother hopped out to take a leak.

Extra-time threw in and I was not minding the sheep that had manifested and encircled the car. If they had been wielding guns, I would still not have cared. Dublin were three points up in the dying minutes, Mam was professing her usual "Meath come back, they always come back, come on outta that Dublin."

My brother was tearing the arm off a toy soldier he'd found under the seat and I made a mistake that I would regret for years to come. I made a pact with God that if he made sure that Dublin didn't draw then I would stop plaguing him about my parents getting back together. I was willing to exchange all previous prayers to ensure that there was no draw today. But I guess I wasn't explicit enough in asking that the result go Dublin's way.

When Kevin Foley's shot sailed past the Dublin keeper, John O'Leary, with two minutes to go, I panicked. I made the pledge again – 'please God, don't let it be another draw, you can forget everything else I have asked you for.'

When David 'Jinksy' Beggy's point went over, prayers were answered. Only they weren't mine. Meath won. There was no reconciliation, and it was to be a few years before I could get a Dublin jersey of my own.

Gráinne Daly lives in Tallaght, Dublin. She played camogie for St. Anne's, Bohernabreena and recently, in her twilight years, has started to kick a football. Her earliest years were spent in Kingscourt, Co. Cavan so she grew up with two counties to support, but in recent years the Dubs have done more to deepen her smile lines.

Monaghan At Odds With Times

Anon

Suggestions made in a report appearing in a July 1951 edition of the Dublin publication 'Times Pictorial' to the effect that attendances at GAA matches in Co. Monaghan were dropping owing to unseemly conduct at matches provoked a strong denial from Mr James Cahill, chairman of the county board.

"In five years, there has only been one case of a referee being struck," Mr Cahill stated.

He said he had never in his experience heard of a referee being "mobbed". Neither had he heard of a referee being "terrorised" into suppressing reports of bad conduct.

"We in the GAA in Monaghan pride ourselves on the contrary," he remarked.

Continuing, he said that annually there were at least 100 games played in the county and incidents between players were less than half a dozen each year.

GAA matches were drawing ever-increasing attendances with a resultant increase in finances.

This was proved by the fact that in 1938, the county board was £300 in debt with the medal fund in arrears to 1925. This debt had now been cleared and a substantial balance was now on hand, so that they were able to train their team last year (1950) without calling on the public to spend some hundreds of pounds on their training.

"Monaghan officials, as I know them, are not worried but are quietly and justly proud of the conduct and standard of GAA games in the county."

Mr Cahill concluded by stating that it was the intention of the GAA in Monaghan to seek an apology and withdrawal from the newspaper concerned.

From the Monaghan Argus Edition of July 28, 1951

Timing Was Everything For My Whistler Dad

Louise Walsh

They say time flies when you're having fun – but maybe that's not totally true for a former Meath referee when time literally stood still for him in a championship match.

Navan man Colm Walsh, my father, was a great GAA enthusiast and used to hop on his bike – when they were cumbersome and had no gears – to cycle to Dublin or Mullingar in Westmeath to watch his beloved Meath play. When the game was over, he thought nothing of cycling home again for tea without any of the Garmin accolades(?) or map my ride apps about now.

Colm was born in 1924 on Watergate Street where his father Christopher and grandfather were the local watchmakers and jewellers. The family was responsible for taking the correct time from the Dublin train and conveying it to all the clocks in the big houses in the areas to ensure synchronised time was kept in the town.

It was a trade that was passed down eventually to Colm's brother Robbie and Colm himself 'served his own time' as a grocery manager, eventually opening up his own shop in the early 60s – a shop ahead of its time which sold escargots and caviar.

Colm loved all things football, both GAA and soccer, though the latter earned him a stiff punishment from the Christian Brothers as the 'foreign sport' was not allowed at that time.

Growing up he joined the Parnells and the O'Growneys before becoming one of the founding members of the Navan O'Mahony's club.

Ahead of his passing in 2017 at the age of 92, he recalled memories of his football days both as a player and a referee at a time when weather didn't stop play.

"Navan O'Mahony's was founded in 1948 and the following year, we won the Junior Championship. I remember I was playing as a forward against Drumree.

"It was a December day and it was snowing. It was such a bitter cold and mucky day that the only ones cheering on the sidelines were the subs. We won by three points as far as I remember."

As an official, he umpired the Meath senior championship final in 1950 that saw North Meath beat reigning champions, Skryne, by two points.

"I remember that match well because there were four Carolan brothers on the North Meath team which was, I'm sure, pretty unique for a family," he recalled.

But it was remembering being a referee in a championship game that made him giggle. It was really a game of two halves.

"My brother Robbie, who was a watchmaker, gave me a new watch especially for the match that morning, so I gladly put it on and thought no more of it.

"There was a chap who used to always come into the shop to me after a game and berate me if I played a couple of minutes over or under time.

"I saw him out of the corner of my eye just before I threw the ball in to start the game. All went well in the first half and I looked at my watch when I resumed the second half with the second throw in.

"What I didn't realise was that my new watch had not been wound properly by my brother. I assumed it had been as he was the expert on such things. However, some time into the second moiety, I glanced at the watch to see how much time was left and to my horror saw that it had stopped.

"Well, what could I do? I had no option but to guesstimate how much time was left. I blew the full-time whistle at what I felt should be the end of the 30 minutes and left the pitch with head down as fast as I could.

"No one said a word. Still, I had a sleepless night and thought I'd be for it the next day when (no pun intended) like clockwork, I saw the time critic enter my shop.

"I took the bull by the horns and asked, 'well how did I do yesterday?' as I waited for his bad news verdict. 'You were spot on with the time Colm!', he said, 'in fact, it's the best you've ever been.'"
Louise Walsh is the daughter of Colm and is a freelance journalist working as a producer of the Late Lunch Show on LMFM Radio. She is married to Eoin and has three children.

Living Through 'The Troubles' As Irish Exile

Barrie Henriques

In so far as it is possible to do so, given the length of the Welsh railway station, Llanfairpwllgwyngyllgogerychwyrndrobwllllantysiliogogogoch, with its 58 letters in its name flashed by the steamed-up carriage window, as the double-headed British Rail steam engine pulled 18 passenger carriages across the North Wales coastline to the city of Manchester.

Myself and many thousands of luckless young Irish lads and girls had spewed from the bowels of The Cambria at the Holyhead Ferry port earlier, terrified, heart-broken, innocent, and jobless as we stepped into the great unknown.

It was a month of October in the 1950s; I was 17 and a bit; there were plenty older, some carrying brand new suitcases, others with message bags with very little content. I looked at the departure schedule displaying the destinations, time of departure, and platform.

I found the Manchester departure platform as well as many others to places like Rugby, Coventry, Leeds, Newcastle, Birmingham, London (3 times), Liverpool, and more.

The noise of hissing steam, billowing black smoke, steel-rimmed baggage trollies, language that was totally alien. Later in life I was to find out that the Welsh were notorious for speaking their own language whenever there were strangers in their midst, and there were at least 2000 reasons to maintain that dictate.?

The rail staff were shouting and roaring; to my mind not a single syllable of the Queen's English passed from their mouths. There were plenty of British police around the place. There was an inert fear of lawmen in the vast majority of Irish people. Did it have something to do with the Irish DNA, a throwback to the times our country was a part of the so-called greatest empire in the world?

Like myself, a large number of the people were stepping onto British soil for the first time in their lives. These mostly were people who first saw the light of day less than 20 years on from the departure of the crown from the 26 counties. At the Customs galvanised shed I stuttered through answers to nonsensical questions. What would a 17-year-old young lad have to declare except his fear and abject sorrow?

To compound my fears, they disfigured my brand-new brown suitcase, purchased by my Mam – who could scarcely afford it – with a dirty big ignorant hieroglyphic in white chalk.

I was terrified exiting the shed as I felt the Customs guy had put some sort of secret code to alert the police that there was something in my suitcase for further investigation.

I found a carriage that filled up in double quick time. I might have been the smartest lad back in down town Portarlington on a Saturday night, but as I offered a silent prayer: "Sweet Jesus and his Blessed Mother help me," incantation, I cowered in the corner seat near the window, and shivered with raw terror.

My fears were further cranked up when, on arriving into Manchester Exchange station, the priest who was due to meet me failed to show up. It was 4.20 am on a wet October morning. Eventually I was spotted by a member of the Legion of Mary, and taken to a family in Higher Blackley. It so happened that they ran the Astoria Irish Ballroom on Plymouth Grove on all weekends and Holy days.

What a culture shock that was. If you are of an age, you will understand the drill; all the lads on one side of this massive ballroom, the Astoria, and all the girls on the opposite side. It was where hard-working young Irish single people went for reasons that soon became apparent to a fast-learning raw kid who thought he knew it all.

It was where Irish boy met Irish girl. It was where people got better jobs because a lad knew a lad. It was also where the finest of Irish lads were succoured by bastards of Irish agents, whose mantra was to get enough lads to work on 'the lump' – no tax, no cards, no compensation for injury, and most certainly no records of fatalities in any ledger. The agent would convince them that with him, they could get better wages and better conditions. From a later time I got to find out that the worst enemy an Irishman had in England was the same Irish agent.

It was in the Astoria where I met a lad from near Tuam. He was what locals in that part of Galway called "a buff sham." For some rea-son he found out that I was a footballer, and I was a very close relation of one member of the 'Terrible Twins', Frank Stockwell.

In his mind I had to be a footballer...my luck was turning, and my trepidation abating.

He told me that he was living in Bolton and there was a sizeable Irish Community there. They had a new GAA football club called Shannon Rangers. Subsequently, he sent a lad in to Manchester to take me out to the meeting in Bolton the following Sunday evening.

People can say what suits their argument, but I have no doubts whatsoever that the GAA fraternity are a breed apart. Hypothetically, I think it is a fair bet that but for the existence of the GAA outside of Ireland, many, many of our finest boys and girls would never have blossomed into the great people they eventually became abroad.

It afforded people an identity, a base, a reference. It encouraged them and gave them confidence. Stories of great success are myri-ad, many of them because of the influences brought into their lives through a GAA ethos.

I hadn't found a job after six weeks yet the people I was with were really decent and caring. Pierce and Flo Coogan kept me in their home with no charge until I started to earn. They were the grandparents of the BAFTA Award winning actor and author, Steve Coogan. I pray that they have found comfort and peace in the arms of their creator with whom they were totally besotted.

The upshot of my visit to Bolton was an agreement to join their GAA ranks – the first and best decision I made. It ticked a number of boxes. It brought me back into the GAA family, which I thought had died when the Cambria pulled away from Dun Laoghaire pier. To add to my good fortune, a week later I got a job in the reservations depart-ment of Aer Lingus on Deansgate in Manchester.

The Rangers were a family; I had a great stroke of good fortune join-ing them. The first match I played was against a Manchester based club, Harps and Shamrocks. It was played in the Harris Stadium, named after a World Champion cycling sprinter. Originally called the Fallowfield Stadium, it played host to two FA Cup finals, rugby interna-tionals and rivalled the best sports stadium in Britain at the time.

I'd bought a new pair of boots, socks and knicks with what money

I had earned and got a bus out to the Stadium to meet with my new teammates. I was by far the youngest player and was surprised that they had picked me to start. There were six Gallagher brothers from Cavan playing; a giant of a man by the name of Tommy McTiernan from Roscommon, Gerry Geoghegan from Belturbet and Jack McDonnell from near Tuam who was the captain.

My first impression was that I was a chap among men. These lads were hardy boys. Their hands were as big as shovels, their skin burned to a Bermudan tan and I felt that if anyone laid a hand on me, they would regret the decision. I remember the game lasted no longer than 15 minutes or so, because two English 'Bobbies' invaded the pitch and refused to let us play on.

With thumbs gripping the breast pockets of their tunics, they stated: "Right gentlemen, we have to ask you to leave the Stadium," reminding me as they did so of the Dixon of Doc Green series on television.

"For what reason?" asked a giant of a man whom I later found out to be another Gallagher and chairman of the club.

"We have not contravened any law to the best of my knowledge," he stated.

"Don't get cheeky. You're in contravention of the Lord's Day Observance Society Law Reform Regulations which are enforceable by law," one of them responded.

"For your information sir, the act prevents the playing of outdoor games where a fee is being charged," he added, the latter a reference to the fact that there was a charge at the gate for supporters.

There was no professional sporting entertainment in Britain at all on a Sunday that time. Amateur games and events were OK but not where there was a subscription at an entrance.

Our chairman, thinking on his feet, insisted that there was no fee involved, and what the police observed was a voluntary collection for an injured colleague.

He sought agreement to finish the game but the Bobbies informed him that they would have reinforcements in the stadium within a very short time if we didn't cease playing.

It was game set and match to Her Majesty's forces.

In all honesty, I was delighted to get out of there as I had visions of extradition or a spell in Wormwood Scrubs. I had slipped over a couple of nice points in the time that was played and these scores had earned the admiration and verbal kudos of the Rangers team and followers.

The match was re-fixed for the following Sunday in the same venue. This time the clubs were ready. There were no officials at the entrance. Players and supporters of both sides made their contributions to offset the rent of the stadium and the referee and umpires' costs. Two different Bobbies were close by but they didn't interfere.

As the crowd left after the game which we won by a few points with yours truly scoring 1-4, all was very quiet, although many were seething at the police presence at our game. One member of the opposing team made a caustic reference about occupation of our country within police earshot, and they jumped in like lightning – it was the chance they were waiting for. Within seconds, there was a 'Paddy Wagon' and the miscreant was whipped away.

The fear I had at Holyhead returned like a tsunami. I had just got my job with Aer Lingus, and I had a fear that I would not be reporting for work on Monday. Fortunately, it didn't happen and we lived to play many other days. However, it narked us that at virtually every subsequent game, there was always a few uniformed police hanging around, maintaining a presence.

Which leads me to another game I was involved in shortly after that. It was played in a rugby pitch in Middleton – a satellite town of Manchester. For a totally different reason altogether, the police also halted this game. It was laughable really as the mother and father of a row started half way through the second half. The referee did his best to quell the viciousness, but unable to do so he left the pitch and caught a bus home.

It was then that a Paddy Wagon arrived with six 'Bobbies,' truncheons drawn as they alighted the vehicle. Apparently, locals had reported that "the Oirish were killing each other with sticks," and felt that someone was going to be murdered.

It was tough but nothing comparable to a Laois senior final around the mid-fifties when Clonad and Cullohill locked horns in O'Moore Park. That particular game wasn't finished as a continuous shuttle of ambulances brought the injured to the county hospital. One nurse who was working there remarked that they finished the county final in the Emergency Ward that year.

In England, the hardest part of GAA activity was sourcing venues. Great servants like Tommy Scully (Clare), Fr. Emmet Fullen (Derry), Harry Purcell (Wexford), Chris Johnson (Ardee & Liverpool) did Trojan work to keep the GAA alive. Fr. Emmet said to me one time that it was "easier to push a rope up Croagh Patrick than get pitches to play games."

Shannon Rangers won the county final in 1960. We had a very good team, but couldn't add to our previous laurels. I left that great club, Gallaghers and all, to head to London for a new job with our national carrier.

Aer Lingus had a big team in London doing airport handling, bus shuttles and a throbbing HQ in the West End. At a staff social, it was muted that we should start our own GAA Club. A Committee was elected with Des Kennedy (Portlaoise) as Chairman; Tommy Gleeson (Tipperary minor from Gortnahoe 1957) Secretary; Malachy Faughnan (Father of Conor CEO AA) President. Tom Hanley (Tipperary) was Vice Chairman and Brendan Fogarty (Killeagh, East Cork) was Treasurer.

The presence of Her Majesty's police force at games and even training in places like Wormwood Scrubs, Hackney Marshes, Acton Town was equally apparent in the capital as it was in the North West.

The London GAA Board current HQ at Ruislip was only open parkland at the time. That suited most of our team as Ruislip was just a hen's kick down the M4 from Heathrow. It didn't suit me or a few others who worked in the City as it took 90 minutes to get there on the 'Rattler' (underground) from my home in London E11. New Eltham was the GAA HQ at that time and it provided a real GAA 'mardi gras' every Sunday. It was like a congregation after last Mass in any town on a Sunday at home.

Around the same time the Troubles in the North were getting worse. Bombs were planted in the UK and were getting closer to London. Life for the 'Oirish' was none too welcoming. Suddenly "Paddy" was being bandied about as a mark of disdain, suspicion, mistrust. Even when I rewound my time in Manchester, I could now see why the Bobbies were watching our activities.

It seemed to me that the infiltration by British Security forces was a constant. There is no doubt that there was a very strong Republican allegiance in the body politic of the GAA. All of those trains taking the annual 60,000 jobless to all of those stations from Holyhead had its share of strong Republican supporters. Our culture was celebrated – our music, writing, dancing – in the major English cities by the locals during the fifties and sixties.

However, all that changed when the troops crossed the Irish Sea. The lads at Heathrow Airport would say that their check-in areas in Terminal One was constantly under observation. And then there were the bomb warnings, particularly in the Aer Lingus offices in Regent Street and Poland Street in the West End. In one week alone, I remember evacuating our Poland Street office three times.

It was a harrowing time being Irish in England from the late 60s to the signing of the Good Friday Agreement in 1998. I knew plenty of lads from different GAA teams in London who answered their doors at night to be confronted by British Secret Service operatives. Much of the time, it was a "just making enquiries" approach. I am aware of at least one lad, who was employed in an Irish Company, who was lifted and his wife and kids didn't see him for a week.

Every establishment with an Irish interest was targeted. Aer Lingus, Bord Failte, Coras Trachtala, CIE, Kilkenny Design Workshop (Bond St), Construction Companies (there were plenty), pubs etc. were all raddled with the same stick.

Everyone was nervous. Conversations were guarded and the usual friendly, chatty Irish were becoming very reticent, very guarded, and very frightened. I was married with two children, and my Kilkenny nurse – trained in London, was somewhat worried. We toyed with the idea of "coming home". My mind was dramatically made up for me in the most terrifying way imaginable.

On March 8, 1973, I was a member of a jury in the Old Bailey in London. Even though I was working for an Irish company, it didn't afford a legitimate reason to abstain from jury service. We were sitting on a 'conspiracy to defraud' case, involving Greek and Chinese plaintiffs. After five days we retired to the jury room to consider the evidence. Let me add that another member of the Aer Lingus GAA club was also in the Bailey on another case, whilst there was a lad from Leitrim and another lad from Louth on my jury.

Having been in the room for an hour or so, the foreman came in and asked us to follow, informing me on the way that there had been a bomb threat. I went to the cloakroom to get my coat. As I re-entered the main building my whole world exploded. The front of the Bailey, a very sturdy, well-built structure, came towards me in a tornado of shattered glass.

As I picked myself off the floor some 20 yards from where I was previously standing, my first thoughts were for my wife and children. I was very fit at the time and started running towards my home, some seven miles away in the East End of London.

To this day I can still hear my wife's screams as I come through the front door.

"Oh Mother of Jesus, what happened to you? What happened your face, it's covered in blood?"

My face was a mass of blood and shards of glass. I was lucky not to be blinded. Unfortunately, others in the Old Bailey that awful afternoon were not so lucky. Neither my Aer Lingus colleague nor the Leitrim or Louth jurymen suffered a life-threatening injury.

That evening, Dolours and Marian Price and their mentor, Gerry Kelly and Hugh Feeney were arrested at Heathrow Airport and charged with planting the bomb. Four innocent Irish lads with wives and children were in the Old Bailey that day. I suffered serious mental trauma from that day for a very long time afterwards.

As a family, we were on our way home six months later. Undoubtedly the GAA had sustained me in my life in and around the two places I had lived in England, as it would continue to do so for countless more despite the tough times that followed for the Irish in Britain, especially those with GAA connections. We'd had enough of being spied on as Irish abroad.

We came home and once again that great indigenous association enriched our lives as we reintegrated as a family into life in Ireland.

Barrie Henriques was born in Tuam, Co Galway in 1940 but became known nationally as a sports journalist operating out of Callan, Co Kilkenny after returning from London to buy a pub there. Married with four children, he has edited the Kilkenny GAA yearbook for over 30 years.

Why My Mother
Backed Down In 1960

Collette Bonnar

With the dark recessionary days of the 1950s relegated to the history books, Ireland was looking to a bright future as the sixties dawned. Down had got through to their first All-Ireland senior football final and they were set to play Kerry on September 25, 1960. The spirits of the sporting fraternity were high. If Down won, they would be the first team to take the Sam Maguire cup north of the border.

There was no television in our house at the time and national and worldwide news was transmitted via the Pye radio or the newspapers. The first battalion of Irish soldiers were sent to the Congo in July of that year where a bloody war was raging. In June, Patrice Lumumba became Prime Minister after the Congo gained their independence from Belgium. The Irish people had a vested interest in the conflict as many feared for the safety of our young soldiers who were on peacekeeping duties there. Every news bulletin was intently read or listened to.

However, as September wore around, the All-Ireland final was eagerly awaited. The excitement in Down was at fever pitch and it was reported that a small farmer had offered his 25-acre farm in exchange for two match tickets!

In our farmhouse in Donegal on the evening before the final, the usual group of GAA die-hards had gathered to discuss the impending game the following day.

"I think I'll have a wee flutter on the game myself," Mammy announced after she had served the men the customary tea and homemade scones. A hush fell over the small gathering; Mammy's only involvement in the GAA was washing the football jerseys on a Monday morning after the previous day's game in Lifford.

Hugh Doherty, one of Lifford's star players, was the first to speak.

"I didn't know you were a betting woman, Ellen," he remarked, his voice dripping with amazement.

"Normally I'm not... but I got a little tip... a sort of an omen so to speak and my money is on Down," she replied firmly.

"Well, no harm to your tip or your omen but the men from the Mournes have no chance against the giants from the Kingdom," Hugh Doherty replied confidently.

Mammy took her purse from the drawer in the kitchen table and planted a shiny half-crown on the dresser. "Put your money on Kerry and match that," she challenged, equally confident.

"Well, Ellen, I'll do better than that, I'll bet you four to one, that Kerry wins," Hugh answered as he withdrew a red ten-shilling note from his wallet and placed it alongside my mother's half-crown.

"Sure, we'd all love to see the Northern team win," added Sean Finnigan, "but Kerry are the hot favourites."

"Sporting history could be in the making," Mammy declared casually as she refilled the teapot.

"History might be in the making but it won't happen at this All Ireland," said Hugh Doherty as his eyes wandered to the cash on the dresser. "Besides you do a grand job washing the jerseys on a Monday morning," Hugh added which earned him a withering look from my mother.

As Daddy glanced at Hugh, his expression said it all; "Sure, what would a woman know?"

After all this was the GAA.

The talk finally turned to the war in the Congo and the recent military coup that deposed Prime Minister Patrice Lumumba. As the night wore on, the group began to disperse.

"Thanks for the tea, I'll be in tomorrow night to collect my winnings," Hugh Doherty said as he flashed Mammy a wide smile as the men took their leave.

"What kind of a notion have you taken, Ellen?" Daddy asked as he locked the back door for the night. "A half-crown is a lot of money, what came over you? Who gave you the tip? Everyone knows that Kerry are the favourites."

"Just wait and see," she replied mysteriously. "I feel in my bones that the Down captain, Kevin Mussen, will lift Sam tomorrow in

Croke Park." Then a dreamy look stole over her face. "Wouldn't it be just brilliant if they were the first Northern team ever to win the All Ireland and bring the Sam Maguire across the border."

"Mmm, dream on," Daddy replied, "but I don't think so."

The following day after much shouting and screaming around the Pye radio, the cheer went up when the final whistle was blown. Down won 2-10 to 0-8. My father and my three brothers looked at Mammy in disbelief, unable to take it in that she had won her bet on the underdogs. Finally, Daddy asked: "What made you decide to back Down?"

"All will be revealed tonight when the men call to replay the game and Hugh officially hands me over my winnings," Mammy replied, beaming from ear to ear.

Later that evening, the usual gang called to our house to carry out the post-mortem on the match. Hugh Doherty was the last to arrive.

"Well fair dues to you, Ellen," he declared nobly as he presented Mammy with the twelve shillings and six pence. "How come you were so sure they were going to win?"

Reaching under the cushion on the settee, Mammy's face broke into a smile that was bordering on smugness as she pulled out a copy of the national newspaper dated September 15, 1960.

The front page was packed with the latest news of the war in the Congo while the emblazoned headline read: LUMUMBA BACKS DOWN.

Collette Bonnar is daughter of the late Barney McDermott and wife to Denis Bonnar until his untimely death a year ago. A former bank official, she lives in Stranorlar in Donegal and is a member of the Gateway Writers Group in Lifford. Collette also writes the weekly short story column for the Donegal news and the Strabane Chronicle.

'He had an eternity to kick that ball, but took far too long'

Wexford's Liam Griffin

Vienna Tenor Hits High Notes As A Hurling Goalkeeper

Tom Birch

Invariably in life, you tend to remember the circumstances when you get an opportunity to climb the ladder in your chosen career. As a tenor looking for a little 'security', the day the Viennese Opera company 'Theatre An Der Wien' offered me a contract was one such moment.

In its own way, it's like one of the Gaelic footballers getting a deal with an Aussie Rules franchise or a League of Ireland player getting a big move to a Premier League or Championship club over in England.

Getting this offer was such a big deal that the theatre company insisted that I sign a contract – and this was where I was confronted with a real dilemma.

You see as an English-born, Aussie brought up outdoor type, I love all sport and had always sought to play games at various levels right through my twenties. Now about to turn 30, I was being asked to sign something that effectively barred me from playing anything more physically challenging than tiddledywinks or darts.

Of course, you can see it from the opera company's point of view; they have big productions planned and if you walk in with a leg hanging off or your face disfigured, you are not going to be able to go on stage and perform.

I looked down the detailed list they gave me and soccer, rugby, Aussie Rules, cricket, American Football, basketball, boxing, cycling, diving and equestrian were just ten of a long list of barred sports. I was so disappointed that my opera singing opportunity was coming at the expense of my active sports life... unless I wanted to swim (which I didn't) or play snooker, which I don't really consider a sport at all.

I was in despair on what should have been the happiest day of my singing career, especially as the Theatre An Der Win is the second biggest company in the music mad city of Vienna and was a platform that performers eagerly sought out.

As happens when you are signing professional forms, it is wise to get legal counsel to make sure you are not signing your life away too cheaply. So, I stuffed the pages in my pocket and instead of going home, I headed straight to the nearest Irish bar in the city for a few drinks to drown my sorrows. What a serendipitous decision that was!

I wasn't long in the premises when I struck up a conversation with another patron, Des Reilly, who as well as being a great club mentor and referee, has since become a very good friend. Out of the blue, I heard myself telling Des my whole story as if he was some sort of counsellor who could advise me on what direction to take.

Like all Irish people, Des always seems to find an answer to the most difficult of questions if only by directing the conversation with a question of his own.

"Was Gaelic Games on the list your new employers gave you as sports you can't play?" he asked me as he drained his pint and signalled to the barman to get another one ready.

I pulled out the contract and while I was convinced they had every game under the sun in the list, sure enough there was no mention of Gaelic Games.

"There's your answer," he said sizing me up. "Sign the contract and switch to the GAA. You look the type that will take to our sports like a duck to water."

"Sports," I queried, noticing that he had used the plural of the word.

"Yes, we have a club here in the city called Vienna Gaels and you can play either football or hurling with us if you join. Come down next week and I'll introduce you to the relevant people."

And so a chance encounter in a bar had not only sorted a professional dilemma for me but actually changed a large part of my sporting and social life.

I signed my contract the next day and began preparing for roles such as Don Jose in Carmen. I also presented myself down at the Gaelic club and with my background they felt that I would be more at home playing football than hurling.

I enjoyed the training but something inside felt it wasn't action-packed enough and I asked if I could try my hand at "the hurling."

Once I had the rules explained to me and after a few months of practising how to rise the ball between the hurley and sliotar, I couldn't wait to get down to the grounds for training.

Coming late to the game, I worked out that maybe the best position to try out for was goalkeeper. The old timers in the club raised their eyebrows when I mentioned that but nevertheless gave me a hurl with a bigger bas and said "go ahead and see how she goes."

I am now in my fifth year as goalkeeper for the club and the involvement has been one of the most joyous things I have done in sport. Yes, I've had a few broken fingers – that sliotar can be unforgiving when pelted at you at 100 miles an hour from 15 yards out – but you don't sing with your hands, do you?

I've also had a few stitches inserted for various cuts but (touch wood) so far I've not sustained any serious injury that would interfere with my tramping the boards of the professional theatre. When they asked me what happened after my latest injury, I told them I fell over and suffered a gash playing with my daughter at home.

Unlike the counties in Ireland where you play in local leagues and championship, here on the continent, we rely on inter-city tournaments five or six times a year for competitive fare because there is normally only one GAA club per country. We may be in Berlin or Amsterdam or Prague or Brussels or Paris to play in the one year – and believe me in those games, there's skin and hair flying.

Those weekends become fairly big affairs. For instance, our club hosted one recently in Vienna and we had 350 players here for that hurling and football tournament. The organisers normally run two levels of competition as often there are top class young hurlers working in different cities or recently relocated on Erasmus years who clearly are a step or two above the level I play.

However, it doesn't take away from the enjoyment that at our most recent weekend in Amsterdam, we won the second-tier competition. I was so proud to pick up silverware after a great team performance and a shootout following extra time when the goalkeeper (me) managed to save a couple of shots in the sudden death climax to the competition.

Even at 35 years of age and even though my Irish connection has helped me perform at Wexford Opera Festival last year and (as I write) this year as well, I am so grateful to have discovered the game of hurling and the Irish culture that goes with it.

I grew up loving Aussie Rules but my one regret is that I wasn't introduced to hurling when I was really young. It truly is a wonderful game, and instead of impeding my singing career, I believe it has enhanced it. I love the challenge being a goalkeeper gives me and, like all who play between the sticks, it helps if you are a little mad to start with for that position.

Wexford last year was a special place and my only regret is that the Faythe Harriers and other local hurling clubs had finished their competitions due to Covid 19 a few weeks before I arrived. This year and in the future, I want to train with GAA clubs in Ireland and get to experience first-hand how teams prepare for their big games.

And if you meet any opera directors on the way, I'd appreciate it if you avoid mentioning the fact that one of their tenors is a mad-keen active hurler! Otherwise, they just might include Gaelic Games in the 'banned List' and I'd be out of a job.

Tom Birch was born in Hampshire in England but spent most of his youth growing up in Australia. Now married to Amy, who is EA to the Irish CEO of Lauda Europe and Malta Air (Ryanair group), they live in Vienna in Austria with their daughter Elisa, who attended her first cúl camp this year. Tom has sung the role of Don Jose in over 40 performances of the opera Carmen and among his other notable parts is playing Macduff in the Verdi operatic adaptation of Macbeth.

Zero Hour As County Final Ends Scoreless

Liam Flynn

As often happened in the decades of the last century, county finals were often held over to the following year due to weather problems or a series of replays in the earlier rounds or semi-finals.

And so it was in Longford that the 1946 senior football final between Ballymahon and Dromard was played on Easter Sunday, April 7 in Pearse Park.

This turned out to be a very unique final in that the game ended in a scoreless draw after the 60 minutes action.

According to newspaper reports, the game was played in a gale and just at the throw in "a terrific shower made the ground conditions appalling."

Ballymahon played against the elements in the first half and their defence put in a herculean effort to thwart the Dromard forwards. Similarly on the change-over, it was the Drom defence who were the heroes as they defied their opponents and the elements to keep out the threat of scores.

Just once they seemed to be in trouble when Ballymahon was awarded a penalty and it seemed they were close to their first ever senior title. Liam Flynn, the two-goal hero of the junior final took the spot kick. Apparently, the tactic was to blast the ball directly at the goalkeeper and then bundle man and ball over the line if he managed to save it. The plan failed and so a replay was needed to prise daylight between the two teams.

In the replay which Dromard won, there is the memory of seeing a player, Paddy Sheehy, wearing a pair of new white boots, in the kickaround before the throw in.

The winners got off to a whirlwind start with an early goal boosting their chances. They led 1-4 to 0-3 at half-time and though they didn't score at all in the second-half, Ballymahon could only raise one white flag and lost by 1-4 to 0-4. The result was achieved by Dromard despite the fact that they only scored in one of the four 'halves' across the two games which constituted the final and replay.

More long-term loss for the club was the fact that the following week, starting midfielder Tom Cowan departed to begin a new life in England, one of a number of young men who left the locality in that time of dire economic need in Ireland.

Ballymahon also reached the senior county final in 1950 where Mullinalaghta beat them by 2-2 to 0-4. It was to be another 52 years before Ballymahon reached and won a Longford senior football championship in 2002 against Clonguish on a 1-11 to 0-12 scoreline. Efforts to complete a double against the same opposition the following year failed, but again, only after a replay in which Clonguish emerged victorious by 0-11 to 1-1.

The Late Liam Flynn was a native of Ballymahon, Co Longford. Coming from a family steeped in the GAA with his brother Jimmy a long-time Chairman of Longford Co Board, he too played and served in many positions in his club.

The Crucible And Croker
– My Unforgettable
Sporting Occasions

Ken Doherty

I've had two experiences out on the pitch at Croke Park – both memorable but for different reasons.

The first was after I had won the World Snooker Championship in 1997 at the Crucible in Sheffield and after a huge home-coming reception through the streets of Dublin, the GAA kindly offered me the chance to walk out onto the centre of the pitch with the trophy before that year's Leinster senior football quarter-final between the Dubs and Meath.

Obviously as an out and out Dub, I wanted to put only blue ribands on the trophy. That's what my mother had on but in deference to the Royal County, I also put on a set of green and gold ribbons.

The reception I got from both sides that day was so memorable that I can still almost experience it just by thinking back to that electric five minutes where I walked on, waved to all sides and walked off again.

The Hill gave me a particularly great reception and I was tempted to run down to that end and put the Cup over my head – but I demurred because it would have been showing favouritism.

The place was packed and the match turned out to be a nail-biter going right down to the wire. Dublin won a penalty in the last seconds of the game which, if they scored it, would have drawn the match instead of losing by 1-13 to 1-10. The kick was given by Wexford whistler Brian White after he adjudged Meath full-back Darren Fay had foot-blocked a shot by Mick Galvin.

Unfortunately for the taker, Paul Bealin, his shot after 73 minutes thundered against the underside of the crossbar and cannoned back to safety, leaving the Meath players delirious in victory and the Dubs crestfallen in defeat.

According to folklore the crossbar was still shaking when the Meath fans invaded the pitch to salute the victory some minutes later.

The other time I actually played, as in togged out, in Croke Park was for a charity event with two teams of so-called stars both from the GAA world and from other sports. Seemingly, I fitted into one of those.

My abiding memory of the occasion was the fact that I had a prominent businessman as a teammate who had an inflated opinion of both his athletic and football prowess. Every time anyone passed him a ball, he either fell over or allowed it slip out of his grasp.

I made up my mind after a few abortive raids down his wing that he could shout all he liked, but he wasn't getting another pass from me.

Near the end, I picked up the ball and made progress deep into the other team's defence. All the while I had this colleague demanding a pass and roaring at the top of his voice in my direction.

I kept going, in hindsight using him as a decoy, and then kicked my one and only point ever on the hallowed Croke Park sward.

This to me was history and as the umpire bent down to wave the white flag, I had a smile on my face as broad as the Liffey.

It didn't stop our friend from berating me for ignoring him in the build-up. "We scored a point," I told him in mitigation, trying to get him to see that things had turned out well.

"I know, but you should still have given me the pass," he said.

Many, many years later, I haven't quite worked out the logic of that repost.

Ken Doherty is an Irish professional snooker player, commentator and radio presenter. Since turning professional in 1990, the Dubliner has won six ranking tournaments, including the never-to-be forgotten 1997 World Snooker Championship in which he defeated Stephen Hendry, thereby inflicting Hendry's first loss in a world final. An intelligent tactician, Ken has compiled more than 350 century breaks in professional competition. Since 2009, he has combined his playing career with commentating and punditry work.

Magical Opening Of Semple Stadium Gate

Mike Hackett

The story I tell here was first recounted to me by John (Seán) O'Connor, former Principal of Piltown National School. It revolved around the great Waterford team of the fifties, when such names as Ned Power, Austin Flynn, Tom Cheasty, Frankie Walsh, Johnny Kiely and Philly Grimes were local and national icons. Their era culminated from a Deise point of view with the winning of the All-Ireland in 1959.

Seán and two of his pals set off for Semple Stadium in Thurles one summer Sunday morning in that time to cheer on their heroes against Cork. Demand for stand tickets was high but one of the pals managed to get his hands on three from his local club. Seán's green Morris Minor car transported the three friends to the game.

When approaching Thurles, the traffic slowed and for a while it was total gridlock. Car drivers entered different fields around the town that had been opened as temporary car parks for the day.

The delay was expected but the length of the virtual standstill caused panic to set in. The three friends began to wonder if they would miss the start, if not more, of the senior game?

After a while, Sean's two passengers decided to jump ship and walk, leaving him all alone to queue to get into a car-park field. Hastily, the others shouted that they would meet him outside Hayes' Hotel in the square when he got there.

When Seán finally parked the car and headed for the square in the middle of Thurles, he knew time was against him. With the huge crowd, his progress even then wasn't as quick as he would have liked, particularly as it had just occurred to him that the others had the tickets.

By the time he got to the square, there was no sign of the pair. It was now close to throw-in time. He headed for the stadium in the hope that he would either catch up with them or meet them at the gates. He was to be disappointed on both fronts.

What was he to do?

As he scratched his head and wondered, he noticed how a man had approached a small door in the wall of the stadium and wrapped loudly on it with his knuckls.

A voice from inside said as Gaelige: "Ce tá ann?"

"Cigire, Cumann Luth Cleas Gael," (An Inspector of the GAA), said the man outside. The door opened immediately and in he went.

Seán decided that he had only one way of seeing the match and taking his bravery in his hands, gave the door a commanding wrap. When asked: "Ce tá ann?" he replied: "Cigire, Cumann Luth Cleas Gael."

The door opened and Seán went in.

"Tá failte romhat," duirt an fear. ("Welcome" said the man behind the door).

Seán was presented with a premium seat amongst the dignitaries, bang in line with the middle of the pitch. He said he never enjoyed a match so much. It was a reward for his perseverance and inventiveness. To increase his happiness, following all his earlier anxiety, Waterford won the game.

The three pals later met back at the car-park field and from feeling guilty that they had let Seán down by not waiting for him, they ended up green with envy at the story he told – the first of many retellings in the rest of his lifetime.

Mike Hackett is a historian and author who lives in West-Waterford – between Ardmore and Youghal. He has written 19 books on social history, maritime disasters, children's stories and two life-stories of friends. A former An Post employee, he also contributes to the Dungarvan Observer, the Dungarvan Leader and youghalonline every week.

Cora Staunton And The Fist Of Fury She Avoided

Art Ó Suilleabháin

Cora Staunton was and probably remains the greatest player that Mayo Ladies Gaelic football ever produced. Her record in the annals of the GAA remain unbroken and unmatched.

She won six All-Ireland Gaelic football club finals with her club, Carnacon, four All-Ireland Ladies finals with Mayo, three National League titles with Mayo and was chosen as an All-Star on 11 occasions. She became a model for commitment and loyalty to a sport that was once only for the boys and men.

Cora played for club and county since she was 14. In fact, a new club, 'The Carnacon Ladies Gaelic Football Club' was established in the 1990s in a bid to harness the energies of this developing force, who bound herself to promoting the emerging participation of girls and young women in the skills of Gaelic football. Indeed, I have often heard it whispered in the stands at a Mayo men's Gaelic football match – "Cora should be in the forwards – she would be worth a few points at least."

My own story about Cora comes from a much earlier stage in her career. I was principal of Carnacon NS, a small rural primary school in Mayo. We were playing a Cumann na mBunscol Mayo match. As a small school with fewer than 70 pupils it was a seven-a-side game and we were allowed to have girls on the team.

This was in the late 1980s when boys still considered Gaelic football as their own domain and the girls were frowned upon but tolerated to make up the numbers. Cora was more than making up the numbers even as a young girl playing full-forward for a small three teacher school in south-west Mayo. She was the only girl on the Carnacon school team, in fact the only young girl on the field. During the first half Cora scored a goal and a number of points as we led the game quite handsomely.

The boys on the rival team were horrified. The two backs in particular received a ribbing from their own supporters that a girl was running rings around them. Early in the second half Cora scored another point. One of the backs had enough; he clenched his fists and announced to his teammate that he was going to settle this 'girl' on her next foray forward.

As her teacher and mentor on the side-line, I had overheard the exchange and I tried to warn her as she headed for their goal. The unfortunate corner-back confronted Cora and made a swing for her that Muhammad Ali would have been proud of. Cora deftly danced around him and his outstretched fist, soloed on and planted the ball into the back of the net with such force that even Stephen Cluxton, at the height of his brilliance, would have had a problem with it.

Needless to say, Carnacon went on to win the match and Cora's reputation began to bloom in the annals of GAA football.

Art Ó Suilleabháin is a native of Corr na Móna in Co Galway on the shores of Lough Corrib. He is a retired director of Mayo Education Centre and Fullbright teacher (2017-18) at the Catholic University of America in Washington DC. A father of six, Art is the author of a number of children's book.

The Viet Celts Are Coming

Connla Stokes

This is a story of how a motley crew of men from Hanoi and Saigon made history by unfurling the Vietnam flag at the 2007 Asian Gaelic Games in Singapore, ambushing everyone, including themselves.

Every now and then, as at least one poet would know, there are places where a thought might grow; Peruvian mines, Indian compounds, lime crevices. A disused shed in county Wexford.

So, for the sake of posterity, let us remember a time when a travelling evangelist met with a modest flock of Irish and English emigres in Hanoi and planted an unlikely thought that would grow, against the odds, in the heat and humidity of the Red River Delta.

And that thought?

To muster a squadron of men, in less than seven weeks, that could, and would, represent Vietnam (for the first ever time) at the next Asian Gaelic Games.

This historic summit occurred on the mezzanine of a mildew scented, all-purpose pub, where drinks were ordered, and where drinks were drunk, as the unlikely thought grew, and then grew some more.

Representing Vietnam at the games greatly appealed to the Hanoi contingent, but there were some practical and logistical concerns. It was 2007, a time when only a scant number of Irish men lived in the city, and even less of those men had played the sport. There were zero O'Neills balls in town, and a 19,000km round trip to Elvery's. Across the capital of Vietnam, there were also no grass pitches with grass growing, never mind the lack of high posts.

Nonetheless, the evangelist – a persuasive man by the name of Peter Ryan, a former player with Synge Street and, at that time, a missionary for the Asian County Board – was assured a Vietnam-based club could and would be formed and attend the games to be held that year in Singapore.

Having completed his mission, the evangelist slid over a bag with two spanking new O'Neills balls and then disappeared into the night. Just like that a club had been formed. Three reasonably wise men – Colm Ross of Ardee, Gareth O'Hara of Ashbourne, Sean Hoy of Enniskillen – were quickly elected onto a dedicatory board. Everyone in attendance made it into the committee, even those who'd only come for the beers.

The first item on their agenda? What to christen the club...

From a hastily compiled short list of monikers, there was one clear standout: The Viet Celts. It wasn't the simplicity of the name that sold it. "We just started to imagine the other teams shrieking 'The VC are coming! The VC are coming'," one of the founders would later recall.

On the same occasion, the inaugural committee also discussed recruitment. To have worthwhile training sessions, the inchoate club would need to convert some able-bodied men to the Gaelic code. They first turned to Minsk FC, a local football team named after a Belarusian two-stroke motorbike, a notoriously unreliable steed, once commonly found belching smoke across the northern mountains of Vietnam.

Known for their epic weekend drinking sessions (whether or not they had won a game, or were even playing a match), Minsk F.C. had a smattering of mercurial Irish footballing talents in the squad, who at least knew the terminology and (some of) the rules.

Among the club's books there were other, more tentative, connections to Gaelic sports and Ireland. A Glaswegian who had played shinty as a teen. A strapping Englishman whose great-grandfather Thaddeus Forde Dockery upped sticks and left Roscommon in the 19th century. A Londoner whose great grandfather was an O'Sullivan who swapped a life in Cork for the English capital's east end. They were all game to give Gaelic a go.

Others were, too, and so a training session was duly arranged. By then it was exactly six weeks until the tournament, and – more alarmingly – the month of May, when the stultifying heat of Hanoi could hit 40 degrees Celsius and render the city's population motionless. Training would be held at a shadeless, sun-baked 'grass' pitch (called 'Thuy Loi' which means, ironically enough, 'irrigation' in the local lingo), which was only free between 11am and 3pm. But that day a dozen men – the mad dogs of Hanoi – turned up, slathered in sunscreen, sweating buckets at the mere thought of chasing a ball.

After a brief explanation of the rules to the uninitiated, and while the rest of the city sensibly cooled off under electric fans, a historic throw in was made. Seconds later, Patrick Cooney of Cork soloed between a stationary American and a confused antipodean before rattling the dust off the well-worn net in a goal (with no keeper).

Over subsequent sessions, dribs and drabs of reinforcements bolstered numbers, mostly out of curiosity, and the promise of post-match refreshments. Some identified their place in the game straightaway. A broad-shouldered, red-haired Australian who bore the surname Lambert was a natural at cleaning out anyone with pretensions of soloing a distance. A schools rugby player raised among the northern pastures of Albion revealed a flair for punting the ball right into the 'breadbasket' of his teammates, which came as a surprise to him as a former front row forward.

Others who joined – a svelte French DJ with baggy basketball shorts; a handful of Englishmen, mostly soccer players and cricketers; an American whose punk band once supported Nirvana in Seattle; a man from Dublin 4. Well, they'd all need a little schooling from Colm Ross – the only resident of Hanoi to possess a pair of Gaelic shorts, a memento from his days as a county player in Louth – who had assumed the role of player-bainisteoir.

In the gruelling heat, Ross ran various drills and led pitch-side discussions to help the non-Irish V.C. wrap their heads around the basics. At the 'club house' (a local beer joint that operated under the shade of a Banyan tree down the road), there was a new vernacular to be taught, too: 'Steps!', 'Drive it in!', 'Take yer point!', 'Clatter'im!'

Word of the VC's formation had spread beyond the Hanoi parish to the port town of Haiphong, 120km to the east, where an electrical engineer by the name of Bernard Casey, once a champion hurler for Kilmacud Crokes, was stationed and tanning himself for free, "like yer man out of the Harp ad", as someone astutely noted. He gamely made a weekly trip and helped to inculcate some of his old school footballing skills into the minds of the recent recruits, including two Vietnamese soccer players. Let it be noted that two men by the names of Huy (pronounced 'whee', and fittingly a 'pocket rocket' of a player) and Toan were the first Vietnamese to kick the leather off an O'Neill's ball in Hanoi, and the first of many more.

To supplement Colm's crash course in Gaelic football, the club's inaugural chairman, Sean Hoy had asked a friend in the Old Country to send out some DVDs of classic matches. When the package arrived in Hanoi, the VC duly assembled at Finnegan's – the city's only Irish bar, owned by a Vietnamese woman called Moon, and managed by a young man called Fergus from Kildare.

The non-Irish were especially eager to sup on canned Guinness (for poetic inspiration) and feast their eyes on this exotic sport. Sadly, the official GAA disc wouldn't play on a machine hardwired to read bootlegged films from China. Class was dismissed (though the drinking continued).

With the tournament fast-approaching, ESBI, Terotech and Enterprise Ireland all made welcome donations to the campaign coffers. The club's treasurer, Gareth O'Hara crunched the numbers and declared there was just enough funds to cover some cheap red jerseys and subsidise AirAsia flights and shared rooms in the hallowed halls of YMCA Singapore for two teams.

Just a few more able-bodied men were needed to round up the numbers – a hasty communication was dispatched to Saigon. Three Irish emigres – all unknown quantities to those in Hanoi – would answer the call and agree to unify the country under a single flag.

The northern squadron all arrived in Singapore only to have more questions than answers. "Can you drink the water from the taps in Singapore?" asked a young man representing the Flemings of Castleisland, foreseeing the chronic dehydration to come. Another young man from Roscrea continued to explain the rules to his English and Australian comrades on the steps of YMCA, despite not being sure of them himself (he'd been reared for rugby, not Gaelic, in the Irish midlands).

As the whole squad walked wide-eyed through the bright lights of the Lion City it would be soon discovered the price of a pint was eight times the Hanoi average. An emergency meeting by the squad's leadership group was held. It would be agreed there was no shame in smuggling cans from 7/11 into bars for the duration of the weekend.

Little did the VC know what awaited them. On the eve of the tournament, a lavish reception with free-flow Guinness was held for all of the teams. Not believing their luck, each member of the squad felt duty bound to horse down a rake of pints before hitting the town.

There are no reliable accounts of when players returned to their beds, but suffice to say, the sun rose much earlier than requested. Yet every groggy, Guinness-scented Viet Celt was accounted for at the tournament, which went better than expected. One of the two teams even managed a 100% record in the group stages (winning all four games).

The AGG was a 7-a-side tournament in those days, leaving ample space for the heat-hardened VC's singular 'brand of play'. While the opposition teams often stuck to points, the VC continued to go for broke. They had also unearthed a secret weapon. One of the three Saigon players was Bernard Hartigan – son of Bernie Senior, and nephew to Pat, the two Limerick hurling legends. A fine hurler himself (a demonstration of his skill with the sliotar would be witnessed on the Sunday), Hartigan junior spent the weekend running rings around defenders and finding the top corner again and again.

But really it was the VC's collective, incomprehensible mishmash of talents and playing styles that proved to be Kryptonite for many of the opposing teams. Some of their antics didn't always go down well with the purists on the sidelines. At one stage, the shinty player of Glasgow, also a nifty winger when playing soccer, drew boos as he continually dribbled the ball on the ground. The French DJ was even throwing in some basketball moves while the Australian Lambert – despite stern words from exasperated referees – never managed to modify his AFL tackle technique and repeatedly 'broke up the game', instigating a shemozzle or three.

On the second-day of play, the great-grandson of Thaddeus Dockery certainly exemplified the foolhardy, diehard spirit of the VC – after splitting his head open, he rushed to a nearby hospital, flirted with a nurse called Mary, fell in love (with another patient's girlfriend), received his stitches while apologising for the stink of his socks (the same pair he'd worn the day before), and returned to the field of play (waving off a concerned referee), all in the space of two hours.

But arguably it was after heroic losses in the quarter final stages of the men's cup and bowl competitions, which ended their tournament, that the V.C. really hit their stride. After ample pitch-side pints, bouts of cramp, a few well deserved power naps, the whole platoon returned to the YMCA to plot one final ambush at the after party, an open-theme, fancy dress affair.

Before departing Hanoi, the Londoner with Corkonian roots, and whose grandfather had fought in World War 1, had purchased military clobber for one and all. So donning army surplus pith helmets, and clad in olive green shirts, the V.C. proudly marched toward the entrance of a beach club, brandishing a large red flag with the golden star, singing in unison: Viet Nam, Ho Chi Minh! Viet Nam, Ho Chi Minh.

Alas, when entering the club, they would discover none of the other teams had yet to arrive in their kimonos, silk pyjamas and Hawaiian grass skirts. An emergency meeting was held and the leadership group agreed the squadron should retreat to the bar, where drinks were ordered and where drinks were drunk.

"Let's just do that again at 1am when everyone is here," someone shouted. "Then they'll hear the VC coming," said another.

And that thought would grow, too... and the rest is history!

Postscript: After the AGG of 2007, the 'thought' of Gaelic football in Vietnam would continue to grow from year to year, with the VC introducing the game to a broad mix of nationalities in Hanoi. In 2008 a ladies' team (dubbed the 'Duracelts') would form, and at a later stage formally merge with the Viet Celts and start attending the AGG on an annual basis.

In 2010, a visionary from Mullingar by the name of Jim Kiernan would initiate a 'youth programme' and with the assistance of a Dubliner, Dave Cunnigham, and many others promoted the game at Vietnamese schools, which continue to play the sport to this day.

The sport also migrated south. A Saigon Gaels men's team formed in 2011 and a women's team in 2013. As for the 'VC', well, by all accounts, they're still a wild bunch, but they also got a bit better at football. In fact, in 2018, the Viet Celts men's football team won the Southeast Asian Games, besting Singapore in a final played in the savage heat and humidity of a May day.

Proudly watching from the sidelines were Colm Ross and several members of the original 2007 VC veterans, who first nurtured the thought of Gaelic in the Red River Delta, helping it to grow, and then flourish.

Connla Stokes is a Dubliner residing long-term in Vietnam, where he works as a journalist and writer. Having played rugby as a teen and soccer as an adult, he eventually got around to playing Gaelic in Hanoi with the Viet Celts. He is now a card-carrying member of Saigon Gaels in Ho Chi Minh City, where he's thinking about taking up hurling.

'I'm not giving away any secrets like that to Tipperary. If I had my way, I wouldn't even tell them the time of the throw-in'

Clare's Ger Loughnane

Trains And Boats And Pains

Ann Curran

I wonder how many players would cycle 80 miles (almost 130 kilometres) just to play a match. Well, that's what a legendary Westmeath player did back in the early days of the last century. How did it happen? Well, let's reel back to the beginning.

After a somewhat stuttering start the GAA finally got on a firm footing in Westmeath in 1903, with Mullingar Young Irelands winning that year's senior football title. From 1904, however, Westmeath's dominant force was the Riverstown Emmets club. Based in a little townland close to the village of Killucan, this club, in the period 1904 to 1914 annexed nine senior football titles, as well as senior hurling and junior football titles 1909.

Two of the most enduring and noteworthy members of this team were the Leech brothers, Lar and Ger. The unique record which Lar holds is that he twice captained Westmeath teams which won Leinster titles. The inaugural Leinster junior football championship of 1905 was won by Westmeath under Lar's captaincy, and when the title was won again in 1915, Lar completed a unique double.

Ger also served his county but is remembered for a different and singular feat. The Leech brothers had a select occupation which is now only a memory – they operated boats up and down the Royal Canal. These boats were used to convey goods and passengers between Dublin and Tarmonbarry in Longford, where the canal joins the River Shannon, serving towns such as Kilcock, Mullingar, Ballymahon and Longford along the way.

It happened that on a Sunday morning when the Westmeath team were due to play a match in Dublin, Ger Leech, who was selected, found himself on his boat near Ballymahon. No problem. He had his trusty bike with him, and he headed for Castletown-Geoghegan railway station, a 20-mile trip, to catch the Dublin train. Unfortunately, he didn't make it – he was just in time to see the smoke of the train as it disappeared down the track towards Mullingar.

Undeterred, however, he got back on his bike and took off for Dublin – a mere 60-mile spin. Local lore has it that he made it in time and played the match. After an 80-mile trip on his bike, it would be nice to be able to say that he gave an outstanding display. Maybe he did, but the local 'bealoideas' has no recollection, other than he lined out.

Still, it was an outstanding feat, the like of which will probably stand alone in the ranks of the GAA in Westmeath or anywhere else indeed and will probably never be replicated.

Ann Curran, nee Leech, is a granddaughter of Ger Leech in this story. A farmer's wife she lives in Fennor, Collinstown, Co Westmeath with her husband Paddy and their two sons and daughter. She has a wide range of interests including GAA, reading, gardening, farming and music.

'The Barbed Wire All-Ireland' Played In The Welsh Croke Park

Ben Dunne

This year all the talk in GAA circles was the playing of the two All-Ireland finals in July but in our house, we have been familiar with a July final for the 'All-Ireland' between Louth and Kerry which took place over a hundred years ago.

The reason it's so special is because our grandfather, Thomas Kelly (known as Tommy), and his brother and our granduncle, James (known as Jimmy), played for the Wee County against the Kingdom in a Welsh field at Frongoch in a final which became known as the 'All Ireland Behind Barbed Wire'.

Given that it occurred only months after the Easter Rising of 1916, it is worth explaining the circumstances in which the game came about. The Crown Forces in Ireland decided in an obvious state of panic to round up known Republican activists and sympathisers from all over the country but they didn't have the jail capacity in Ireland to accommodate all of them.

Accordingly, they decided to put 1,800 Irishmen on boats and sent them to England and then on to the Welsh village which now lies on the now disused Blaneau Ffestiniog railway line close to the village of Bala in Gwynedd, North Wales.

The place was used as a similar base to intern German soldiers during World War 1 when it was divided into a North Camp and a South Camp with the two separated by a road that ran through the middle.

Among the well-known Irish historical names to be housed there were Michael Collins, Arthur Griffiths, Richard Mulcahy, Sam Maguire and Terence McSwiney as well as famed Kerry footballer

Dick Fitzgerald, after whom the stadium in Killarney is named.

Another person of note sent to Frongoch was Jim Nowlan, who was actually President of the GAA at the time of his incarceration and has the unique distinction of being the longest serving president of the association from 1901 to 1921, a period of 20 years. In 1927, he was honoured by his own county when they named their county grounds Nowlan Park in Kilkenny City after him.

My granduncle Jimmy was captain in the Old IRA B Company Fourth North Division under the command of Frank Aiken and my grandfather was in that company as well. They were quite inseparable, whether it was playing football for Hitchestown GAA and Louth or fighting for Irish freedom.

There were men from every county in Ireland in the internment camp and after a number of weeks in which they were largely confined to prison cells, they were allowed out to exercise. This the young men embraced with gusto and an effort to formalise sporting activity was made when a Games Committee was established in the South Camp with fellow Louth man, Joseph Stanley from Drogheda, the Hon. Secretary.

The field where they played in the South Camp was christened 'Croke Park' by the Irish lads and under Stanley's watch good records were kept of the games played there which have survived to the present day. After it became clear that the prison authorities would not countenance hurling because of the fear that the hurls might be used as weapons against them, it was overwhelmingly agreed that there would be an All-Ireland football series.

Many of the men, our own forbears among them, were good Gaelic football exponents and according to my Granduncle Jimmy, they used to look forward to games as if they were playing in competitions at home. My grandfather was different to his brother in that he never spoke of anything that went on while they were interned, though he would laugh at Jimmy's accounts and especially when he was leaving the house. My mother Ann recalls that every time when Jimmy would be about to exit, he'd say goodbye and always shout "Up The Republic" back into the people.

The games began with a round-robin league competition among the various huts and dormitories with teams named after leaders in the Rising. After six games, two teams were left standing, with Louth captained by Thomas Burke and Kerry, nicknamed the Leprechauns and captained by Dick Fitzgerald, taking part in the Wolfe Tone Cup Final.

According to reports it was compulsory for all the internees to attend with a humorous note advising them to "leave their wives and sweethearts at home." The match, refereed by Maurice Collins, started at 2.30pm and after two 20 minutes halves, with my grandfather and granduncle manning midfield for Louth, it was Kerry who came out on top by the minimum of margins.

Volunteer and later well-known author, Séamus Ó Maoileóin, explained the importance of the whole experience after the final when he said: "There was never half as much spirit, fun and energy seen in the all-Ireland finals as that which was displayed at Frongoch."

Michael Collins, who would later become Minister for Intelligence and Finance in the First Dáil and Chief-of-Staff of the Provisional Free State Forces during the Civil War, was there for the final and took part on the same day in the athletics programme. In fact, it is recorded that his team won the 100 yards sprint relay with Collins clocking under 11 seconds for the event. He also won the long and triple jumps on a great sporting day for the Irish banged up in Frongoch for that period.

Frongboch Final Line-Ups

Louth – William Atkinson, Dundalk; Sean Butterly, Milltown, Dunleer, Tom Matthews (Vice-Capt) Ardee, James Layng, Dunleer; Arthur O'Neill, Dundalk, Nicholas Butterly, Milltown, Dunleer, James Jennings, Dundalk; Thomas Kelly, Grangebellew, Dunleer, James Kelly, (Do); Daniel Tuite, Dundalk, Michael Donnelly, Cooley, Thomas Burke (Capt), Drogheda; Peter Clifford, Dundalk, Patrick Kerr, (Do), Owen McGeough, (Do).

Kerry – Dick Fitzgerald (Capt) Killarney; Tralee, Willie Horgan Killarney, Mick Spillane, (Do) Michael John O'Sullivan; (Do) Pat O'Shea, (Do), Paddy Cahill (Vice-Capt), Tralee, Willie Mullins, (Do); James Wall, (Do), Michael Doyle, (Do); Dan Healy, (Do), Michael J and James Moriarty, Dingle; Michael Knightly, Castleisland, Tommy McEllistrim, Ballymacelligott, J Byrne, Adfert.

Ben Dunne is a native of Grangebellow, Dunleer Co Louth and is a local postman in the Drogheda area. He is an avid GAA fan and would love to see Kerry open the new GAA pitch in the county playing against Louth as in Wales.

Dropped By His Own Club, He Starred For Opponents In Final

John Dowling

My uncle Tommy Dowling of Killeen, Moutmellick, Co Laois was a larger-than-life character with few equals on or off the GAA pitch. He was born on Good Friday in April 1913 during the tumultuous events of the Dublin lock out led by Big Jim Larkin.

His sporting exploits unusually extended well beyond his native parish. In 1930, he helped Emo to a minor football title. In 1934, he was very much to the fore in forming the Derrydavy club and played a big role as captain when they won the junior hurling championship at the first attempt.

The following year Derrydavy reached the intermediate final only to be beaten by Portlaoise. In 1939 Tommy helped Mountmellick junior footballers qualify for the county final where they were narrowly beaten by Mountrath.

Two years later in 1941 he created a record in the Mountmellick club by winning both junior football and hurling titles – the hurlers beat Clonsalee, Raheen on their way before accounting for Ballinakill in the final while the footballers, with Tommy as captain, overcame The Heath, Portlaoise, Ballyroan, Kellyville and ultimately Ballyfin. They also won the Feis Shield and medals in 1942.

The following year saw Tommy at his notorious best. His Mountmellick club reached the intermediate football final at O'Moore Park which was not played until March 1944.

In the interim, Tommy, now in his thirties, had spent some time away in England working and on return was considered not to be as sharp as in former years. Despite his history of always delivering on the day and his unique ability to lead others on to greater things, the local selectors decided not to pen his name in as part of the starting side.

Not unusually at the time when often a team was only announced once the players had congregated in a dressing-room before the match, Tommy set out from home for the game believing that, like always in his career, he would be on the pitch for the throw-in.

Arriving at the dressing-room, boots in hand and hungry for action, he was pulled aside by one of the braver backroom men to be told that he'd have to settle for a place on the subs' bench.

Uncle Tommy was both shocked and angered at this bombshell and needless to say all hell broke loose. The commotion that ensued alerted the opposing team's mentors that all was not well in the Mountmellick camp.

The Heath team had taken to the field and after a few minutes play, Tommy was approached by them and asked if he would like to play for them.

The hero of so many Mountmellick moments accepted the offer and there was an air of unreality among both sets of supporters when they saw him running onto the pitch sporting the Black and Amber of The Heath. In a blaze of glory, the dropped Mountmellick talisman led his normal opponents to a famous victory over his own club team.

That year he won a senior hurling medal with Portlaoise. Over the years he played minor and senior for Laois, and amassed 14 county titles in a star-studded career.

In the early 1930s while studying in Cork, he won a Cork senior hurling championship medal with the famous Blackrock club, an honour achieved by very few Laois men in their lifetimes.

In his funeral homily, former Minister of Justice Charlie Flanagan, mentioned Tommy's life-long devotion to the party but largely dwelt on Tommy's character and how his verbal jousting and sharp turn of phrase was always present whether in pursuit of sporting or political goals. A true non-conformist, he was a naturally gifted storyteller who was never known to have lost an argument, always enjoying the first word and never missing the last.

For a man who grew up to journey across Canada as a freight operator for the national railway line, he still managed to pack a lot into his Gaelic sporting life in Ireland when he returned.

The farmer, insurance rep, beet agent and much travelled raconteur once announced to a large gathering in Mountmellick that

"Ireland was the best place on earth to live", adding that he knew because he had seen the two sides of life during his time in North America.

John Dowling, of Derrydavy, Mountmellick, Co Laois died suddenly on June 28 this year, months after he had sent on this piece about his much-loved uncle Tommy and was delighted that it would be part of this GAA collection. Ar Dheis Dé go raibh a anam dílis.

The Floating Ball

Jamesie Murphy

In 1938, Tullogher were playing Glenmore in the semi-final of the Kilkenny Senior Football Championship at Thomastown. The pitch there is quite close to the river Nore.

On the day, the river was in full spate after torrential overnight rain with the torrents of water swilling from bank to bank. Two unusual things happened during the course of the match.

Firstly, the Tullogher football got punctured and was deemed useless for competition. Then with about 10 minutes left in the game, Glenmore, playing with their ball, led by four points and had by far the better of the exchanges.

An altercation broke out and blows were exchanged and then a Tullogher player grabbed the football and with a mighty kick lofted it into the river, where it was immediately swept away – never to be seen again.

The match had to be abandoned and a replay ordered, which was won by Glenmore in the inland pitch at Barrett's Park New Ross and refereed in fine style by Sergeant Stephen Keher (Eddie's father).

Jamesie Murphy is now 86 years old and is a former hurler, footballer, referee and club historian.

Fights, Camera And Action
As Terry Wogan Looked On

Maria Nolan

Several years ago, when I was secretary of the Rapparees/ Starlights Club at Bellefield, Enniscorthy, we received a request from the BBC looking for permission to film a hurling match at our grounds.

Bellefield GAA grounds has second-pitch status within the county and was frequently used when our county ground Wexford Park was under renovation or unplayable.

Legendary Irishman and BBC broadcaster Terry Wogan, RIP, was in Ireland filming for a television series he was making entitled 'My Ireland.' He was in Wexford and wanted to film a hurling match. He met up with the late Billy Rackard, one of the famous Rackard brothers of Rathnure, who brought him to Bellefield. On offer was a game between Billy's home club Rathnure and Half Way House, Bunclody, who were hurling in the senior championship at the time.

Billy introduced me to Terry and asked if I would look after the camera crew and accommodate them in any way I could. Naturally, I was more than happy to oblige.

The main cameraman, whose name was Scott, sought a good vantage point to film. I took him onto our balcony and offered what to my mind was the best and safest view of the entire pitch.

He said he'd prefer to be closer to the action and pointed to a spot on the sideline. I enquired if he'd ever filmed a hurling game before at close quarters, explaining that the sideline might not be the best place to position his very expensive equipment. I suggested it might be better if we discussed options with Mr. Wogan as I felt he would have a greater understanding of hurling sidelines.

Scott was indignant: "I'll have you know I filmed football games all over the world and have never had the slightest damage to myself, my camera or my equipment."

"That may well be," I said, "but it's my job to see that you film from the best and safest position, which is why I still think we should get Mr. Wogan's opinion."

Terry was an absolute diplomat and totally understood my concerns; on the other hand he didn't want to go against such an experienced cameraman. With a typical look of mischief on his face, he whispered to myself and Billy: "Eh, any chance we could ask the lads to take it easy out there?"

We burst out laughing and Billy quipped: "Terry, do you realise that right now both sets of selectors are in their respective dressing rooms banging hurls on tables and working their players into a frenzy telling them that they want them to go out there and put their lives on the line... for the honour of the club ...and the jersey... and the parish... and their parents ...and their families... and all who went before them... and you want me to ask them to take it easy?"

"Well, when you put it as eloquently as that," Terry replied, "it seems like it's every man for himself out there including our cameraman Scott... so let the fun and games begin!"

Feeling vindicated by staying on the sideline, a triumphant Scott set up his equipment with great aplomb, causing much amusement and comment from spectators.

Comments such as: "I hope he didn't pay too much for all that stuff," or "is he really expecting to stay there for the whole game?" or "there'll be skin and hair flying here in a minute and that fella better be able to run fast," and lastly "that poor soul hasn't a clue if he thinks he's gonna be left there."

About 10 minutes into the game there was a slight fracas in front of him on the sideline between two players which a delighted Scott filmed up close and personal. He even turned around to give me the thumbs up sign message to emphasise that he had been right in choosing the spot.

I waved back with a knowing smile ...and waited.

Unbeknownst to anyone, I had taken the precaution of having two men on standby to run to his aid as soon as the real row broke out, which of course it did, with about 20 minutes to go when everything, especially the honour of each parish, was at stake.

Players ran from every corner of the pitch to add to the melee that had begun over a sideline ball just in front of our cameraman. Hurls and fists swung in all directions, mentors jumped over players to get into the debacle under the pretence of separating the offenders, spectators scaled the wire not to be excluded from it, the referee and linesman threw their arms in the air and left them to it.

A shocked Scott belatedly understood our reticence as he tried desperately to gather his equipment and escape the bedlam. With a look of sheer terror on his face, he had to defend himself as well as his valuable equipment in making good his escape.

In the middle of the fracas, I glanced over to where Terry was sitting on the balcony and was amused to see him convulsed in laughter.

Luckily, my two trusted bodyguards did their job and managed to extricate Scott from the danger before he became part of the passion play being enacted in front of his lens. No damage was done to man or camera.

As a postscript, Scott was more than happy to do the remainder of his filming from the balcony alongside Terry, who tried manfully to keep a straight face while in his company for the rest of the game.

Enniscorthy native Maria Nolan is a staunch GAA follower, having served as secretary of Rapparees/Starlights for over 20 years is the current PRO and Healthy Club Officer. Married to Jim, she is a Department of Agriculture employee, who also writes prodigiously and has had short stories, poetry and Travel published.

'Pat Fox out to the forty and grabs the sliotar. I bought a dog from his father last week. Fox turns and sprints for goal, the dog ran a great race last Tuesday in Limerick. Fox to the 21 fires a shot, it goes to the left and wide...and the dog lost as well'

Micheál Ó Muircheartaigh

Who Kildare's Wins On
The Road To Ardee

Mae Leonard

I was on my way to Ardee with three fine-looking men. One was my husband, the driver, the other two were Kildare footballers. We were on our way to a match as spectators and the footballers were availing of a lift with us.

I am not exactly sure what team Kildare was about to play but it must have been Louth. The talk was football, football, football. And I was wishing that I had stayed at home. Until, that was, when one of our passengers began to hum a song. It was very familiar. I dug into my memory bank and joined him humming and came up with a couple of lines: -

'For the sake of health, I took a walk last week at early dawn

I met a jolly turfman as I slowly jogged along.'

Where had I heard that before?

"The Turfman from Ardee. Dermot O'Brien," my husband said.

Dermot O'Brien! Of course. And wasn't that ballad just perfect for the road we were on? And add to that, the fact that Dermot O'Brien was born in Ardee.

Gosh, I remember as a teenager thumbing around to the different places he and The Clubmen played. My friends and I were massive fans of his music. If my parents knew at that time how far we went with only our thumbs to get us to the different ballrooms and back, I would never have been allowed outside the door. Thank God, we were always lucky and there was never even as much as a scary moment in all those risky journeys. It never even entered our heads that we could be in any kind of danger.

We danced and sometimes gathered around the stage to sing along with Dermot O'Brien – North to Alaska, The Rocks of Bawn, The Merry Ploughman and of course, The Turfman from Ardee. Yes, indeed, Dermot O'Brien was a wizard on the accordion. He could make it talk.

"Louth," one of the lads in the back shouted. "He played football for Co. Louth. In fact, he was captain of the team that won the 1957 All Ireland. And a funny thing, he was suffering with an injury from a previous match. His shoulder, I think, and he needed some medical attention on All-Ireland Sunday so he travelled to Croke Park by car rather than go on the bus with the team. The story goes that he was late arriving and the official on the gate refused to let him in! He wouldn't believe him that he was the captain of Louth."

The other lad on the road to Ardee with us piped up: "He got in, of course, and I remember them talking about him at home, he used to tape two of his fingers together so that he wouldn't injure them. He needed them for his accordion."

The smallest county in Ireland beat the biggest county that Croke Park Day in 1957 with Dermot O'Brien at the helm. He was in huge demand as an entertainer from then on but in 1960 the inevitable happened. He broke a finger and had to call it a day on his football career and eventually focussed on his livelihood of music.

I remember him well.

As we turned into Ardee for the Kildare football match we were singing :

'The axel never wanted grease but one year out of three
It's a real old Carrick axel says the turfman from Ardee'

Once inside the GAA grounds we found a good place to sit but before we could settle ourselves, a Kildare official called my beloved aside. They were short a player. Would he? Could he? And with a bit more persuasion my well-known Limerick hurler was in a Lilywhite jersey playing football for Kildare where we had come to live.

Kildare won that day in Ardee and who was the man who scored the winning goal?

You guessed it. But he was playing illegally as he had not signed the transfer papers. Who was to know? Mícheál Ó Muircheartaigh, that's who. We heard it on the radio on the way back to Kildare. "I thought Joe Leonard scored the winning goal but he modestly denied it."

You should have seen our faces on the road home from Ardee!

Mae Leonard is a proud Limerick woman who has lived all her married life in Kildare. Once upon a time she played camogie for Limerick and captured the heart of a Limerick hurler. The well-known journalist is also an award-winning author of short stories and poetry.

Rivals Won Because We Had A Girl In Our Goal

Tommy Coady

It was the early sixties when Paulstown played Goresbridge in an underage hurling final seven-a-side. The fact that it was two local teams competing meant there was great rivalry and the game drew a large attendance. With a number of the Paulstown players injured, our manager, the late John Byrne, decided he would play my sister Anna in goal, as John knew her strengths from the camogie fields.

The game itself was very evenly matched and Anna played a significant part in it. At the full-time whistle, Paulstown was victorious by three points. There was great excitement when we received the winner's medals but then came the bombshell when Goresbridge lodged an objection. It was lodged on the grounds that Paulstown had a girl playing in goal and the Goresbridge forwards would not go near the goal because of that.

Unfortunately for us, Goresbridge won the objection and the match had to be replayed and we were not so lucky the second time, as we lost the game. Anna went on to play senior camogie with Gowran and had many great victories. She also lined out for the Kilkenny juniors before heading to train as a nurse in Romford, Essex. Anna is now retired from nursing and lives with her husband Michael in Moate in Co Westmeath. They have three grown up sons, Brian, John and Mike.

Tommy Coady is a native of Paulstown, Co Kilkenny and married to Therese and living in Lucan. Now retired, he spends most of his time gardening, following the GAA and going to the races. An avid fan of Kilkenny hurling, he has written many tributes to teams over the years and is particularly proud of the four-in-a-row song he composed as a tribute to that brilliant team.

Tracing My Hurling Career
With Grandson Theo

Joe Leonard

Some years ago, at the rear of his home on the Curragh of Kildare, I was trying to impart and demonstrate some of the skills of hurling to my young grandson, Theo. He posed a question which caused me a lot of thought and deep reflection – "Grandpa," says he, "when did you finish hurling?"

Those of us who played hurling from a young age can easily remember when we finished with the game in a physical sense. However, most of us are still hurling in a mental sense. Nowadays, when watching those super fit muscular young players on our TV screens, we follow the play with the same mental intensity we did in our playing days.

My grandson, young Theo, wouldn't be interested in listening to my philosophical ramblings so I told him the story of my last game.

The 60s and 70s were times when emigration from Ireland was prevalent. In the early 70s, one of my younger brothers, John, who had recently married Evelyn, decided to leave the green fields of Limerick and head for the distant plains of Australia. They started their new life in Melbourne.

In 1977, I was offered a job on a two-year contract in Saudi Arabia. I thought that such a move was the end of my hurling career, probably a better way to finish than being dropped to the subs bench. So, when that contract ended, I decided that on my way home it would be practical to detour via Australia and visit John, Evelyn and their first-born son, Dermot.

After the hugs, kisses and welcome at Melbourne Airport, John casually said to me: "You're playing a hurling match next Sunday".

It transpired that the inter-state GAA games were being held in Western Australia and that the State of Victoria, being short of hurlers, were happy to add me to their panel, irrespective of my ability or fitness.

Now, John had been a good hurler in his younger days, his greatest achievement was that he played on Limerick's Sexton Street CBS Team which won a Harty Cup. My admiration for his win was tinged with a slight envy. My appearance with Sexton Street CBS in a Harty Cup final ended in defeat by St. Flannan's of Ennis.

"Do you know where Melbourne is?" I ask Theo.

"Australia," he replies.

"And do you know where Perth is in Australia?"

The blank look on his face had me reaching for an atlas.

Together, we found Melbourne and traced the long long road all the way to Perth in Western Australia. And I continued my story.

It was the longest distance that I and the other players on the plane had travelled to play a game of hurling. Three and a half hours flying time. A journey that took us south of the Murray/Darling River, across the Great Victoria Desert over Lake Eyre and the Great Australian Bight and finally touching down in Perth on the shores of the Indian Ocean.

Though the people in Perth were warm, friendly and inviting, our State of Victoria Team resisted temptation and focused on the next day's match against New South Wales. After all, we could only muster 14 players and I found myself positioned as one of the two-man full forward line. If our team was described as a 'motley crew,' one could readily agree.

"Grandad, Grandad, what does a 'motley crew' mean?"

"Well, young Theo, listen to this."

"Our centre-back was an old man. He was at least 55 years old but his skill and talent were still obvious and his two wing backs were fit agile young lads whose lack of ability with a hurley suggested that they came from parishes in Ireland where only football was played. That's what you could call a 'motley crew.'

"On the rare occasions that the sliotar reached our full-forward area, I managed to scramble it over the goal line. We lost the match but all players were happy to have participated in a unique game in an exotic location.

"Theo, your Grand-Uncle John wrote to the family back in Ireland and told them of my participation in the game. He reported that: 'My brother Joe scored a goal in Perth Australia.'"

The match result did not play on my mind but my emotions were twofold. The first was a deep sadness that so many Irish, young and old, were forced to leave their families, friends and homeland and relocate to a far distant land.

The second was admiration and a sense of pride that they brought an important part of their culture and tradition with them and were prepared to organise and nurture a GAA club and an organisation that would be a haven of friendship and welcome for future Irish immigrants to Australia.

Buíochas dos na hÉireannaigh sán Astráil.

Joe Leonard is a native of Limerick and the eldest of a family of eight where hurling was the sole focus of interest growing up. He played on the Harty Cup team with Sexton Street CBS and also lined out at centre-back on the Limerick team that won the All-Ireland minor title in 1958. His hurling career continued for a number of years later with the Limerick Senior Hurling Team.

'The first half was even, the second half was even worse'

Pat Spillane reflects on an Ulster Championship clash

The Hat Man Of The Hill

Aidan Grennan

The man on the hill looked kind of familiar when I saw him that Sunday in O'Connor Park, Tullamore. Yet a second look told me he didn't look familiar at all. Could I have seen him at a classic Leinster final – on a scorching July afternoon – or at a run-of-the-mill league game in dreary November? I couldn't decide either way.

It was June 1985, and I was at the Leinster Senior hurling quarter-final double header. Laois were taking on Dublin while Westmeath had the frightening task of tackling Kilkenny. Being from Offaly, I could enjoy the day's games, without a breathing apparatus. I hadn't to endure the torture of watching Offaly being taken down to the wire, or indeed taking us down to the wire, as they often did in the early '80s.

The Man on the Hill got chatting in the way only GAA followers understand. "Who do you fancy today?" he asked. Not knowing what county man he was, I played cautiously. "I think Laois will do it in the first game, but if Dublin get a good start, who knows? After that, we can pencil in Kilkenny." By 'pencilling in Kilkenny', I prayed he wasn't from Westmeath.

I formed the notion this man was an Offaly native, and was, like me, just in to view the opposition for a few weeks' time, in the Leinster semi-finals. The draw declared the winners of Dublin and Laois would meet Wexford, while the Faithful county would meet the winners from Kilkenny and Westmeath. Unless a miracle greater than the sun dancing over Fatima in 1917, it had to be Kilkenny.

Just then, as the Dublin and Laois midfielders lined up for the throw-in, my friend dived his right hand into his pocket and produced a Laois cap! My hurling fan was a Blue and White man, after all. Indeed, once the ball was thrown in, he shouted on every Laois hurler, never once referring to his match programme.

On and on he shouted, occasionally roaring, as if he were a soccer commentator from Uruguay, at the 1950 World Cup final against Brazil.

My man was kind of hoarse by the time the short whistle sounded. And, when the long whistle sounded, he could have used the stronger brand of Lemsip. Laois had won well, and he smiled from ear to ear, like a present-day emoji.

The first game brought the customary analysis among those fans around me and others queueing for the toilets. When the mystery man returned, he had two choc-ices. Neither came my way. Astonishingly, he opened one and hid the other in his pocket!

Westmeath and Kilkenny each paraded their 15 hurlers, and soon the national anthem rang out. Just then came another surprise. With my mystery supporter croaking like a harvest frog – despite having devoured his second choc-ice – he now removed the Laois cap and replaced it with a Westmeath one! I couldn't make sense of all this. Was he a Laois man living in Westmeath or a Westmeath man living in Laois? Or maybe his parents originated in both counties.

As the late Michael O'Hehir often said 'we'll follow the play', and we did. Kilkenny, as expected, put Westmeath to the sword, closing out the game with a huge score of 1-30, to 1-10.

O'Connor Park had emptied considerably by the end of the second match. Dublin fans had begun leaving at half-time, while several Westmeath people were moving towards Kilbeggan, by the time Kilkenny had opened their shoulders, with 25 minutes still on the clock.

Meanwhile, me and my colleague of 'dual caps fame' stayed on to the bitter end, chatting as we left the venue as to how the semi-finals would go. We both agreed Laois would trouble Wexford. (They did more than that...they beat them).

Beating Kilkenny in any championship season is a noteworthy occasion for most counties. In 1985, Offaly rallied from nine points down in the second-half, to level with the Cats: 3-18 each. Offaly had their homework done for the replay, and won by six points: 1-20 to 0-17.

As me and my newly-found friend advanced towards the gates on the Arden Road, the third surprise of the day was lying in wait.

He removed the Westmeath cap and tucked it into the same pocket that housed its Laois companion. It was time I satisfied my inquisitive nature by finding out the full story.

"Don't mind me asking," I began, "but how are you connected to Laois and Westmeath?"

His reply again brought forward his emoji face. "I'm not connected at all. I'm a staunch Offaly fan, but I love supporting the neighbours!"

So that was it, then. As dedicated a hurling man as you'd find anywhere.

"Well fair dues to you," I said. "You had me confused."

As I journeyed towards my car on Convent Road, the words of the late Galway footballer and author Jack Mahon, came into my mind: "The GAA will never die." As long as we have supporters like the Man Of The Hill, it's true, our games will live forever.

Aidan Grennan is a native of Rahan, Co Offaly. Married to Martina for 40 years, he has a huge collection of GAA books and books of general interest. In 2018, he published his first book 'Memories of Rahan.'

'Anthony Lynch the Cork corner back will be the last person to let you down - his people are undertakers'

Micheál Ó Muircheartaigh

The Making Of The Green Above The Red

Sean Hallinan

Less than a quarter of a mile from my home stand the ruins of Towerhill House which belonged to the Blake family.

The Blakes were descendants of one of the Twelve Tribes of Galway and are credited with having reintroduced Gaelic Football to County Mayo, by sponsoring a two-hour match on their lands in 1885.

This is verified by a report in the Connacht Telegraph dated December 26, 1885 which covers a game played between Carnacon and Ballyglass at Towerhill the previous Sunday which unbelievably (between close neighbours) ended with a party! "Colonel Blake and his lady looked on, admiring the revival of one of our ancient national sports, and the former generously ordered from his cellar a barrel of porter to refresh both the vanquished and the victors!"

In a following Telegraph match report dated January 29, 1887 it stated that the local team, Towerhill, wore the Red above the Green that was to become the colours of the Mayo county team. The positioning of the stripes of the jersey was by no means an accident – it goes back to the very foundation of the GAA itself.

Colonel Blake insisted that Towerhill and Carnacon teams line out in strips that featured Green above Red, in reference to Dr Croke's fear, expressed in his letter to Michael Cusack, that if the Irish did not stand up to express their nationality, we might all just as well "clap hands for joy at the sight of the Union Jack, and place 'England's bloody red' exultantly above the green."

The January 29, 1887 newspaper report states that Towerhill and Cornfield "met in a field in Towerhill Demesne. The ground was very tastefully marked out, the 'Green above the Red' the Towerhill motto, waving gracefully all round, the same badge worn by the guards with strong wire enclosing the whole area!"

Towerhill won the match as the report goes on to state "at the expiration of play, after taking on three fresh men, Cornfield scored nil while their opponents, under the colours they love best and which their eyes are hot to see, realise the position they gave it that day, secured two goals".

The nationalist fervour of the above lines indicates that the adoption of the 'Green above the Red' was indeed a strong political statement by the Towerhill men. The report goes on to state that amazingly "at least 2,000 persons were present, among whom many were the elite of this and surrounding parishes."

The above strong sentiments are the reason that the Mayo colours are 'Green above Red.' This was strongly reaffirmed by Dick Walsh in the 1940s who was county chairman. Dick, a native of Balla, had been an ardent republican who had served time in jail after the 1916 rising. Dick was a TD up to 1951 when he was replaced by the All-Ireland winning Mayo captain, Sean Flanagan.

The 'Green above the Red' colours so valued by Dr Croke and Colonel Blake were undoubtedly selected in response to the Young Irelander Thomas Davis' poem... (*See Poetry section, Page 356*)

Mayo GAA teams and their legions of supporters can indeed be very proud of the heritage and tradition that lie behind our county colours. Mayo teams have valiantly tried in recent decades to ensure the green above the red reach the very summit and win Sam each September.

In 1989, I took some Fuchsia from Towerhill and scattered it on the sward of Croke Park after our All-Ireland defeat by Cork. In return I also brought a small dug up scraw home and embedded the bit of soil on my front lawn! Some say charms don't work... and yet we live in hope... we are getting close... the dream lives on!

Sean Hallinan has worked for years in the Museum for Country Life, Turlough Park, Castlebar and his hobbies include following GAA games and writing. See poem, Page 388.

A Galway Win, A Holy Picture And A Wholly War

Theresa McGann

The scene is my home village of Ballindereen in Co. Galway, the year is 1956 and the occasion is the All-Ireland Football final between ourselves and Cork.

There is only one wireless for those of us who have not gone to Croke Park.

Michael O'Hehir's commentary on Radio Éireann allows us follow every kick of the ball. All roads had led to our near neighbours in the village at O'Connors' Shop and Pub.

On that particular Sunday many, many men have congregated around the open kitchen window and are either sitting, standing or kneeling outside in the street to hear the commentary.

It's pre-television times and we're all excited that we can tune into what's happening in the game being played on the far side of the country.

We're even more delirious when Galway win. It's a joyous scene as older folk hug each other in glee while the younger set jump and dance with joy around 'The Cross' – there were few cars then to interrupt us.

The following week's Connacht Tribune had extensive coverage of the victory, with a team photo in black and white, where all players signed their autographs under or over where they were pictured.

In my keen teen enthusiastic mind, I said to myself "this picture has to be framed."

So (God forgive me) I took down a holy picture of some great saint, removed it from its frame and placed the Galway team photo inside.

What followed was a 'holy' war in our house for a time. I took my punishment for my sacrilegious act but to her eternal credit my dear mum Mary Ann (R.I.P), never asked me to replace the sacred picture... and the 'boys' hung proudly on the wall for many's the year.

I would like to still have it as a memento of my childhood cheeky stunt but unfortunately it got lost over the years.

Nine years later, I had my holidays booked in advance from my job as a midwife in London to ensure I'd get home in plenty of time for the 1965 All-Ireland final where Galway were going for a two-in-a-row against the same opposition as the year before, Kerry.

I took my flight on Aer Lingus to Dublin on the Friday afternoon. However, the weather was atrocious and the severe heavy rain prevented us from being able to land in Dublin. Instead, we were diverted to Shannon Airport.

By now it was well into Friday night and overnight hotel accommodation was arranged for all the passengers. The motley crew re-assembled at the airport early on the Saturday morning. Aer Lingus had decided to take west and south bound passengers by taxi to their destinations. That posed a dilemma for me, as first and foremost on my mind was getting to the match on Sunday.

If I went home to Ballindereen in Galway, I would need to cycle to Ardrahan to get the train to Dublin on Sunday morning. That didn't appeal too much, so my 'yuppy' head took over and I decided I'd fly back to Dublin instead. Galway won of course and I was on a high like all the other maroon fans when I arrived home for the remainder of my holidays.

My poor Dad John Flaherty (RIP) was a great man to tease me and said to everyone he met – "What do you think of a cailín who was in Shannon on Friday and didn't come home to her own house until Monday."

They had a laugh at my expense but sure we all had the last laugh together when we won the three-in-a-row the following year against Meath... and yes, I got to that final too but took a less circuitous route on that occasion.

By then, I was working in Portiuncula Hospital, Ballinasloe as midwife having come back from England. I opted for night duty so I could be free to go to the All-Ireland. I even got a Hogan Stand ticket from a patient's husband who couldn't make the journey because his wife was still in hospital after she'd had a section.

That was my luck, I had a great seat beside a priest. I still have the programme and it cost one shilling.

PS There is no sport to equal the game of hurling.

Theresa McGann (nee Flaherty) is in her early eighties and is thankful to have so many memories following Galway's county and club teams down the decades. A former nurse and midwife, she has three grown up sons and five grandchildren.

Gaels, Gales And Winning Appeals

Pádraig MacMathúna

Back in the day, when I attended county board meetings, there was no such thing as an appeals committee, which are part and parcel of how business is done today.

It meant that a full county board meeting would sit to hear all appeals. One case I remember involved Shannon Gaels, whose team all cycled to Kilkee to fulfil a fixture.

This was a 20-mile cycle and, as it happened on the day, it was into a strong head-wind.

Normally in that time, if you had a bike, you'd do the distance in an hour and a half. Against the wind, the journey took over two hours. It meant the team was late arriving at the appointed pitch and were feeling more tired than usual.

Despite this, the Gaels won the game and were aghast when the opposition objected, citing that they hadn't fielded in time, as per the rules. Cruelly, the opposition was awarded the victory in the boardroom.

Pádraig MacMathúna is a native of Cooraclare and turned 88 in June, 2022. He spent all his working life in Ennis with Clare County Council. Pádraig has served as President and Irish Officer for Clare County Board and was a long-time editor of the county's annual GAA book.

Rome Ruled OK But Bill Hayley 'Bate' The Ban

Mick McCarthy

It was in the early 1960s that hurling took off in Rome. Up to then, there would have been the odd game among the Irish expatriates in the city, most of whom were young clerical students, but it was a rare enough event. At that time, up to 200-300 Irish seminarians were housed in the various colleges, both Irish and international. Most of them would have been in their early-to-mid-twenties.

They were all doing university degrees in the city. The largest student centre was the famed Irish College, catering mainly for diocesan clergy and a sprinkling of others, but the Franciscans, Dominicans, Augustinians, and Holy Ghosts, were also well-represented. These foundations were part of the residual legacy of the Irish narrative going back over 400 years.

Their student numbers were an indication of the thriving Church back home that had over 5,000 priests in service then. The numbers also spoke volumes about the financial health of the Irish Church, as it cost a small fortune to run these colleges annually. And it did not stop there. One also had to factor in the cost of running residences or villas outside of Rome where the seminarians spent their summer holidays.

Gaelic football was the more popular game among the students, not just because most of them came from footballing counties, but because of the difficulties with transporting hurls. Not only were they awkward to carry but they also raised a few eyebrows with airport customs officers. Many a Gael got a bit of a quizzing from officials as he tried to explain what a hurley was all about and why he wanted to travel with it on board. And then there was the odd inter-cultural gap, best illustrated by the classic story of the clerical student in Rome travelling by bus to a hurling match in another part of the city. The bus was jam-packed, and he had himself, his sports bag and a pair of hurleys to manoeuvre through the other passengers. Progress was painfully slow when suddenly an elderly lady stood up and offered the young man her seat. Apparently, she thought he had trouble walking, as she mistook his two hurleys for crutches! The incident became part of the Rome-GAA folklore while the student later went on to become a bishop in South Africa.

It was in 1960 that the students had to put a collective shape on themselves as word came through that an Aer Lingus hurling team was keen to visit Rome for a challenge match. This was unprecedented and tremendously exciting at the time. Once the students arrived in Rome for their studies, many of them did not return home for four years until they were ordained priests. The very prospect of a team travelling from Ireland for a match, or a series of matches, was a great lift to the spirits. It was all the brainchild of Captain Gus Madden who ran the Aer Lingus office on Via Barberini, in the heart of the city.

Gus was a larger-than-life, popular character, and while he was a hugely successful ambassador for the Irish airline, he was also ambassador extraordinaire for the whole of the Rome-Irish community. His enthusiasm for the hurling project was infectious and he soon had a committee of half-a-dozen clerics meeting in his office to plan for the event. A trial game was organised to pick the best 15 from among the Rome players. Unfortunately, Irish expatriate numbers were low in Rome in those far-off days with the result that an all-clerical team was chosen.

The next challenge was to secure a pitch in the city big enough to accommodate hurling. Tipperary's Monsignor Tom Ryan, then based in Rome and Secretary to Pope John XX111, managed to secure the sports grounds of the American Pontifical College on Monte Mario, overlooking St. Peter's. It was the American seminary in Rome for students.

It had a beautiful green sward, far superior to most of the other options where wear-and-tear and sunshine had burnt the ground, leaving the surface dusty and rock-hard. The only criticism one could make was that the grass was perhaps a little too short for pick-up, but it was ideally suited for the ground hurling that was a classic feature of the game just then. All was set.

Gus and his committee travelled out to Fiumicino Airport to welcome the Aer Lingus 20-man strong team. Also present was the representative of the Irish Ambassador to Italy, Louis Cullen. The latter's presence gave the occasion a certain formality. It was also a recognition of the times that were in it as Aer Lingus, the national airline, was a burgeoning semi-state company destined to rise quickly to about 5/6000 employees at its peak.

It was also an expression of the new Ireland that was taking off due to the Lemass-Whittaker vision, coupled with the massive inflow to the country of foreign capital and investment. The occasion was probably a first in terms of the native game at that level, not just in Rome, but in that part of Europe. About half-a-century earlier, in 1910, Tipperary and Cork hurling teams had, in fact, travelled to Brussels, Fontenoy and Malines for exhibition games as part of a European tour but two world wars had disrupted further initiatives. Gus was always proud of his particular achievement in the 'sixties' and, with the characteristic broad grin, boasted, "You can write it down!"

A surprisingly large crowd turned out for the match. Naturally they were partisan in the extreme, giving full vent to their support for the students. As was customary at the time in big games, a cleric threw in the ball to get a game started and Mgr. Tom Ryan obliged. However, Aer Lingus proved to be the stronger side and took the honours.

Dermot Sheedy, then playing with Clare and working in Shannon, was the man of the match with a tremendous exhibition of skill and finesse. Jim Hogan, the Limerick County goalie, also impressed hugely with some brilliant saves. Many of those watching had never heard of hurling, not to mention attending a match, so to these the contest was somewhat of a puzzlement. But they were hugely impressed by the speed of the game, the fierceness of the engagements and the overall passion of the hour. For the majority of those Irish attending, it was nostalgia at its most potent, rekindling youthful memories and underscoring what they were missing living 'in foreign parts.' One well-known Cork friar was heard to comment contentedly that the game was as good as a holiday at home to him.

A second game was due to be played in a few days but in the

meantime the young Aer Lingus team could see the city and how it could turn art and history into reality. Robert Hughes, the great Australian travel-writer once wrote that Rome is a gift to each of us from people who are dead and yet can never die. True, the city never fails and keeps on giving. But one has to factor in that historically Irish people had a particular relationship with Rome.

In the 60s their world then was viewed through the prism of their pietistic and high-moral Catholicism of the time. To the vast majority of Irish, Rome meant the Pope, pure and simple. The city was the spiritual centre of their world. When, if ever, they got an opportunity or could afford to go there they wanted to see him. As for it being the artistic home of Michelangelo, Bernini, Brunelleschi, Caravaggio or the stomping ground of Caesar, Marcus Aurelius, Nero, Caligula or Cicero, or any other of the mighty, forget it. Or even that it was the hallowed burial place of two great Irish leaders – Hugh O'Neill of Tyrone or Rory O'Donnell, Earl of Tyrconnell – not a bit of it.

All of this was underscored by the famed Mickey Grimes, who was a member of a Limerick-Rome pilgrimage in the 1950s, when he exclaimed during a Papal audience: "Holy Father, the people of Limerick would go to hell and back for you!" The Pope was the focus of Irish attention. So, true to form, the Aer Lingus hurling team was down for a special audience with himself in the Vatican, all arranged through powerful Irish clerical connections, and they were powerful in those days.

However, while the team was hosting an evening session in the German bierkeller at the foot of the Spanish Steps for a throng of Irish clerical students on the night before the audience, Mgr. Tom Ryan informed the team that, unfortunately, the audience with the Pope had been cancelled. There was huge disappointment, but worse was to follow. When the drinking eventually eased later in the night, the Aer Lingus lads were presented with a bill that they just did not have enough money on them in Italian lire to cover.

Con Clarke, Chief Executive of Customer Services with Aer Lingus, who was heading their hurling party, had to turn to Mgr. Ryan to explain the embarrassing situation. But it was no bother to the future bishop who was glad to ease the team's disappointment over the audience. He had his assistant sign a cheque and the event became one of those "Do you remember the night ...?" Con certainly does.

The second match a few days later was another affair altogether. The students had learned a lot from the first encounter. They had never played together as a team before the first match but were a different meld this time. They knew what they were up against and played to their own considerable strengths.

Inspired by Tipperary minor star, Tom Gleeson, and Laois dual county player, Sean Conlon, they came through clear winners after a hard-fought contest in rather damp conditions. Another formal reception followed, attended by His Excellency Michael Flynn, Irish Ambassador to the Holy See. In his address, he spoke of the importance of the visit of the Aer Lingus team to Rome as a significant cultural initiative and how it strengthened the common bond of all Irishmen.

The games certainly gave a fillip to the small Irish community in Rome at the time and their success ensured that they would become an annual feature of the Irish calendar in the city. However, the biggest on-going challenge facing Gus and his committee was the procuring of a suitable pitch. There were very few sports grounds or facilities in Rome with a pitch 140 or 150 metres long and nearly 90 wide. All were either soccer or rugby pitches that were in or around the 100 metres mark and were just too short and narrow for hurling.

At one famous meeting in his office the matter came up for discussion. Various suggestions and proposals were tossed about. Someone foolishly raised the question of 'The Ban' and the incongruity of playing GAA games on a soccer or rugby pitch. This was a throwback to the prohibition on GAA members not attending foreign dances or foreign games. What would be the reaction in Croke Park if they heard that the Rome crowd were actually playing hurling on a rugby pitch? "More importantly," said the Columban, Fr. Frank 'Fontenoy' O'Leary from Kerry, winding Gus up all the more; "How will I explain it to my lads in the Black Valley? They'll think I'm gone raving Communist altogether."

This was all too much for Gus. He just exploded. His precious bottle of Irish, that was always a feature of these meetings, and the couple of glasses on the table went flying. "Listen," said he in his most passionate, eloquent style ever, "Bill Hayley bate the ban! This is the 1960s. Nearly every house in Ireland with kids listens to Radio Caroline and not to Athlone. Nobody gives a tuppence any more about the ban. Everybody goes to foreign dances and wherever they like to Twist, Rock Around the Clock, or whatever bloody jigging they want to do. We're nearly 2,000 miles away from Ireland, so we play wherever we can. That's the end of that."

And so it was. Rome had spoken or, at least Gus had!

A number of the students used to play rugby with local clubs at Aqua Acetosa and the Italians gladly loaned the pitch to the Irish for the day. They also turned up to watch the hurling matches and were just gobsmacked by the speed of the game and the skill-levels of the players. But they also felt that the whole thing was just too downright pericoloso for them. When they heard about 'The Ban' with its prohibition on foreign games and dances for players, they readily admitted that they were quite prepared to live by it and leave hurling to the Irish!

Aqua Acetosa became the venue for what had become the annual matches in the mid-sixties. Some bright spark called it Rome's Vinegar Hill, as the Italian name literally translates as Vinegary Water. It too was the scene of many a hard-fought battle.

The Aer Lingus team won in '64 but the students took the honours in '65, '66, and '67. As became the norm, there was a second game every year at the American College, but the first game was the one where the colours were won or lost. Dermot Sheedy's place as a county player on the Aer Lingus team was taken by his colleague in Shannon, the great Bernie Hartigan of Limerick. Bernie was a power of a man and gave some outstandingly stylish performances that had everybody enthralled. They also had Pat Walshe from Kilkenny who showed that he had inherited the Cats' magic, but Mick Phelan, Val Harte, 'Boogie' Smith, Paddy Kenny, Con Clarke, and, of course, the laughing cavalier of the team, Limerick's star-goalie, Jim Hogan, were also up there with the best. Con became Dublin's County Board Chairman in the early '90s and he still won't disclose where in Rome he got the gabhail of relics for Heffo's army that got them started on their path to glory.

In 1965, Aer Lingus sent out a rugby team to Rome. Two matches were played, one against the clerical students and a second against Frascati club. Curiously enough, Aer Lingus did not send out a Gaelic football team in those early days.

The times, they were a'changing. In December 1965, the Second Vatican Council closed in Rome. It was a watershed moment. The Council heralded renewal and modernity. But the conservative Irish Church leadership were less than enthusiastic. They soon found their Church being outstripped by a new, emergent, dynamic Ireland that was rapidly shedding the regressive moral strictures of yesteryear. Seminaries closed at home and those abroad faced the same fate. It was the end of an era.

Invariably this impacted on the clerical-dominated hurling scene in Rome. Seminarian numbers were not only on a diminuendo but were drying up altogether. However, a new generation of young Irish were arriving in the city. Some came to study, some to work, others to take up permanent residence. Many were attached to various European political and cultural institutions, while others had business interests. They brought their passion for their native games with them and soon the embers of the clerical fire that had once burned so brightly were now being re-kindled by this new generation. They missed the opportunities of home and were keen to indulge their sporting talents in ways they knew best.

Nostalgia can be a strange dynamic and can lead to even stranger results. Joe Phelan, who had played hurling with Limerick and Armagh in the 1960s, found himself in Rome in the 70s working with FAO, the UN Food and Agricultural Organisation. Few could boast of it, but Joe recalled visiting the famed Circus Maximus of an afternoon and having a most enjoyable bit of a puck around with his young family! That surely was some cultural overlay, not envisaged by the imperial architects of that great stadium.

In 2003, Croke Park decided that the Railway Cup hurling final would be played in Rome. This was a generous acknowledgement by Sean McCague and his administration of the exponential development in recent years of GAA clubs throughout Europe. His predecessor, Joe McDonagh, with the help of an international committee, had initiated a European County Board structure and this later morphed into Gaelic Games Europe that has representation on Central Council and at Congress. It has over 100 clubs scattered through 24 countries and runs competitions for men and women in the various sports and grades.

The prospect of the Railway Cup Final coming to Rome was hugely welcomed and looked forward to. In early November, Leinster and Connacht travelled out for the final. The match was played at the Giulio Onesti Sports Complex in the city watched by not just the sizeable Rome-Irish community but also by Gaels from other clubs throughout Italy and further afield. Noel Skehan's men took the title, winning by three points.

The occasion was a memorable one and even though the Railway Cup as a competition was ailing at the time the match did wonders for the Irish community in Rome. Many looked on it too as the coming of age of the European GAA organisation.

Rome Gaels took a major step forward in 2012 when Chris Taggart from Tyrone formally established the Rome Gaelic Football Club. Funding was provided by Declan Crean of the Scholars' Lounge, a famous Irish pub on Via del Plebiscito, near Piazza Venezia. In a novel development, the club subsequently established links with the Societa Sportiva Polisportiva di Lazio, the second largest multi-sport club in the world after FC Barcelona. It is now known as Lazio Calcio Gaelico. It's a thriving club and won the Pan European Junior B title in 2017. It also organised the first European Gaelic football tournament in Rome in 2019.

It is hard at a distance to fathom what these clubs mean to those living abroad with their families, friends and communities. They strike huge cultural chords that are profound and personal and help to shorten the distance for people between wherever they are and home. They deepen their own sense of Irishness, not in any chauvinistic way, but in engendering a pride and value in their own culture. They also enhance the situations they find themselves in, as Gaelic games were largely unknown throughout Europe until quite recently. The numbers of non-Irish now getting involved in them speaks for itself.

Just to return to Robert Hughes, the travel writer who said that Rome and its treasures are a gift to each of us by people who are long since dead but will never die. The same could be said of our national games – they are a gift to each of us from people who are long since dead, but they too will never die.

Michael Cusack in his wildest dreams could never have thought he would hear of the Eindhoven Shamrocks, the Madrid Harps or the Seamus Heaneys in Moscow. Our games are his gift to each of us, and every club, no matter how humble, no matter where it is, ensures that The Man from Carron will never die.

Mick McCarthy was born in Parteen in east Clare and was a member of the local GAA club. He played hurling with Limerick CBS and captained the Rome clerical team for three years while studying there. He then worked in Africa before returning to Ireland in the mid-seventies and joined RTE. He has fond memories of producing editions of 'Up for the Match' for a number of years before retiring.

'I used to think it was great being a wee nippy corner forward, but it's better now being a big, fat one'

Meath's Ollie Murphy

Anguish Of Mother's
Lost Camogie Medal

Florence Wise

My mother, Rosaleen Swan, won a GAA Camogie Cup Final Medal back in the 1930s and boy was she proud of it for the rest of her life? Not loud and proud but in her own quiet way proud.

Mum was a very modest lady but was so thrilled with her contribution to the winning of this particular cup final that she wore it pinned on her going away rigout at her wedding in 1939. And it also had pride of place close to her heart on her overcoat later that year as herself and her new husband (my father) Patrick McGrath sailed towards England and the oncoming war.

Growing up her family lived in O'Connell Gardens, just off Bath Avenue in south Dublin. My mum's father, John Swan, was keen that all his children kept fit through sport so they were all encouraged to join teams in a sport which interested them.

The camogie team Rosaleen and her sister Eileen belonged to had been organised by a local doctor in Sandymount who had daughters who wanted to be involved. The team were keen, excited, and so friendly. Their ability to enjoy a game meant that they gave of their best through that season to reach the cup final.

As far as this particular Sandymount team were concerned on that eventful Sunday, it was just another match so much so that they all cycled miles and waited outside the ground for the gates to open.

They had few, if any supporters but this was just another match, wasn't it? nothing new? While they waited, a coach drove down the road filled with a team in smart uniforms and a very posh group of supporters. The girls looked at each other, err, have we come to the wrong place? Maybe there is a match before ours? No, this was the opposition.

To cut a long story short, they gave their all, and won whatever competition this was. Despite our research we can't figure it out, perhaps it was some sort of local final.

My Mum's contribution was to give the telling pass to Eileen, who scored the decisive goal. They were all so proud of themselves, and afterwards got on their bikes, some on the bus, and went home. Just another match, eh?

My Mum and Dad returned to Ireland around 1943 and the little medal was still her prized possession. Settling down in a modest flat at 4 Mespil Road, Dublin, facing the canal, they lived there while my father surveyed the area for a plot on which to build a home while also attempting to rebuild his career.

One winter's evening in 1949, they went out to a Brown Thomas function leaving their little boys at the time (Paul, Errol, Brendan and Patrick) with their eldest daughter Florence (me) and a neighbour to keep an eye on them. Sometime through the evening, the boys got their hands on the medal and posted it through a little hole in the floorboards. Panic set in when they couldn't retrieve it.

When my parents returned from the function, they were in high spirits after having enjoyed a wonderful night; with my mother particularly happy after winning a pair of crocodile skin shoes in a raffle.

It was as good a time as any to tell her of the lost medal. She went quiet at the news while I felt a guilt over the missing gem because I blamed myself for not supervising the boys properly.

The following evening Dad brought a small magnet home with him. Tying it onto a piece of string, he dropped it through the small hole and tried swinging it in various directions. Everyone crossed their fingers but after half an hour of fruitless endeavour, we gave up. It seems that somewhere between the floors, the priceless medal had come to a standstill away from human recovery. The little treasure which had featured on my mother's biggest days in life, could very well still be there.

In my fancy, I see the medal as having been found years later... maybe when the house was being refurbished. My hope is that the person who retrieved it has minded it well because it was my mother's and she was so proud of it.

As proud, in fact, as if it had been a Celtic Cross instead of being from some local GAA Camogie Final all those years ago.

Florence Wise (nee McGrath) is the daughter of Rosaleen and now lives in Malvern, Worcestershire in the UK. She has been married to David for the past 57 years and they have one son, Simon. Florence had a career in local government in Economic Development & Tourism plus a spell working in Brussels. Her husband and herself are both keen travellers, visiting Australia, China, USA, Malaysia and in later years, exploring Europe and Ireland in their trusty caravan.

'*Brian Dooher is down injured. And while he is, I'll tell ye a little story. I was in Times Square in New York last week, and I was missing the Championship back home. So I approached a news stand and I said: 'I suppose ye wouldn't have the Kerryman would ye?' To which, the Egyptian man behind the counter turned to me and said: 'Do you want the North Kerry or the South Kerry edition?' He had both... so I bought both. And Dooher is back on his feet...'*

Micheál Ó Muircheartaigh

Unique Collection Of Ring And Other Stars' Memorabilia

Ricey Scully

Just like his hurling hero of yesteryear Christy Ring, Cork man Denis O'Sullivan sets the standard high when it comes to his own game of collecting memorabilia about Gaelic games and sporting heroes.

The quietly-spoken former member of the armed forces is on a daily mission to add to his 10,000 immaculately preserved cuttings, his 500 match programmes, his hundreds of radio and video recordings.

On top of all that he has well over 100 club and county jerseys in pristine condition not to mention an array of hurleys picked up over the years from various parts of the country.

The 67-year-old Ballynoe resident in north-east Cork has kept pace with the times by having a surprising amount of invaluable material in the growing games of camogie and ladies football as well as hurling and football.

"I never got to meet Christy but was a hurling fan always and he is the one player who even today is synonymous with Cork and hurling lore. It started there and I'm proud to have his commemorative jersey in my collection as well as countless photos and cuttings on him.

"There is no doubt he forms the single biggest segment of what I have but then I branched out to the other GAA sports and I've built up a lot of camogie and ladies football paraphernalia as well.

"And I get material from other sports as well. Liam Miller, who played Gaelic as a youngster before going on to play for Manchester United, Celtic and Ireland died young from cancer and recently his mother Bridie recently sent me five jerseys which I will cherish as part of my collection as well.

"Most of the jerseys I have represent either clubs or county colours and there are historic ones too like the Michael Hogan jersey – that is one of the special ones for sure," he added.

Unlike many people who pursue a collection hobby, Denis loves to share the joy of his wide-ranging stock with the public and has gone round to clubs to mount exhibitions for them.

Probably the biggest display of his collection was staged at the end of August this year (2022) when his local village put on a full exhibition of his work in the community centre – seldom has there been a busier Saturday in the precincts as people came from far and wide to view his array of Gaelic assortments.

He admits that it all started almost by accident. He was in Collins Barracks in Cork during his days in the army about 35 years ago reading a book about Christy Ring when a great man from Cloyne, Jackie Farmer "asked me if I was interested in Christy Ring. When I told him I was he gave me a load of paper clippings."

Over the years the word spread about Denis and different collectors have dropped him in stuff they wanted kept for posterity and reckoned it was safer if it was in his hands rather than their own. And how right they are. People were gobsmacked at how his indexing of tapes and videos meant he could source and play them within 30 seconds of being asked if he had a particular recording.

It is this painstaking approach to ensuring every item is properly preserved which makes Denis's collection a veritable treasure trove for GAA fans everywhere – not just for now but into the future as well.

He said there must have been confusion with the GAA in Cork because when he offered to display his content as an attraction for them, they came back saying it didn't suit at the time.

"I haven't heard from them since but the offer stands from me to show this archive I've created either in Páirc Ui Chaoimh or Croke Park. I haven't collected all these wonderful memories just to keep them in my own house. There are thousands of hours of reading and listening materials which I'm sure ordinary GAA fans would love to see and hear."

A neighbour of his in Ballynoe, Leanne McDonagh-Power, is a talented artist and has painted a number of photos Denis has in his collection. "They are unique paintings and her creativity gives my entire collection a great lift," commented Denis.

Denis O'Sullivan is former member of the Irish defence forces and is a keen collector of sporting, and in particular, an exhaustive GAA archive. Denis is from Ballynoe, North Cork and is a lifelong GAA fan.

Ricey Scully is a former Offaly footballer and hurler at all grades. A native of Clara, Co Offaly, he is a former well-known band leader and local government worker in the midlands. Married to Mary, he is the father of four grown-up children.

Ring And Mackey's Verbal Joust

Seamus Walsh

The question has often been asked as to what was said between Mick Mackey and Christy Ring in the famous photograph taken by Justin Nelson at the Munster Hurling semi-final in Limerick in 1957.

The following account was related to me by Mick Mackey's brother, James (Todsy), in Castleconnell, Co Limerick in 1984. Todsy won two senior county championship medals with Ahane in 1946 and 1948 in the company of his two brothers Mick and John.

I was chairman of the Ahane club in the millennium year and Todsy was a great friend of mine for 25 years. This particular game was played in the Gaelic Grounds in July, 1957, between Cork and Tipperary. An incident happened three minutes before half-time which caused controversy afterwards. 'Musha' Maher sent in the ball and, as Cork goalkeeper Mick Cashman caught it, he was bundled over the line by the Tipperary forwards.

Umpire Mick Mackey reached for the green flag to signal a goal, but the other umpire seemed to be in disagreement. The referee ran in and awarded a 70 to Tipperary and disallowed the "goal".

Ring scored a goal early in the second half and shortly afterwards was forced to retire with a fractured wrist. Making his way off the field, he said to Mackey: "You never lost it Mick." Mackey replied: "And neither did you, Christy". And that was it contrary to what a lot of people think. Cork won the game by three points, 5-2 to 1-11.

Séamus Walsh is a native of Clonlara, Co. Clare, and is ex-chairman of the Ahane club in Limerick. He served as umpire in three All-Ireland senior hurling finals with Limerick ref, Pat O'Connor.

SAID AND DONE: This is an iconic GAA photo but what was said between Cork legend Christy Ring and former Limerick great Mick Mackey, acting as umpire in the 1957 Munster hurling championship semi-final game? See 'Ring And Mackey's Verbal Joust', Page 128

LOST AND FOUND: **Following this presentation of the Fahey Cup in Roscommon, it disappeared for several years only to surface again recently.** ***See 'Mystery Of Stolen Fahey Cup Solved', Page 24***

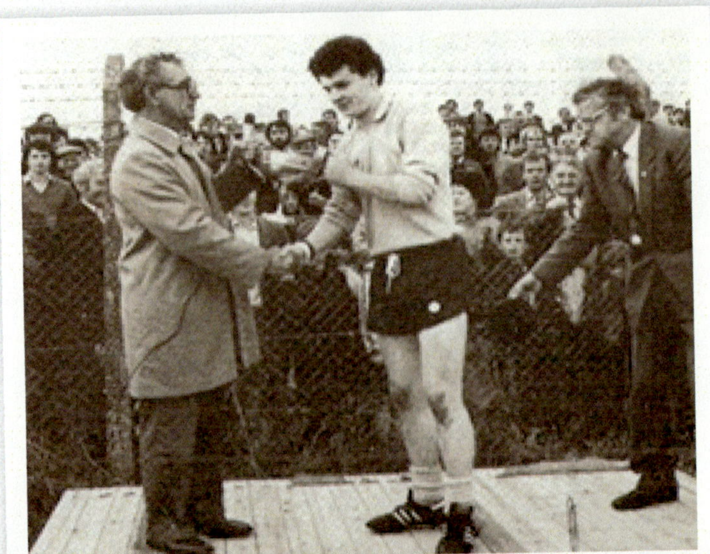

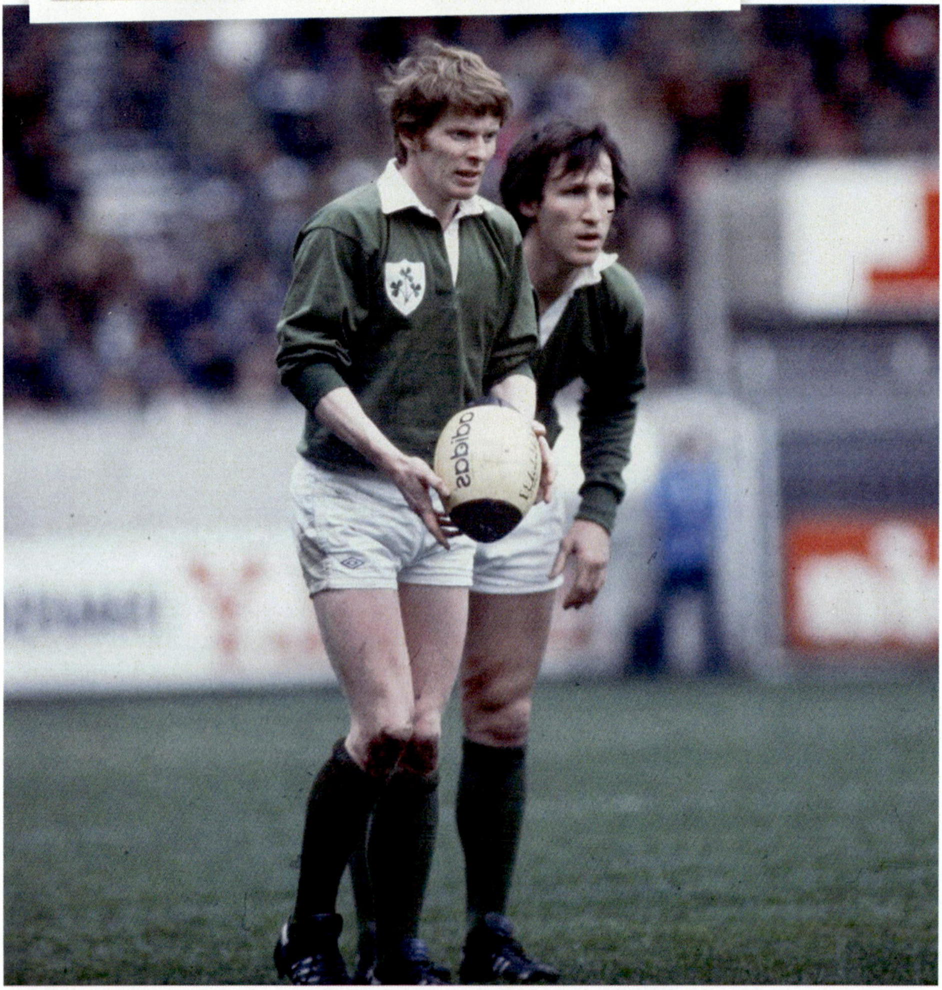

OUTSIDER LOOKING IN: **Famed Lions and Ireland rugby outhalf Ollie Campbell writes about his unique GAA experiences.** PHOTO: SPORTSFILE
See 'My GAA Stories From Outside Looking In', Page 25

SAMBO STYLE: Antrim's Terence 'Sambo' McNaughton takes the fight to Limerick during the 1996 All-Ireland semi-final at Croke Park. *See 'The 'Waiting Game' I Played With Lone Soldier On Dark Country Road', Page 29* PHOTO: SPORTSFILE

DARING BREED: Ireland's most beloved playwright, John B Keane, reserved praise for the lowly junior referee. *See 'Junior Referees – A Daring Breed of Men', Page 35*

RIGHT ON CUE: Former World Snooker Champion, Ken Doherty, shows his skills as a Gaelic footballer in an Alan Kerins Project charity match between Galway and Dublin selections in 2011.
See 'The Crucible And Croker – My Unforgettable Sporting Occasions', Page 65
PHOTO: SPORTSFILE

BLAZING A TRAIL: The Viet Celts' squad on the pitch at the AGG in Singapore, 2007. Back row, left to right: Colm Ross, Dan Burns, Gareth O'Hara, Dan Dockery, Michael Clifford, Matt Lee, Clint Lambert, Emmet Fleming, Patrick Cooney, Brian Lalor, Fergus Broderick, Bernard Casey, Connla Stokes, 'Seattle Steve' Christensen, Sean Hoy, Steve Kinlough, Pham Duc Toan. Front: Paul 'DJ Polo' Mariage, Colin Campbell, John Symons, Bernard Hartigan, Richard Rastall. Missing: Brian O'Reilly. *See 'The Viet Celts Are Coming', Page 71*

CORA'S CRUSADE: Former Mayo star, Cora Staunton, is still breaking glass ceilings down under in Aussie Rules but her former teacher remembers how she outshone the boys in Primary School. *See 'Cora Staunton And The Fist Of Fury She Avoided', Page 69*

PHOTO: SPORTSFILE

FRONGOCH LINE-UPS: The so-called 'Barbed-Wire All-Ireland' played in the Welsh 'Croke Park' shows the Louth and Kerry teams. *See 'The Barbed Wire All-Ireland Played In The Welsh Croke Park', Page 81*

GAME FOR A LAUGH: The late Terry Wogan had a laugh because he knew what to expect when the BBC filmed a club hurling game in Wexford, but his cameraman didn't. *See 'Fights, Camera And Action As Terry Wogan Looked On', Page 89*

THE ROMAN LEGION: Continental action from the 1960s when a team from Aer Lingus played a clerical students' team domiciled in Rome. *See 'Rome Ruled OK But Bill Hayley Bate The Ban', Page 111*

CAMOGIE CONUNDRUM: A lost medal is the story of Rosaleen Swan, who was captain of the Sandymount camogie team in the 1930s before emigrating at the start of the following decade. Rosaleen is pictured, bottom right, sitting while her sister Eileen with blonde hair is beside the coach at the back.
MEDAL MYSTERY: Rosaleen, pictured alongside her husband Patrick McGrath (right) with her camogie medal pinned to her coat, was distraught when it subsequently got 'posted' underneath floorboards never to be found again.
See 'Anguish Of Mother's Lost Camogie Medal', Page 121

COLLECTOR SUPREME: Cork's Denis O'Sullivan proudly shows off a photo of his idol Christy Ring outside his house in Ballynoe, Co. Cork.

ARTISTIC TOUCH: Leanne McDonagh-Power has painted a number of photos Denis O'Sullivan has in his collection. "They are unique paintings and her creativity gives my entire collection a great lift," commented Denis.

See 'Unique Collection Of Ring And Other Stars' Memorabilia, Page 125

Galway's Golden Age And Darwin's Theory Of Evolution In Sport

Paul Holland

I was born in 1954. My awareness of GAA, and of the world in general, was something that evolved as we evolved from the dinosaurs. My child's perception had me thinking that Roy of the Rovers played hurling, that there were 15 on a normal Gaelic team and 50 on a county team. By late 1962, my intellect had grasped that the Cuban crisis was a major threat, that death was serious and that the two best teams in Ireland played in the All-Ireland final. By early 1963, the Gaelic codes and the mechanics of the competitions were 90 percent clear to me. It was just in time.

In August 1963, we had no radio so my father, brother and I went to a neighbour's house to listen to Michael O'Hehir's commentary on the All-Ireland football semi-final, Galway against Kerry. I recognised the iconic name of Mick O'Connell and also recognised that Galway weren't doing well.

It was Kerry 0-4, Galway 0-1 at the interval. Curiously the referee's name, Eamon Moules from Wicklow, made an impression on me, maybe it's because I needed some distraction as the score was now 0-7 to 0-2. And then, out of the blue, O'Hehir went hysterical. "He's 21 yards out, 14 yards out, 10 yards out, It's a goal! A goal for Galway!"

Suddenly, Galway were on fire and Kerry had no answer. The gap closed. A minute to go and Galway were a point ahead. We were on our feet in ecstasy, crowding around the radio. Final score was Galway 1-8, Kerry 0-9.

We were on a high for days afterwards. My enthusiasm abated a bit when I was informed that the final would be on Sept 22, many weeks away. Down and Dublin somewhat ominously expressed delight that Kerry had been eliminated. A sage 14-year old remarked to me that if Dublin managed to beat Down, Galway would be home and dry.

Dublin managed quite well, thank you. In fact, the manner of their victory, which I also listened to on the radio, had me worried. Our neighbour obligingly acquired a television and, on Sept 22, the entire male population of the area (young, old and infirm included) crammed in to watch the first All-Ireland football final to be transmitted live on TV. I remember the grainy picture and my father remarking that this was a better view than one would get in Croke Park. My memory is of furious uncompromising exchanges. Dublin were no pushover but, although Galway had to fight for everything, they managed to be 0-6 to 0-4 ahead at the break.

We worried about chances missed but were in high hopes when Eamon Moules threw in the ball for the second half. In those days, almost half of the respective teams lined up for the throw-in. There was a frantic tussle – only after three attempts at resuming did someone finally break away with the ball.

On that day, I learned that life is cruel. Dublin were level within a few minutes and, next thing, it was a goal. "Are they (expletive) asleep?", someone yelled. As if they had heard, Galway suddenly took things seriously but, every time they pointed, Dublin restored the margin. Two points behind, and Mick Garrett fell with the ball in the Dublin parallelogram.

"Penalty!" we all shouted. Eamon Moules didn't think so; I've never forgiven him. To rub salt in the wounds, a Dubliner (John Timmons, I think) pointed a free from a distance that would have taxed a hurler. This couldn't be happening, Galway players were crying with frustration and disbelief. We left in disgust at the sight of crowds invading the pitch. Final score was 1-9 to 0-10. With my childhood naivety, I thought next year (how many youngsters, before or after me, thought the same thing, but in vain?).

JFK died and 1964 came almost as an afterthought. Some compensation was gained when Galway beat Dublin in the Wembley Tournament. Subsequently it was a stroll through Connacht. My brother went to England on a summer job, my father and I went to see Galway v Meath in the All-Ireland semi-final. Galway had a goal allowed, Meath a goal disallowed. It was as tight as that! When the final came and I again watched on television, it was clear after about 10 minutes that Galway were going to win. Michael Donnellan, a former Galway star and father of John, the Galway captain, passed away in Croke Park. Mick Higgins, the winning Galway captain of 1934, died at home during the match. The story goes that Michael and St Peter waited in suspense until Mick arrived to tell them the final score, 0-15 to 0-10.

In 1965, Galway played Sligo in Tuam Stadium. Self-confidence and dearly-bought experience saw them through, just about. Sligo could/should have won the game. Down were our opponents in the All-Ireland semi-final. On a miserable day, Galway had a slight edge. Down came strong in the second half. Galway defended heroically and a shot screamed just over rather than under the crossbar. Down were bitterly disappointed having been fully confident of victory. The final against Kerry was tighter than in 1964. Late in the second half, a Kerry forward on a defence-splitting run was pulled to the ground by Pat Donnellan. Not surprisingly, he retaliated. The net outcome was three players sent off and Galway winners 0-12 to 0-9.

By now, Galway had targets on their backs and even Galway supporters were half-feeling that it was nearly time for someone else to be winning. Some mothers, wives and sweethearts were thinking that maybe it was time they saw more of their men.

Connacht was won, not without a scare from Mayo on the way, and Cork put up a worthy challenge in the semi-final. Hopes were high although Meath looked formidable. As it happened, Galway ran riot winning 1-10 to 0-7. Mattie McDonagh got his fourth All-Ireland winners' medal. Again, I was watching on television at a neighbour's house. Final whistle, we all stood up, cheered and scattered. No discussion – winning had become routine. Many of the people in that room did not live to see Galway's next senior football final victory.

Over the same time, Galway won and lost Grounds Tournament finals. They won the League title of 1965 in New York having beaten Kerry in the home final with a controversial goal at the death. In 1966, they lost the home final to Longford. In 1967, they were trailing after the first leg of the final in New York. A Sunday paper carried an alleged quote from Enda Colleran: "Relax all you Galway fans back at home. We hear you're worried..." With damned good reason. New York easily won out in the second leg and became League champions.

Galway had a Golden Summer of Victory. Now it was Autumn but we didn't know it. In 1967, Mayo beat Galway in Connacht and Michael O'Hehir remarked that this Mayo team might really go places (They won leagues within the next few years). In 1968, Galway again met Down in the All-Ireland semi-final. This time, Down had the edge. A fortuitous goal for Galway threw everything back in the melting pot with first a victory, then a draw, looking likely. It wasn't to be. Down went on to win the final.

In 1969, Galway had Mayo on the ropes at Pearse Stadium. Another attack, the Mayo defence was split and the ball rolled towards an empty net. One of the forwards, thinking he was making assurance doubly sure, kicked at the ball but somehow managed to hook his foot around it instead. A grateful defender booted the ball clear, Galway lost momentum and finally conceded a free that levelled the game. Mayo won the replay and Galway's hopes for 1969 had gone in the same direction as the Apollo moon rocket.

Meath defeated Galway in the 1970 All-Ireland semi-final. Then we had the heartbreak of final losses in 1971, 1973 and 1974 to Offaly, Cork and Dublin. In 1976, the flame fluttered and died when Dublin beat us in the semi-final.

History often revolves on little things... 1963 stung Galway and maybe we owe our three-in-a-row titles to Dublin and Eamon Moules. I often wonder what made the difference between our often close-run successes of the mid-sixties and subsequent close-run failures.

Did retiring players take the team's killer instinct away with them? Were the latter teams simply not good enough, perhaps only borne along by the aura Galway had at the time? Or maybe they were as good or better than the winning teams but the ground had changed in a new era where different talents were needed to win All-Ireland titles. Darwin's Theory of Evolution applies as much to sport as it does to organisms and species.

Paul Holland is from Lisheenkyle, Oranmore, Co Galway. A retired science, maths and computer teacher, he has travelled extensively, including expeditions to both the North and South Poles as well as Campbell Island, which is the most distant land on earth from Ireland.

'He'll regret this to his dying day, if he lives that long'

Dublin fan after Charlie Redmond missed a penalty in the 1994 All-Ireland final

Encounter With My Would-Be Assassin In Croke Park

Aidan Clancy

My father Matt Clancy was enjoying the crisp October Sunday weather with a weak sun warming Croke Park as he sat on the steps of the then northern terrace.

In fact, he was wondering whether life could really be much better. Apart from being young and fit and healthy, he had a good job and "a few pound" in his pocket, in fact "a good few pound" to see him through the week and, if needs be, a week or two after that as well. He felt secure in every way.

It looked like the troubled times that followed Irish independence were now over. Ireland was finally free, an independent nation... well almost. The gallant efforts and sacrifices of my father and his IRA volunteer comrades were finally being rewarded. It gave him a great sense of pride but a pride that had been badly wounded by The Split – that ugly chasm that had set comrade against comrade, brother against brother in the Civil War.

It all seemed so senseless, so pointless, so futile. Even so, my father felt that now he could do whatever he liked to do, go wherever he liked to go without fear or trepidation ... well nearly, it was now 1924 and people on all sides had moved on from that dreadful time of internecine bloodshed.

My father was very comfortable with his job as a farm labourer at Blackrock College in Dublin. The college looked after him well. He was earning £1-15s-6d per week with bed and board thrown in. He had just finished a hard two weeks' ploughing the best land in the country with a pair of horses that were second to none.

The soil in the farms at Deer Park, Merrion and Kimmage Manor had the best of black clay soil that seemed to have no bottom. Wasn't this a far cry from the four pence (4d) a day he earned when he went to work at 10 years of age for Mike Neary (which he always pro-

"

nounced Nary) down the Castletown Road in his native 'The Island' back in Offaly.

It wasn't that my father resented Mike; in fact, he always spoke highly of him and often recounted the way Mike had taught him the ways of farming life. Mike gave him welcome employment and a place to stay which made a bit more room for his parents and the seven younger ones still at home in the two-roomed thatched cottage. Still, Mike Neary's farm was a far cry from the splendour of Blackrock College's almost endless acreage of great land and its modern machinery and the finest of well-bred horses.

Exiled in Dublin, my father had a yearning to visit his mother – just for a day or even a few hours, but could he chance it? He had written to her and sent word of himself with his two sisters who also lived in Dublin. The girls went home on the train as far as Bal-lycumber Station and from there journeyed to 'The Island' every Summer. They would come back and tell my father about how good things were at home but after nearly three years in exile, he longed to go there himself.

There was a reason he didn't dare to go home and in some ways, arriving in Croke Park to support Offaly junior hurlers playing in the All Ireland final against Cork, was also a big risk.

This was the 1923 final, but it had been held over to this day, October 12 1924, some 30 months or so after the Civil War started. It lasted less than a year by ending in May '23, but it left him wonder-ing if the intervening year had allowed the rawness of the pro and anti-treaty sides to heal.

Absentmindedly, he watched as the Cork team came out. He scanned the crowd to see if there were any Offaly people he knew near him. In particular, he was looking for any of his neighbours who he knew were all hurling mad. Lads he had played with and against when the 'The Island' played Rahan during what he would refer to as his own "heyday" of hurling. All those fellas were fine hurlers but maybe not up to the level of the players now warming up in front of him in the Offaly colours from further south in the county.

This was Offaly's first day of glory and with many newspapers claiming the standard on the day was of senior status, my father said he was at all times cognisant of the potential danger his presence might put him in.

His thoughts kept reverting to the summer Sunday two years previous when he played his last match for his home team. That was also the last day he set foot in 'The Island.'

He recalled that the match against Rahan had been a tough hour's hurling. When he told me about the game many years later in the seventies, at that remove he was no longer sure of the final score, but he had a feeling that The Island might have won. What he was certain of was that the match ended in a row, like many's a match against Rahan. But, perhaps understandably, his memory of the detail of this final match was more than a bit clouded by the events that followed later that Sunday.

The match had been played in the field in the townland of Ballina, a couple of hundred yards from his own home. When the match ended and the hullabaloo quietened down, he made a bee-line for home.

To his great dismay when he opened the door into the kitchen, he found his mother cradled in front of the fire in tears, not something she was wont to do.

"Matt, you have to go away immediately," she implored between loud gasps of anguish. "Go down to Ballycumber Station this minute and get on the next train to Dublin and go and stay with your sister Bridgie."

My father was confused but as an anti-treaty activist, his antennae would have been attuned to fear the worst around every corner.

His mother explained that "a young lad from Rahan had slipped away after the match and came in here in a hurry and told me that 'The Boys' will be coming to get you tonight."

Matt and his mother knew exactly what that meant – reprisal killings were all too common in those black days of 1922. There was no time to spare and it didn't take long for him to pack his few items of clothing and a few other things to bring to Dublin with him.

His mother had already told Paddy, his younger brother, to yoke the pony and the trap which was by now standing in 'the street' in front of the house and ready for off.

His mother told him: "Your father has 10 shillings in a tin under the bed – bring that with ya" and in what seemed like a blink of an eye, she was standing at he half door waving after him. Matt, my father, was gone out the door a fugitive of his time.

And so at Croke Park this autumn Sunday two years later, the Offaly and Cork match had finally started and the two teams were going hell-for-leather. My father's attention was on the game and he watched the three Cordials, especially Will, his favourite player in the county, do the colours proud in a tit-for-tat first half.

There was a big crowd that day and after a while he forgot his inhibitions and began roaring on the Offaly lads and at times shouting out instructions to them. There was nothing in it when the half-time whistle blew, he remembered clearly it was 2-1 apiece.

The brief respite from the action gave him another chance to look around. It was then he noticed a vaguely familiar face making his way through the crowd towards him.

A Killoughey man he seemed to remember. Killoughey was another Offaly hurling parish but a good way from 'The Island', somewhere off down near the Slieve Bloom mountains. The thoughts of Killoughey instantly stirred up an uncontrollable feeling of terror in him, not because of the matches he had played against them, but because this was an area where much of his own active IRA volunteer activity took place.

In fact, he had spent a number of months on the run in that vicinity from The Tans and the RIC. Croke Park hadn't been unscathed by the Troubles and he told me that at that very moment, the scenes of Bloody Sunday shot across this mind.

 But surely nothing like that was afoot on this occasion…

He relaxed when the man held out his hand in greeting and said: "I don't know that you remember me at all, Matt…".

He said the man gave him the warmest of extended handshakes. It was full of happiness and delight and any fears he had about reprisal immediately left his mind.

The man smiled, then composed himself for a moment and whispered into his ear. "I want to explain why I'm so delighted to see you here today."

He hesitated for a moment, then went on: "It's because myself and another lad were given a revolver and ordered to go to shoot you the night of the Rahan match".

Before my father could fully comprehend everything that was being said, the Killoughey man continued: "I tell you truthfully, I was never as glad of anything in all my life when your mother told us that you had left when we knocked that night on your door".

When my father mentioned this story to me maybe half a century after that day for the one and only time, I could see the change in his eyes and his demeanour as he recounted the encounter at Croke Park.

He said he and the Killoughey man repaired to a local hostelry after the game and drank the night away. He spoke movingly of their shared feeling of elation not just at their improbable meeting but, also, their shared disgust and utter frustration at the many unspeakable events of the civil war that they were both trying hard to forget.

That day changed my father – he saw it as a sign that he was no longer a fugitive in his own land. In the interim, he had made a new and better life in Dublin but within a week he travelled down to see his mother and family again and knew there was no longer a price on his head.

He continued to live in Dublin for many years afterwards and would go to Croke Park almost every Sunday there was a match there regardless of who was playing. The year 1966 was a big year in Ireland, as the country celebrated the 50th anniversary of the 1916 Rising.

Although married and with a large and still quite young family (he was 60 when I was born), my father could resist the call of his own place no more and uprooted me, the youngest of his family and my mother to spend his remaining years living happily on Offaly soil. The rest of the family, who were much older than me, stayed on in Dublin.

My father died in 1986 aged almost 90 and other than telling me about his meeting with the Killoughey man in Croke Park, I don't believe he ever referred to the incident to anyone else.

As I watched him grow older through my own adult eyes, I detected many times when I know that day sustained him – for one, it brought an end to the Civil War within his own head.

I don't think there was a day that passed that he wasn't grateful to his would-be assassin for putting his mind at rest on the day Offaly, under the captaincy of Jack Halligan, won their first major national honour as All Ireland champions against Cork by 3-4 to 3-2.

Aidan Clancy was born and raised in Dublin until at the age of 10 went to live in Cloghatanny, Clara, Co Offaly where he stayed until his late teens. Since then, he has lived in Dublin, spending a lifetime in the civil service where he worked in a variety of roles with a deep commitment to public service, perhaps inspired by his father's earlier sacrifice for his country. Aidan is married with two children but still loves to keep in contact with that area of Offaly his father loved so deeply.

Uprooted Tree For
A Dressing-Room

Murt Hunt

As a true blue GAA man all my life, it is a proud moment to have over 60 years football enjoyment and things have changed a lot in that time.

Watching a recent match, I was fascinated with the gear that most players have now, various brands and colours of boots, socks and the now familiar bicycle shorts, also the fantastic changing rooms with showers, etc. and the wonderful manicured pitches.

It brought me back to my own football days, when we were not so fortunate to have these luxuries. We had pitches with an uphill and downhill and usually togged out behind a fence or tree.

Indeed, one local team was the envy of the neighbouring clubs as they had an uprooted tree as a dressing room and it provided shelter from the elements. I remember running home from the bog one summer's evening after a hard day's work footing turf, grabbing a bite to eat and running into town to play underage football for my local club. Had I football socks or boots? No. Had I togs? No. But I was accommodated by a few mates and finished with two different football boots, both hurting like mad and my mother's home knitted brown woollen socks.

My good friend Michael RIP had a pair of second-hand boots to sell and gave me first refusal, the only problem being that there was a hole in the toe of one boot, but gladly he was left footed and I was right footed. My right boot was like new and I had wet and muddy feet all the time with the left. Did I mind? Not in the slightest.

Many a goal and point were scored with that good boot until eventually there was a hole in both boots. I was in secondary school before I graduated to a fairly good pair. A boy named Casey had finished up school and left his boots behind, so I borrowed/stole his boots and socks and togs.

I won a Connacht colleges medal as captain and represented my club at all grades with those boots. I bought my first new pair in England and played for St. Anne's in Manchester for a few years, before coming home and playing for my local club again.

I broke my wrist twice, was knocked out twice and now suffer from arthritis from my football injuries. Would I do it all over again given the opportunity? You guessed it, of course I would, even with only one good boot.

Murt Hunt is a native of Lecarrow, Ballyhaunis where he still lives. He is an ex-Guinness employee and is a part-time farmer. Murt recently celebrated his 75th birthday with his family in Boston, USA. He has a family of six, four girls and two boys and 10 grandchildren, his wife Anne R.I.P. having died at age 43 in 1994. His hobbies include gardening, GAA, crosswords and writing poetry and songs.

Radio Broadcast That Called Me Home From London

Brendan Kelly

Your destiny is not in the stars but your own hands, according to the playwright William Shakespeare. And I'm inclined to agree with the old bard on that although in my case, I was more inclined to drift along with the tide of day-to-day living as a young lad in exile in London.

That was until something happened inside my head on Sunday September 7, 1975 when I woke up and realised I would not be making the journey to Croke Park to support my beloved Galway who were playing Leinster champions Kilkenny in the All Ireland senior hurling final.

Had I been back living in my native Laurencetown, near Ballinasloe, there would have been buses, cars and trains taking us all east to Dublin to cheer on the county which had not got that far on the hurling front since 1958.

Instead, I was living in a flat in London and wondering how I'd find out anything about the game. Remember these were the days before mobile phones or internet coverage and even before the time that Ambrose Gordon used to bring back recordings of big games from Ireland to London pubs on a Monday night.

A friend of mine, Mick Nevin from Eyrecourt, who played hurling with St Gabriel's and London, lived nearby and was as interested as me in seeing how the great John Connolly and co would get on in Croke Park.

Fortunately, he called to my flat early that day and suggested we both go up to Roundwood Park in Willesden in the London borough of Brent which was a good spot for transistor radios to pick up RTE's radio signal.

By the time we arrived in the place, there was a fair crowd already assembled, mostly Galway people but a few from Kilkenny as well as a handful of men from other counties just interested in the game itself.

I'd say there was a big group of 50 or so trying to listen as four lads climbed up on branches of trees seeking to find the clearest reception. And so it was that the crowd drifted one way, then another, up and down the footpath under the trees as the band waves ebbed and flowed between the four transistors and between the commentary box in the Hogan Stand and this 25-acre patch of North West London.

The match started out well for us and when Frank Burke scored an early goal to give us a 1-3 to 0-3 point lead, for a short time, Mick and I felt this might be our year. By half-time Kilkenny were 0-9 to 1-3 in front and when Eddie Keher began motoring and hit us for 2-7, well, it was no contest as they ended up beating us by 2-22 to 2-10.

We waited until the very end of the transmission and the crowd began dispersing when the lads swung down from the trees and we had radio silence. As the few Kilkenny supporters in our midst shouted and celebrated another successful Liam MacCarthy voyage, a few curious passers-by and drivers rolled down their windows to ask what was going on.

Myself and Mick didn't feel inclined to answer them as we were pretty crestfallen to be beaten by 12 points. Like all good Irishmen, we headed straight for the nearest pub, the College Park on Harrow Road, deciding we'd have a few pints to drown our sorrows.

As we approached the pub, we could hear huge excitement inside and for a minute I thought it had something to do with the All Ireland. However, on entry, we could see that the fuss was over a game of dominoes which had reached its conclusion among a group of Jamaican lads. We passed them on the way to the counter where we called for our drinks and looked around to see a small knot of Sunday afternoon drinkers watching an old black and white John Wayne film on the television.

In that moment as I looked around at the group playing dominoes and the older set watching a movie I had something of a Eureka moment.

After taking a slug of the pint, I said: "Mick, I'm not going to spend the rest of my life here. I'm going home as soon as I can."

We both imagined what it must have been like back in Ireland on an All-Ireland day and even though Galway lost, we knew people would be out talking about the match and later still, the chat might turn to what could happen next year.

For us as GAA lovers, this was a sacred day in our calendar, yet in this London pub, it had no relevance at all.

"You know what," Mick said after considering our line of chat – "I might do the same myself." As it turned out he didn't, but he remains a great GAA man and he hops on a plane any time Galway get to Croke Park.

Later that night when I met up with my girlfriend Anne Fitzgerald, I told her we should plan to move home. That time jobs were pretty scarce on the ground in Ireland and I was getting good pay working on the buses in London, initially as a conductor and later as a driver. Anne also had a good job working in the office of McVitie's biscuits factory in Harlesden. So, it was one thing talking about going home, and an entirely different matter to actually contemplate doing it.

When we got married in England in '77 the thought was still in our heads even though by then we also had bought a house for £13,000 and put a lot of time and effort into doing it up and making it a very comfortable dwelling.

Our eldest son Kevin arrived the following year and all the while life got in the way of some of the hazy plans I made the day Galway lost to Kilkenny. It took the wise counsel of a neighbour over from Tipperary to get us focused again.

Talking one day as Irish people do when they bump into each other, he congratulated me on my son and said if I was to ever seriously think about going back, I should do it before the young lad went to school.

"I'd every intention of going home myself with the wife and our two daughters but once they started making friends at school, Ireland was fine for a summer visit but London was home to them," he told me.

By the time of our encounter, his twin girls were sixteen and he knew he was destined to live out his days in England's capital as an Irish exile.

Shortly afterwards destiny beckoned us again when Anne's brother told us when we were home on a visit that he had built a house in Galway for £33,000, which coincidentally was the same price a local auctioneer had valued our property in London.

Eventually, we arrived back to live in Galway a decade after I had left our family home of mother, father and 12 children as a 17-year-old to earn my keep firstly in Dublin as a barman and later in London on the buses. I had also begun work on the building and my first day I was enrolled as a 'carpenter' by a foreman I knew well and went on to progress up the ranks in the construction world.

We were only a month home when the Pope arrived in Ireland and in Galway and it was a great time to be Irish. And an even better one to be Irish and living in Ireland.

We settled in Craughwell and when our second son Shane arrived by then we were part of the community. As the years went by, we became embedded in the local GAA club and I had the honour of working on various committees as well as serving as chairman for a number of years.

The club's facilities have grown exponentially over the years and it is of immense satisfaction to see not just my children but now my grandchildren becoming part of the fabric that Anne and myself have been involved in for over four decades.

I often think of the Robert Frost poem 'The Road Not Taken' and wonder would I have ended up like the Tipperary man and spent my life in London had Mick and myself not gone to Roundwood Park that September Sunday and felt the need afterwards to be surrounded by our own sporting and social culture.

To paraphrase the poet, we took the road less travelled home... "And that has made all the difference" to our family.

Brendan and Anne Kelly are Galway natives who have two sons, Kevin, who is married to Karina and Shane, who now lives in Vancouver. They have three grandchildren; Laura, Eoghan and Ronan. Brendan is a well-known Formwork sub-contractor and has been involved in many major contracts all over Ireland, including Dublin Airport's Control Tower and the old Hill 16 in Croke Park.

The GAA's Role Of Team Doctor Can Be A Broad Church

Dr Liam Farrell

My native village of Rostrevor dates to pre-Christian times, and the Farrell clan have been here all along, a savage race as ancient and atavistic as the peat; to us the good old days means hunter-gathering. The ancestral Farrells used to own all the land, until it was stolen from us by the Druids.

Gaelic football is our passion; my son Jack now wears the same red and black worn by his father and his father's father before him, and I am one of the team mentors. Mentor was Telemachus' adviser during Ulysses' suspiciously protracted return from Troy, and I am sure that if deep-browed Homer could have foreseen how Mentor's name would be hijacked by a bunch of overweight balding men running up and down the touchline in unflattering pink lycra, he would have been both charmed and delighted.

The role of team doctor is a broad church. Of course, I treat injuries and advise on fitness etc but when the honour of the parish is at stake, the Hippocratic oath becomes but a trifling matter.

Recently, we reached the county final and on the big day, I introduced myself beforehand to the referee, assuring him that my medical skills were available to both sides if needed; to paraphrase Shakespeare, 'thus winning him with honest trifles to betrayals of deeper consequence.' It proved a wise investment.

Rostrevor was two points ahead with only minutes left, when one of the twin Magees (I still can't tell them apart) went down from an accidental boot to the ear. In emergency medicine every second counts, and I burst on to the field to gasps from the crowd.

Sprinting desperately, I arrived just in time...just in time before the brat got up. Pushing him back down with one heavy hand while putting on a Robert Jones bandage with the other (this was a cunning and time-consuming choice).

Aware of the thin line between safely running down the clock and the referee smelling a rat, I timed it carefully. I tied the last knot with a flourish and seconds later the final whistle blew, the other mentors surged forward and carried me shoulder high on a glorious lap of honour, and we drank the blood of our enemies and exulted in their lamentations.

"Let me have around me men that are fat," I thought, wise advice from Julius Caesar.

Footnote; Dedicated to my good friends Tom Magee, Dominic Tinnelly, Paddy McEvoy, Paul McGrath, Peter Bailey and Brian Fitz-patrick, with whom I have spent many happy years running up and down the line.

*Dr Liam Farrell is a Rostrevor native and author of 'Are you the f**king doctor?' He was a family doctor in Crossmaglen for 20 years. His columns have appeared in the British Medical Journal, the Lancet, the Irish News and the Belfast Telegraph. He was Columnist of the Year at the UK Magazine Awards 2005, the Irish Medical Media Awards 2002, and the UK Medical Journalists 2011. He presented A Country Practice for BBC NI and Health Check for UTV. He curated the #IrishMed and #WritersWise tweetchats, and received the Advancing Health through Media award at the Zenith Global Healthcare Awards 2018.*

Was I The First Sponsored GAA Player?

Patsy McGovern

Word had been circulating for about a week that a new curate was coming to the parish and that he was a Leitrim player. The year was 1965 and I was 10 years old. A few days later he arrived into the school, tall and athletic in appearance. Nervously we stood up and recited the well-rehearsed 'Failte Romhat a Atháir.'

"Well tell me, do any of ye play football?" he asked.

Immediately 52 hands shot up into the air. He signalled for us all to follow him. You can only imagine our excitement when he took a real leather football out of the boot of his Volkswagen Beetle.

"Right," says he, "let me see who are the best footballers," and he kicked the ball high into the air above our heads.

With grazed hands and knees after our first serious training session, we returned to the classroom. He then began to pick out players and anxiously I held my breath, until finally he pointed to me.

"I have a challenge game arranged for ye for next Friday week against Aughnasheelin National School," said the curate.

Aughnasheelin was in Leitrim but it was only a few miles up the road; our parish was on the Leitrim border. The Master had no interest in football and I knew he did not like any of this. "I'll get a loan of jerseys," he said.

Needless to say there were no sports shops in those days and even if there were, no one could afford to buy anything!

"Tell your mothers to empty out the four-stone flour bags, wash them and bring them into the Mistress here in two days' time," he continued.

My brother Noel was also one of the pupils selected to play and although Mum had an almost empty four stone bag, she also had to cut open a new one, much to her annoyance, so we'd have one each.

The bags were emptied, washed and taken into the mistress, who then took our waist and leg measurements.

She must have worked until the small hours every night sewing up the 20 pairs of togs. On the day before the match she gave each of us our togs in a bag. They were perfection itself. As none of us had football boots of our own, we played in our working hobnailed boots.

The day of the game came round at last. When we arrived, the other team were already fully kitted out with jerseys, togs and football boots. The curate told us to change quickly and to follow him onto the football field so he could line us out in our designated positions. The curate himself was the referee because of his football experience.

Just then I heard a titter from behind and my teammates began to move in, out and sideways to look down at me. My brother Noel was standing close to me and I sheepishly asked him what was wrong.

"Look at your togs," he muttered. Glaring up at me in slightly faded, but still very legible lettering were the words – Odlums Flour.

I can still clearly remember staring down at the words. It was then the turn of all the opposition to pick on me and scoff at my predicament. They did so with gusto.

I couldn't wait for the game to start in the hope that the action would divert their attention from me. No such luck! After about 10 minutes, the opposition had almost as many goals. Half-time came and in fairness the curate did not criticise us. Neither did he do so at full-time.

We returned home a battered, beaten, deflated lot. I threw the togs into a drain, swearing never to set foot on a football pitch again. The incident continued to cause amusement at my expense in the school for months and resulted in several fights.

About a year afterwards, my mother bought me a leather football for my birthday and from then on I was hooked on the game. The curate continued to play county football for Leitrim and is still hale and hearty, nearly 50 five years later, living in North Leitrim.

The Master and Mistress have gone to their eternal reward. I often look back at those early years at the national school and in my home club. There were very few facilities. I often think about that game, the mothers who emptied out and washed the flour bags and the dedicated Mistress who made the togs.

However, to this day when I'm shopping, my heart still skips a beat if I happen to see that little owl staring out at me from the Odlum's Flour pack. From time to time, I meet some of my old school mates and also players from the Aughnasheelin School and we reminisce about our school days and I can laugh about that day in particular. I have a good story to tell – I always say that despite the embarrassment I surely must have been the first sponsored GAA player!

Patsy McGovern is a native of Corlough, Co. Cavan. He served in An Garda Siochána for 35 years. Married to Mary they live on the border of Donegal and Leitrim. Patsy has a keen interest in GAA and rugby and has been an active member of Melvin Gaels GAA Club, Kinlough, Co. Leitrim for over 40 years.

Objection Over Player Leaving Field To Hit Fan

Pádraig Mac Mathúna

Objections were a big part of the GAA during those decades of the last century and many games were won and lost, depending on the skill of those presenting the case.

A memorable example, which was upheld from a hurling match, was when a club put forward the case that a player named James Carney had rendered himself illegal for the rest of the game when he left the field of play to strike a spectator – without the permission of the referee (to leave the field that is). The case was upheld!

* * *

In a game in Clare between Corraclare and Ballyvaughan in the 1950s, one of the Corraclare cars broke down on the way to the game. This resulted in the club only having 13 players available at the venue for the start of the game.

To comply with the rule that they needed a full 15 by the start of the second half, one of the taxi drivers went in to make up numbers, though they still only had 14 instead of the required 15.

This man had never played football in his life but despite this and the fact that they were another man short, Corraclare won the game on the day.

Unfortunately, they lost it in the boardroom afterwards when their opponents objected and cited the requirement of 15 players on a team by the start of the second half, noting their opponents had only 14 by then.

Proud To Be From 'All-Ireland Scenery Champion'

Michael O'Brien

Many of our sporting organisations are feeling the financial pinch since the Covid 19 Pandemic. The big four that immediately come to my mind are Horse Racing Ireland, the FAI, the IRFU and the one that is nearest and dearest to my heart, the GAA.

I have been an enthusiast and a member since I was a small boy. Horse racing is known as the sport of Kings. Kings you associate with crowns, power and wealth. I suspect the kings still have deep pockets. The FAI always seem to be scrapping to survive. They are used to a tough coalface and I suspect that this time they will again muddle through.

The IRFU is associated with the wealthier end of society. On big days at Lansdowne Road sheepskin coats and whiskey flasks abound. The IRFU is now, at top level, a professional sport with a big wage bill and sundry expenses. They will survive.

The GAA is an amateur sport so no big wage bill there. But they do have their administrative staff to pay both in Head Office and at county board level. The development of new stadiums is also very costly while some existing stadiums have large debts. The GAA was built up at parish level by the energies and pennies of the ordinary local people.

Playing field facilities and equipment were 'chicken roost' in my early days. Today, at club and county level, the team panel will arrive with designer tracksuits, branded boots or joggers. Contrast that with the teams of my boyhood who were lucky to have their own togs, football boots and a pair of club stockings.

Every club would have one football, value £5-0-0. Both players and officials came to matches in their Sunday best, lucky to have a £6 suit straight out of Talbot St. Each club had one set of jerseys, those same jerseys being used for all senior, minor and juvenile matches.

Several of my classmates were swamped when wearing the jerseys but, as I was quite a burly lad, the jersey did not quite consume me. The games were usually played in a local field, the property of a local farmer. There were no dressing-rooms and no facilities of any sort.

One just hoped that not many bovine had adorned the pasture during the previous week. Sheep were usually less destructive and usually herded up to a far corner. Referees were appointed at local board level while umpires were usually a compromise on the day. Generally, they all wore their street clothes.

I once observed an official from a rival club, a club poorer than ours, distribute the jerseys.

"Here Noel. Put this jersey on and stand in the goal".

"Where is Jim Byrne?"

" Oh, he won't be here. He has to take a cow to the bull. Mick, will you put on this jersey?"

"Oh, I have no boots".

"Doesn't matter. Play away without them."

So, it went on through the bleak 1950s. Many clubs struggled to put out a full team. I remember one such occasion when our club was hard pressed to field 15 players. A local garda was arrested and press-ganged into playing for us. He removed his police jacket, pulled the jersey over his shirt and tucked his trousers into his stockings. As there were no boots available out he went and the opposition tore into him.

But clubs stayed afloat somehow, mothers darned and washed and ironed football shorts. As far as I can remember, our only set of jerseys were thrown into a club official's turf shed. Games were played and results and performances were topics of conversation in the entire parish for the next few days. Later in the week, talk of the upcoming games dominated. Hard work by the locals kept parish clubs ticking over.

County Wicklow is one of the few counties that never won a senior title at either provincial or national level. However, right now my native club, Valleymount, boasts a pitch and club premises that is located in the most picturesque setting in all of Ireland as has been illustrated in the national newspapers and digital media these past few weeks for all to see. There is no dispute but that the setting is beautiful but it came at a very great cost as I well remember. The major portion of the land on which the facilities sit today were once part of my late mother's family house and farm, the rest belonging to a neighbour.

Both families, along with about 80 other families were compulsory purchased out of the valley to make way for the 7,000-acre reservoir and Poulaphuca Hydro Electric scheme circa 1940. The official line was that public purpose must override private sentiment. A community was vanquished and the reservoir took over. Around the time that the GAA club took over the lease on the property, I was 12, had just acquired my first long trousers, my first bicycle and was in the process of pushing my parents for my first football boots.

My early pleadings fell on deaf ears but my father must have sold an extra wether or two because, one evening, my mother arrived home on the evening bus laden with several brown paper parcels, one of which she handed to me. Upon ripping off the string and wrapping there they were, my beautiful new football boots resting snugly in the box.

The boots were made by Blackthorn in Dundalk. They came up above the ankles and carved into the leather on both boots was the word "Krackshot". I immediately donned the boots, jumped on my bike and took myself across the bridge that spanned the narrow neck of the recent reservoir to the football field.

Most evenings would find me in the field. It was a sort of addiction and also proved, in later years, to be an antidote to a young man's thoughts of girls and their positive differences. Some of my schoolmates began to admire my new attire and often, as I togged out, the odd one would sidle up and sotto voice, would enquire: "Is there any chance of your left boot?"

The thinking was that if you were a right-footed person you would not be using the left boot with the same frequency. So, yes, I often shared my boots. The jersey may have been thrown into the turf shed but not the boots. My 'krackshot' boots were hung on my bed post every night, the smell of the new leather and the bruised grass intoxicating. Each evening I said my prayers to my new boots. Amen.

The football pitch was made up of two fields divided by a cla-sach or 'mearing' ditch. I took my spade to the field to help fill in the mearing ditch. Wicklow is the birthplace and home of Irish forestry so there was no bother getting the material to make a set of goalposts and crossbars. Nets came much later. By the mid-60s I had moved away the 25 miles to live and work in Dublin and even to this day, I always make the distinction between where I reside and where I live.

At the time the field was acquired, Valleymount was a Dublin Diocesan parish that was somewhat despised by ambitious clerics. It boasted a store where, as the poet Patrick Kavanagh put it, you could purchase "meal, pollard and flour.

Horse nails too, coal, porter, stout and stronger brew."

Next door was another family-owned grocery and post office. Next to it was a doorway to the dark – the farrier's forge. The flooded valley hit the farrier's business hard due to loss of farm horses, ponies and donkeys too.

Today my home village has lost its parish status. It is now part of the Blessington Union of Parishes. The shops and post office are long closed, bus services have been curtailed and the pub only opens at the weekend. The one feature to have endured and that sets it apart from other places is the GAA club. Since the lease was put in place more than 60 years ago club officials, volunteers giving of their time, financial help from both the Lottery and Croke Park have built state of the art facilities while cleaning back the site and improving it so that today it can now hold its head high as 'The All-Ireland Scenery Champion.'

My late mother's home stood to the left of the new Clubhouse. I was reared across the Humphreystown bridge, fished illegally in the reservoir, took my first swimming strokes there too (also illegal). I suppose we should be glad to have 5,000 acres of clean water serving our needs, all in a beautiful setting – but at what price.

Michael O'Brien comes from a family of nine siblings, is a native of Wicklow and played minor football for the county for two years. Although living in Dublin for almost 60 years, his heart never wanders far from his beloved Valleymount.

Spectating From GAA's Hidden Sanctuary

Paul Holland

I like to go there. It's the sanctuary just behind the goal. What's more, if it's a match where the attendance is comfortably accommodated in the stand or the sideline terraces, you have the place almost to yourself. In this haven for observers, you see and hear plenty.

The rumble of jumbo jets provided the background music to a club game in Shannon but it didn't drown out the voices of defenders querying the state of the umpires' eyesight. I was soon concerned about my own vision as well as the umpires as they allowed scores which, the defenders pointed out, were wides or followed from square balls, illegal passes, too many steps, obstruction and a million other infringements. The umpires didn't seem overly upset by the insults, one of them saying to the goalie: "You do your job (which he wasn't) and I'll do mine." Still, he had got it relatively easy.

His counterpart in another county had been told that the only white coat he was fit to wear was the type they gave you at the local mental hospital. And, more sinister, another umpire was asked how thick was the brown envelope he had got from Kerry Co-Op?

A ball falling from heaven may be covered by the goalkeeper only for a forward to materialise from nowhere and put it in the net. Likewise, a ball ordained to go over for a point may be grabbed by a wind to direct it just under the crossbar. A slippery ball or one coming with a lethal spin can result in the 'keeper letting in a goal my grandnephew would have stopped.

At times I find myself identifying with the goalkeeper. I recall a match where the attacking team had a superlative player – he was of African ethnicity. If he got the ball, it was disaster for the defending team. Any time I saw him unmarked, I nearly found myself shouting at the defenders for someone to pick him up. On another evening in

"

county Roscommon, it did not matter that I was outside the fence behind the goal. The attacking team, Strokestown, were into high-speed defence-splitting passing movements. The sight of five or six of them charging towards me made me feel like a Roman legionnaire facing the Parthian cavalry at Carrhae.

The backs, whose fate was that of the Romans, employed pre-emptive defence measures at times – like pulling down a forward when an attack threatened. The game was in a rural pitch but the resultant language was unmistakably industrial in nature.

In Stradbally, it was a ladies football game, Derry v Laois. Not a good day for the Laois ladies. Here I was reminded of the inherent risk of placing oneself behind the goal. The Derry keeper might as well have brought a hammock as virtually all the action in the first half was at the other end. Mentally I drifted and was caught by surprise when some action erupted near the square. The second half was the opposite as there were plenty of scores but what sticks in my mind was the attitude of the Laois 'keeper. She kept to the task, stayed cheerful, and called out directions and encouragement to her defenders. When they weren't waving flags, the umpires called out encouragement to her.

The Laois ladies had a work ethic, tried to the end and when I said "well done" to some of them after their trouncing, they were happy that I had noticed that they had given of their best. Elsewhere, at another ladies match, the action had moved upfield leaving behind a forward who had gone over on her ankle. The goalkeeper screamed immediately for assistance for her opponent. Sporting magnaminity of the highest order – and it's nice to witness it when it happens.

In the good old days long before 'Health & Safety', I sat on a stone bench near the goal in Castlebar. Galway versus Mayo in 1968. MacHale Park was overcrowded; people lay on the grass behind the end line. They had to; anytime they forgot themselves and jumped up in excitement, they were bombarded with cartons, rolled-up papers, clods of earth and filthy language. We were inches away from Mattie MacDonagh as he dribbled the ball soccer-style, held off three Mayo defenders and buried the ball in the net. It was Galway's day and, for me, there was the extra reward of seeing myself in a picture of the incident that was published in the Connacht Tribune.

I'm from Galway but I like to go to games around the country. There's less risk of cardiac arrest when you go to matches as a neutral. In summer 2017, I was at the U-21 B All Ireland hurling semi-final involving Donegal and Tyrone which was held in Carrickmore. I sat behind the goal all by myself in the Nally Stand, the same revered stand that stood in Croke Park for years. It brought back memories of days in Croke Park with my late father. And I got some exercise – whenever sliotars cleared the boundary fence, I hopped down to retrieve them and fling them back to the umpires rather than, as Michael O'Hehir put it "take home a souvenir".

Spring 2018 brought me to the beautiful Glens of Antrim and Cushendall, where Antrim faced Limerick in a hurling league game. The crowd was a small one and only a few of us were behind the goal. Antrim started well but Limerick gradually took control.

In the second half, I watched the Limerick forwards walk in a goal, a good one which was greeted with total silence. That goal, I thought to myself, would have lifted the roofs off the stands in Croke Park if it had happened there.

A few months later, to Galway's grief, it did.

A 15-Year-Old's Carlow Senior Debut... Almost!

John Kelly

Back in late September 2000, Carlow was playing Wexford in the All-Ireland SFC 'B', down in Enniscorthy. I have long been a massive Carlow follower in both codes. However, at the time I was only 15, so I persuaded my good mother to drive me down to Enniscorthy.

Once we got there, we discovered we were the only two Carlow supporters present and to make it worse, Carlow only had 14 players.

We got talking to Carlow secretary Tommy O'Neill, as we all came from Tinryland and knew him well. Tommy said that if Carlow didn't have 15 players by the start of the second half, he would get me some gear and stick me in to bring up the numbers.

As a 15-year-old, I was excited but also a little scared. These were my heroes, after all.

Alas, about 10 minutes into the first half, John McGrath came running through the gates with his gear bag and, after a quick change, he was out on the field and with it brought Carlow up to the full complement of players.

His arrival scuppered my senior intercounty football career, which was now officially over before it had begun...

John Kelly is a native of Tinryland in Carlow but now resides in Castleisland, Kerry. A massive Carlow GAA follower all his life, he is currently involved in the GAA in Kerry through Castleisland Desmonds & is chairman of St. Pat's East Kerry hurling club. He works as a healthcare assistant & his passions are music and the GAA. He is married to Marie and they have three children, Rian, Oran and Aodhán.

Reaching The Moment
Of GAA Reason

Jim McNamara

The elders said "he'll be fine, sure we'll take care of him and it will be a day he'll never forget." So in the grey Austin 40 all six of us set off for Limerick and the Munster final between Cork and Tipperary.

Our crew consisted of two older brothers, only one of whom could drive, three neighbours and myself.

Limerick was already full of cars when we arrived about noon. We drove in along the river bank, opposite Barrington's Hospital towards May Roberts pharmacy, until one bright spark noticed a parking space where someone had just pulled out. The day was fine and we took a few treats in a bag, and then headed with the crowd for what seemed miles to the Gaelic Grounds.

Flag sellers, fruit sellers, buskers, a banjo player called Pecker Dunne and programme sellers, all added colour and sound to the journey, intensifying as we approached the gates. A turnstile wheel made a loud click and someone said "the child is free", so instantly I was lifted over the obstruction and landed inside with the older brothers, my first elevation of the day.

Well pleased with this bargain and with his first day driving to the city, the older brother took the lead role in getting us a place to view the match, down near the side-line to be close to the players.

A minor match was already in full swing between Clare and Waterford, but that seemed to evoke little tribal excitement as people around us settled into sandwiches and increasing rumours of who was not going to be on for the big game, the changes of position and what all this meant for the likely outcome.

The rumours settled as a pipe band dressed in kilts, 'The Boher-bui', struck up and came within yards of us, with a massive drum and a lively march that put big feet around me tapping. Then a massive roar of the crowd as the Tipp team ran onto the field. The Blue and Gold players were followed shortly by Reds causing our immediate neighbours to roar even louder.

A sliotar landed from somewhere, but was hit only by the Reds, making me wonder "What's the problem with the Blues?" until someone said: "It's just a warm up." A while later the band appeared again and everyone stood and went silent with a serious look on faces as Amhrán Na bFhiann rang out across the field. A whistle was then blown and the real game was now on.

Lightning fast that little ball flew up and down with players running and reversing on all sides. I noticed a scoreboard at our end was continually being changed by hanging long numbers onto a hook 2-7 to 1-5. It was nearly half-time and one of our neighbours was now shaking his head, indicating something was up.

For the second-half the teams changed around and whatever took place at the break, suddenly our end was where all the action was. After another opening point by Cork, our goalie Tony Wall drove a longer than usual puck out down the field towards our end. We saw two not so tall players run and lift themselves higher than myself competing for that ball. One called Jimmy Doyle, with a twist of the hurley, guided that sliotar down to his waiting left hand. Then with a few turns and side steps we saw the net rattle and a roar of resurrection from the Tipp supporters. A tit-for-tat exchange of points continued, but Doyle repeated his magic twice more and each time with a heightened roar.

As the game came close to ending and with a widening gap on the scoreboard, one of the wiser neighbours suggested, maybe we should get out before the big rush. We walked with difficulty through long legged fans, over the raised bank and down towards the exit gates. As we approached the gate, I felt the space between me and the others tighten, legs and bodies were coming closer. I held on tightly to the older brother's and neighbour's hands, then in a sway of the crowd I lost one hand grip.

Someone then said "lift up the child". I remember clinging on to the shoulders of the two neighbours, but we still had to get through that gate. For what seemed like several minutes I felt the squeeze of upper bodies tighten around me and the air, it was too hot to breathe.

Both scared and excited, someone reassured me we'd be out of there soon and just to hang on up there!

Relieved to land down to earth and find my own feet again, the walk back to the city seemed much shorter. We all now needed to celebrate and a bakery/restaurant near William St called "Finns" was our next stop. The owner, they said, was herself from the mountains and known to give a decent meal to her own people. The smell of still fresh morning baking blended with the sauce on battered fish and a second helping was offered if needed.

On our way towards the car, we passed near the Round House Pub with all its doors open and could hear singing inside. Soon I was climbing onto a high stool, holding onto a shining brass bar, where a lady moved handles that filled pints and glasses of porter. 'Slievenamon' rang out in one corner and nearly everyone joined in, followed by "The Banks" near the door and then the banter continued. "He gave it to yea! The bloody ref gave it to yea!"

"Sour grapes!" the reply, as the intensity of accents raised with each glass of porter consumed.

When we arrived back towards the front of May Roberts, all the other cars had already gone home leaving our Austin van now in the middle of the road, in the care of a curious guard with a book in hand. Whatever negotiations and whispers took place to have the car released seemed to pass over me, but after a while the tall guard approached me.

"What age are you boy?"

"Six guard, but I'll be seven on Wednesday."

Someone said that's when we reach the age of reason. Decades on, I'm still not quite sure where reason meets the excitement of a Munster hurling final.

Jim McNamara is an organic farmer and founder of An tIonad Glas – the organic college in Dromcollogher, Co Limerick. Married with three children, he is co-author of the herb book Cluain Chumhra; Fragrant Meadow.

Going Through The Motions In A Different Era

Pádraig Mac Mathúna

Sometimes motions to the county convention asked for what we would now consider strange things to happen. In the 1930s to the 1950s, in particular during the last century, many were aimed at shooting down anything to do with foreign games.

Here are some examples:

1930 - From Kilrush: 'That GAA use everything in its power to prevent students attending school and colleges where foreign games are played.'

Also from Kilrush that year: 'That we call upon all members and supporters to refuse to support traders who support foreign games.

1934 – From Clarecastle: "That GAA use its influence to ensure that male teachers only are appointed in all national schools.

1937 – From Kilmihil: 'That umpires be selected at county board meetings.'

1942 – 'That the Garda authorities and the Minister For Post And Telegraphs be approached so that GAA results can be phoned from Garda barracks on Sundays and after 8.00pm on weekdays.'

1941 – 'That County Chairman seeks permission from government for the transport of teams to matches in lorries.'

1944 – From Clonbonny: 'That all clubs be compelled to organise a cross-country team and affiliate with NACA board.

1953 – Clohane: 'That when a penalty kick is taken, no player should be allowed to touch the ball until the goalkeeper has cleared it.'

1955 – That one of the All-Ireland finals be played in Casement Park.

1956 – 'That there be a special competition for over-aged minors.'

1957 – Kilkee: 'That there be three umpires at each goal.'

Giving Up A Cap
For Sam And Mayo

Maura Flynn

All that summer, cousin Pádraig had worked hard for the money to buy a cap. Every man worth his salt wore a flat cap in 1950s Ireland. Helping the neighbours save the hay, he hoped they would throw a few bob his way. Some did. Others just told him he was a great lad and his father would be proud of him. But pride wouldn't buy the cap. He saw the one he wanted in McCormack's window in Ballinrobe.

It was a grey and blue check, 'hounds tooth check' his big sister informed him it was called. As the summer moved on so did the Mayo team. It was 1951 and expectations were high.

The win the previous year was sweet, but to do it two years running would put the icing on the cake. Then they beat Galway in the Connacht final and they were on their way. Kerry was a tough one and they just managed a draw in the semi-final, but they beat them in the replay. The road to the final was clear...they would meet Meath in Croke Park.

Pádraig's father promised he would give him the train fare to Dublin, but he was still short some money for the cap. He had seen pictures from last year's final in the Irish Press and the crowd seemed to be a sea of flat caps.

He had to have one.

With only a few weeks left he had almost given up hope of getting the money together when he had a stroke of luck, well a stroke of luck for him anyway. His neighbour's sister died up the country and Pádraig was asked to milk the cow while the man was away at the funeral. No money was promised and the neighbour, Jonny, had a reputation for being tight-fisted. But when he came back from the funeral, he presented Pádraig with two shiny half-crowns, more than enough for the cap. Maybe his sister's death had softened him a bit, but it meant Pádraig would now have his cap and go to Croke Park the same as all the other lads.

At last, the great day arrived. Pádraig made his way to Ballinrobe railway station, carrying his topcoat in case it rained, his match ticket, a brown paper parcel of ham sandwiches... and most important of all his new cap. All his friends had flat caps, and when he put his on, he felt he had reached a new milestone in his life.

It was his first time on a train and his first time out of Mayo. As the train travelled through the countryside he marvelled at the new sights. Big towns. Small towns. Little cottages puffing turf smoke out of small chimneys and tall factory chimneys billowing out huge plumes from Bord na Móna bogs of the midlands.

It was like watching a film looking out the windows of the train carriage – no sooner had the lowlands and bogs disappeared and the magnificent sight of the Curragh racecourse in Kildare with horses being trained came into view.

By the time the train arrived at Westland Row in Dublin his head was spinning with all the things he had seen along the way. When he got off the train, he was swept along with the throng making their way to Croke Park. No need to ask how to get there, everyone was heading the one way. Then the great stands loomed in front of him and he thought his heart would burst with excitement.

It was a pretty even game to start with, but then Mayo pulled away and all the supporters cheered and roared at every score. In the end Mayo beat Meath by 2-8 to 0-9 in front of 78,201 spectators. Pádraig was one of that statistic.

As the final whistle was blown, the Mayo supporters stood and threw their caps in the air. In the excitement of victory, Pádraig did the same with his.

He was never to see his beloved millinery creation again. They say what goes up must come down but while this obviously happened in Pádraig's case, it disappeared into someone else's 'ownership' in that moment of hair-raising emotion.

As he walked down Jones Road on his way back to the train, Pádraic kept his eye out to see if he could spot his prized cap on someone else's head.

Not a sign. And even if he did, how could he prove it? With all the excitement on the train going home the cap was soon forgotten. Anyway, he reckoned on the journey that it was a great swap ...a cap for Sam Maguire.

Many years after the game, Pádraig and his family got a Land Commission swap to relocate from Mayo to county Meath. At every match and mart he went to, he still kept an eye out to see if he could recognise his beloved first flat cap.

He never had occasion to throw his cap in the air again, as Mayo have never won an All-Ireland since. Pádraig has since swapped that flat cap for a halo. I'm sure he will be looking down from on high, and he will still be looking out for his first flat cap that he lost on the hallowed ground of Croke Park.

Well-known writer Maura Flynn McDermott is originally from a townland called Partry in Co. Mayo, nestling between the beautiful lakes of Carra and Mask. She has lived in Westport for over 50 years with her husband John B. and has four grown up children.

'The Gaelic League was founded not upon hate of England, but upon love of Ireland'

Douglas Hyde, first President of Ireland

My First County Appearance Was Also My Last

Jarlath Mannion

I am lucky enough to have a son who played 100 times for Roscommon. So many times, yet I remember his first time like it was yesterday – I was very proud and then as the number of times he played stacked up, obviously some of the later games became something of a blur.

I wonder do people remember my first time which turned out to be my only time? Yes, I played once for the seniors in the primrose and blue and no I didn't just come on – I started in the Connacht senior championship semi-final when there was no second chance if you lost. It was the start and the end of my intercounty career – my fate decided by the mocking of a crossbar on the day.

I was the new up-and-coming centre-forward in 1965 in Mayo, playing on the 'mark'. I worked in Roscommon as a garda. Two weeks before my only game, I was actually working at the first-round game – and watching too as Mayo beat Roscommon.

The next game was Sligo but in the intervening weekend I played with my club Claremorris against Crossmolina. Their centre-back was none other than the Sligo centre-back, Cathal Cawley, who was also a garda and a good friend of mine from our Garda College days. Claremorris were much better and I scored 1-5 on him the week before Mayo played them.

Needless to say, that was the copy-writers dream. The Western People the following Thursday and three days before the Sligo game reported thus: "Who was this Mannion? Is he the best prospect in Mayo for years? Why would he NOT start on Sunday?"

Now Mayo at the time had a brilliant centre-forward, Joe Corcoran, who with the late, great John Morley were seen as two of the best players in the county. Best centre-forward in Mayo? Drop him for Mannion. To give you an idea how mad this was at the time, when

I ran out onto the field on that Sunday against Sligo, Cawley said to me: "Jarlath, where is Joe?"

You can guess how it went. With the teams more evenly matched, Cawley didn't give me a kick – not a sniff of the ball. However, football is a team game and Mayo were winning most of the individual battles on the day and went nine points up.

Then Sligo started clawing their way back but at five points down, I got away from Cawley for the one and only time in the match. I ran straight through and hammered the ball at goal, easily beating the keeper and... it thundered against the effing crossbar.

I hit it so hard its rebounded over my head to Cawley who kicked it down the field and Sligo scored a goal and the gap was down to two points. The die was cast and I was sitting on the sideline subbed off five minutes later with Mayo by then losing the game.

Sligo eventually won but would go on to lose the Connacht Final against Galway. That day for me aged 25 – never having been in the panel before, never being in the panel again – was my one game living the dream. Looking back on it now, I suppose I should think about the one I got, not the 99 I did not.

Forty years later, I sat watching my son score a last-minute goal against Corofin to win the Connacht title for St Brigids, our club in Roscommon. He would go on to win a Connacht title with Roscommon against Sligo and an All-Ireland club title with St Brigids.

I think back to the crossbar 40 years before. Would my life have been different if I had rattled the back of the net? And now I realise nearly 60 years later... the truth is the crossbar doesn't matter anymore.

Jarlath Mannion is a native of Claremorris, Co Mayo and won a senior title with his local club in the early 1960s. His garda work led him to Roscommon where he played with Padraig Pearses before settling in St. Brigids, with whom his son Karol won an All-Ireland Senior club title in 2013 while also representing Roscommon over 100 times. Jarlath is married to Cathryn, who played Camogie with Roscommon, and they have four children – Tina, Emma, Karol and John. Emma represented Roscommon and Connacht in both Ladies Football and Camogie over 10 years.

Lasting Legacies To Comedy And University Football

Fionnuala McNicholl

No matter where we live in the world today, there's something ingrained in us when it comes to our GAA affiliations. Like most who have wandered from their native parish, although I now live in Co Derry, my heart still lies in the green pitches of Tyrone when it comes to team support. From my neck of the woods of North Tyrone, two parishioners were instrumental in encouraging and nurturing the Association we have today.

Already Chairman of the Ulster Council, in 1904, Strabane inhabitant Michael O'Nolan, an Irish speaker, hurler and exponent of the Gaelic League, was appointed the first chairman of the Tyrone Co Board. Although born near Omagh, after graduation from University, Mr O'Nolan joined the Customs and Excise department of the civil service and was posted to Strabane. On arrival, he spent evenings teaching the Irish language in the town and surrounding districts. He also encouraged the playing of Gaelic games, which resulted in the towns first club being set up in 1902.

After marrying a local businessman's daughter, Agnes Gormley, the couple went on to have 12 children, including their third boy, Brian who was born in 1911. He became a civil service officer, novelist, dramatist and satirist, but is better known by his pen name Flann O'Brien and Myles na gCopaleen. In 1912, the O'Nolans moved to Glasgow before returning to reside and work in Dublin, where he remained until he died in 1937, aged 62.

In my home parish of Leckpatrick, on the outskirts of Strabane, George Sigerson was born at Holly Hill House in 1836. His father, a prosperous businessman, owned the local spade mill. George was educated in Letterkenny and later in Paris before returning to study medicine at the Catholic University Medical School and the National University of Ireland.

After graduation and continued study, Dr George Sigerson became one of Ireland's most prolific neurological scientific scholars. Along with his zeal for science, he was an outstanding Irish linguist interested in Irish poetry, literature, music and Gaelic games.

An avid supporter of the Gaelic League and revival, he embraced everything Irish and was an eminent contributor to political life. His home in Clare St., Dublin is said to have been a hive of activity with Irish literature greats and the political activists of the time.

In 1911, Dr Sigerson commissioned a trophy for GAA collegiate competitions. He proposed the trophy design with a silver body resembling a 'mether' (a mead drinking vessel) surrounded by four pillars representing the four provinces.

The Gaelic Football Club of UCD announced the inauguration of the 'Sigerson Cup' which was "to help create a unity between disjointed sections of the national universities."

UCC were the first recipients of the cup at a presentation in the Gresham Hotel on May 11, 1911. Ulster, however, had to wait until 1959, until Queen's University Belfast won, resulting in the Sigerson Cup crossing the border for the first time.

It is the longest-serving trophy for GAA games. Down the years, hundreds of students have been proud recipients of Sigersons medals from their university days, including many current players throughout the country.

Also, in 1911, back in his native Strabane, the GAA club was renamed in his honour to become 'Strabane Sigerson', with the pitch becoming Pairc Mhic Sioghair. In another string to his bow, Dr George Sigerson was a founding member of Feis Ceoil in Dublin in 1892. His final contribution to Irish public life came in 1922 as a member of the Senate on the formation of the Irish Free State. Aged 89, Dr Sigerson died after a short illness and was interred in Glasnevin Cemetery, Dublin.

Although there were turbulent years along the way, including two World Wars, emigration and obstacles throughout Northern Ireland's troubles, Dr Sigerson's legacy is ingrained in the hearts and minds of Strabane towns people and its hinterland.

My late father regaled of travelling by train to Croke Park in 1948 to support Tyrone minors in the All Ireland final. At Portadown station, a crowd gathered waving Union Jacks, knowing most onboard the train were GAA supporters on their way to the match. It didn't deter him or any of the supporters.

As a self-employed blacksmith at the time, a nasty leg fracture put notions of playing aside after spending nine weeks in Tyrone County Hospital in Omagh with his leg in traction. His love of Gaelic games, however, never diminished. Neither did his admiration flounder for his long-gone fellow parishioner, Dr Sigerson. So Dad kept alive Tyrone's anthem, The Mountains of Pomeroy, penned by Dr Sigerson. It was always the first tune he would play after taking his red Hohner accordion from its case. In turn, he took great pride in teaching it to us.

I only wish he had been alive to hear Cathal Hayden of Four Men and a Dog play The Mountains of Pomeroy so sweetly on the fiddle when the band celebrated their 30th Anniversary concert in February 2020 at Derry's Guildhall during the IMBOLC festival.

Accompanying Cathal that evening was the Folk Orchestra of Ireland, of which my nephew was a member. I've no doubt my father would have been proud. I can only imagine the smile on his face to see his Glaswegian great-grandson, aged six, sporting his Tyrone shirt as he, too, plays the spirited tune on a tin whistle.

I think there would be a contented smile on both Michael O'Nolan's and Dr George Sigerson's faces, seeing tiny tots togged in club colours at blitz competitions throughout the country.

Creeping up on almost 100 years since Dr Sigerson's death, I salute you, former parishioner once named among the 125 most influential in GAA history. May your legacy never falter and your words 'The morn was breaking bright and fair, the lark sang in the sky...' never fall silent.

Fionnuala McNicholl is a native of Co. Tyrone who now lives with her husband in Co. Derry. A retired nurse, she has had several stories published in various magazines. In 20129, Fionnuala won Ireland's Own memoir writing competition.

Clash For The Ash

Michael Walsh

My first taste of competitive hurling came about by accident. A group of the lads in my school in the townland of Clash, Toomevara, Co. Tipperary, decided to hold a series of Sunday matches. After getting permission through my brother Matt from the owner to play in a field beside his house, we arranged the first contest.

These were no ordinary matches. A musician was asked to attend and play his accordion as we marched onto the field in single file. All the hurls were placed in a pile in the middle of the pitch and two 'captains' were nominated to extract a hurl in turn until two teams were selected; then we had to stand to attention for the playing of the national anthem.

Games lasted up to two hours, after which the weary combatants ambled home for tea, often nursing cuts and bruises, carrying damaged or broken hurls. As Sunday followed Sunday, some of the local people gathered on the roadside to watch and applaud a good catch, score or save.

Soon, most of that group graduated to playing juvenile hurling for Toomevara and we had an unusual mode of transport. With my father as official driver, the team travelled to all away matches in his open-backed Volkswagen pick-up after togging out at the club, before speeding in all weathers to the various venues.

When passing through the village or town of a team we were pitted against, we would get strange stares. It didn't stop us from winning. We were told that 'lack of comfort' would make us hardy and ensure we would win.

Michael Walsh is a native of Toomevara, Co. Tipperary, but now lives in Dublin with his wife Maura. The couple have four children and eight grandchildren

Memories Of That 'Windy Day' In Doneraile

Mike Monaghan

In 1962, Kildorrery reached the North Cork Junior Hurling Final for the first time. As years went by it is always remembered as the windy day in Doneraile. If 'Met Eireann' were on the go at the time, their chart would have been hitting the red alert button.

I was 13 at the time and my two older brothers Ned (18) and Tom (17) were playing. Tom was in goals and played quite well, even though the story of the game does not hold up very well for him.

We were playing Kilworth and there was no love lost (and there still isn't) between the teams.

Kildorrery decided to play with the wind and led at half time 6-7 to 0-1. On the resumption, Kilworth started banging in goals and with eight minutes to go, the score read 6-7 to 7-1.

I don't know how they held them out for the next five minutes but I have a clear memory of the final three minutes. At that stage, the ball went out for a line ball to Kilworth 30 yards from our goal. Back in those days, there was very little fencing around the pitch and everyone was within a few feet of the sideline.

'Twas mostly Kildorrery people in the area where the ball went out. A highly respectable local man coolly bent down and picked up the sliotar and put it into his pocket. It took a full two minutes before the ball was 'found.'

Play resumed and Kildorrery managed to clear the ball out to the middle of the pitch, where one of their players let fly with an almighty puck and, with the wind behind him, the ball went narrowly wide and sailed about 100 yards behind the goal.

On this occasion, it took another minute to retrieve the ball. The referee of the day was a man called Reggie Nagle from a neighbouring parish, Shanballymore, a great GAA man who always had a soft spot for Kildorrery. And of course, you guessed it, the ball was pucked out and the full-time whistle was blown...right on time. Final score: Kildorrery 6-7 (25) Kilworth 7-1 (22). A never-to-be-forgotten occasion.

Mike Monaghan is a Kildorrery native and is a lorry driver. Married to Kay, they have six children. A life-long GAA man, pride of place in his house is his 'Corn Uí Mhuirí' medal won with De La Salle, Waterford in 1965 and two county medals with his own club in '78 and '81.

Secretary Forced
To Pick Himself For
All-Ireland Semi-Final

George Cartwright

Is there a GAA official anywhere who can match the length of service given to his county than Paddy Reilly from Cavan? Paddy, not to be confused with his namesake the legendary Paddy from Ballyjamesduff made famous by Percy French, was born in the townland of Drumullagh in the parish of Drumlane in west Cavan in 1880. At a young age Paddy moved to Cavan town where he lived all his life residing in later years in Atbara House with his wife and family. Paddy was one of the best-known GAA personalities in Cavan for over half a century and he was often referred to as 'Mr Football for County Cavan'.

He was one of the four men who re-organised the GAA in Cavan in 1903 and in May of that same year he was elected secretary of the newly constituted County Board. He served as an officer continuously for the next 56 years retiring in January 1959. He served as secretary, chairman, treasurer (for 33 years), Ulster Council delegate, Central Council delegate and honorary President. He also served as Chairman of Cavan County camogie board for a period. He was an officer during the golden years of Cavan football in the 1930s, '40s and '50s. In 1954 he was the recipient of presentations from the County Board, the clubs of the county and from his many friends to mark the golden jubilee of his election as an officer. Apart from the GAA Paddy worked in local government, first as a clerical officer, and later he served as secretary of Cavan County Council from 1927 until his retirement in 1940.

Paddy, though a modest player himself, also had the honour of playing for Cavan on one particular notable occasion. This was in the All-Ireland semi-final of 1904 which was not played until May 1906. The Ulster final of 1904 had not been completed and Cavan were nominated to represent the province in the All-Ireland semi-final. They were fixed to play Kerry in Jones' Road in May 1906. When the Cavan players arrived in Dublin it was discovered that only five of the selected team had turned up with 12 absent because of an ongoing dispute with the County Board. Paddy was in charge and as secretary he had the responsibility of putting the team on the field but he was faced with a dilemma. To fulfil the fixture, he began recruiting players from amongst the spectators, many of whom had travelled on the 'Special' train from Cavan earlier that day! He eventually got to sixteen (teams were 17 aside at that time) but as he still had another vacancy to fill there remained only one option and that was to play himself. This he duly did as he lined out at left corner-forward. Not surprisingly Kerry had a big win on a score line of 4-10 to Cavan's 0-1. So not a great day for Cavan football but a memorable occasion for the 12 recruits including Paddy who stepped into the breach unexpectedly and played in an All-Ireland semi-final against Kerry.

George Cartwright is a native of Cornafean and author of a number of GAA books including 'Up The Reds', 'Breifne Abú' and 'The Gallant John Joe'. A former school principal and chairman of Cavan Co Board, he is married to Lorraine and they have three grown-up children, daughters Helen and Emer and son James.

From 'Hiraeth' To A Life-Changing Moment

Helen Calvey

The Welsh call it 'hiraeth' …it is a sense of longing for home and the heartland. My birthplace of Achill Island in Mayo has always had that special connection for me, and 'hiraeth' is a reality that I have identified with at different phases of my life.

One such episode occurred during the lead up to the All-Ireland Football final of 1989 between Mayo and Cork. The endless Achill summer was over; gone were the coke floats and the chips that had more sand than salt. The funfair had moved on, the blackberries were picked, and Paul Henry's canvas fell silent.

Reluctantly, I returned to Dooagh National school nestled on the edge of the Atlantic Ocean. Struggling to settle in, I delighted in the fact that instead of focusing on maths, Irish and English, I would solely be learning about 'Mayo' – the fascinating stories of our history, crest, colours, flags and anthems.

The highlight of those two weeks was the surprise visit by the Mayo midfield supremo, Liam McHale. The whole school assembled in the sparc room on the day of his visit.

It was 'spare' due to the dwindling numbers of pupils in the emigration ravaged 1980s. I can still recall how Liam had to stoop his big frame to enter – a Gulliver among Lilliputians. As I was the smallest in the group, I had a pitch-side seat at the top of the class.

Given my proximity to the home-grown hero, the Máistir gave me a job. It was to emphasise the new words we had inserted into the song the "Boys from the County Mayo".

Thinking it was the most ingenious idea, we swapped out the words "Charlestown too" and turned them into "Achill Sound too" on the second last verse. It was to be sung "Achill Sound too in the County Mayo".

When it came to that line in the song, childish nervousness hindered my delivery. Such was the ferocity of my voice, seagulls in the schoolyard took to the air, adding their cacophony to the already inharmonious sounds coming from the spare room.

Right at that moment, the room had become so hot with us all crammed in that someone fainted. It was utter chaos; the singing was abandoned and children began to spill out through the wide-open door.

Though somewhat panicked, I took my chance to get his autograph.

"And who are you?" he asked with a big friendly smile on his face.

In the moment, I was unable to say my name. Having never met a celebrity before, I was star-struck.

He asked me again and still nothing came. Somewhere in the ether, I heard my name said aloud, and I got my coveted autograph. For years after, the words "and who are you?" haunted me. As for the song, "The Boys From The County Mayo" I only have to hear the opening line to evoke the memory of that hot 'spare room' and I am full of nostalgia for the days of my childhood as the now-familiar 'hiraeth' makes its presence felt.

Years later, I watched as Mayo and Meath battled it out in the replay of the 1996 All-Ireland football final. Having just started university in London, and being far from home, my loneliness was compounded by Liam McHale and Mayo missing out on yet another chance of capturing Sam Maguire.

'Hiraeth'! To encourage some cheerfulness, my sister, having enrolled in an agricultural college outside London, invited me to her campus. Most Irish students in the college were from Meath, Mayo's arch-nemesis from the All-Ireland debacle the weekend before. Queuing at the college bar, I happened upon two ardent Meath fans waxing lyrical about how Mayo deserved to lose, and how McHale warranted his sending off.

I was irritated and about to interrupt when the barman, an agricultural science student from Galway, beat me to the punch. He told the duo that Liam was the best athlete in Ireland and that it was an absolute disgrace he was sent off.

Then, without a moment's breath, he went on to list in encyclopaedic fashion all the medals Liam McHale had ever won. It was the

Meath men's turn to listen open-mouthed, as McHale's basketball haul alone was staggering. Standing there looking on and listening to this total stranger defend my childhood hero, I thought to myself... "and who are you?"

I can now answer that... he is my husband. We live in Corofin, Co Galway, home to many home-grown heroes. Our daughters have witnessed their local Gaelic football team win three consecutive club All Irelands and Galway has also won the Liam McCarthy Cup.

As for me, I still feel hiraeth as I wait for Mayo to bridge the gap back to 1951 by bringing Sam home. I'm still waiting to hear that "music of what happens" as the late great poet Seamus Heaney called it. Child or adult, we all need our home-grown heroes.

Helen Calvey grew up on Achill Island, in Co Mayo but now lives in Corofin, Co Galway. Married to Niall O'Neill they have three daughters Elena, Andrea and Erin. Helen is a National Business Manager with Siemens Healthcare and runs a pony and sheep farm in Connemara. They breed native Connemara ponies that excel in show jumping and farm Blackface Sheep a breed that have roamed the hills of Connemara since 1850.

Slow-Mo Dive
For Original Shot

George Murphy

In a recent club game, the opposition's full forward burst through and sent a stinging shot goalwards. It clattered against the crossbar and rebounded out to the 20-metre line. Their centre forward met the ball and volleyed it. Again, the ball struck just under the crossbar. Our goalkeeper got a hand to the ball and made a magnificent save by putting it out for a 45. After the game, I asked him, "How the hell did you ever get a hand to that rebound?"

He said, "Sure, I was still diving for the first shot!"

George Murphy, Dungiven, Co Derry.

Wee Case Of Smuggling To Success

Seamus McRory

Just after morning Mass in the college chapel, one Sunday in May, 1951, Kevin Beahan was looking forward to his normal Lord's Day hearty, boarding school breakfast of porridge, a round of fried bread plus the weekly treat of one lonely sausage placed strategically in the centre of a piece plate!

Outside the chapel door, an excited priest, Fr John Kenny, asked him to go immediately to the front door of the college where two men wanted to see him. Such invitations could sometimes mean bad news from home. But, the friendly demeanour of Fr Kenny certainly banished such negative thoughts from the young Ardee student as he made his way, through normally, out of bounds territory, to the front door.

"At the door were two good GAA friends from home, Sean Boyle and Tommie McKenna, who told me that I had got special permission to leave the college for the day and that I would be brought to Croke Park to see the first round of the Leinster minor football championship between Louth and Kildare. Not only would I be watching the match, but I would be wearing the number eleven jersey for Louth or, rather, a fellow named in the programme as P. O'Boyle would!

"You see, at that time boarding school students were not allowed out to play minor football for the county. However, the President of St Patrick's College, Armagh, Fr Sheridan, his fellow Vincentian, Fr Kenny and the man in charge of the Louth minor side, Canon McDonnell, were all great football men. So they conspired to break their own rules and had me smuggled out for the match," explained Kevin.

Kevin, over 67 years later, recalled with great pride and clarity, how he felt. The whole occasion had left a joyful, indelible imprint on his memory. He even remembered the car registration number – IY 5051!

In lieu of the missed college breakfast, he was given a sumptuous meal en route. Togs and socks were already in the car and, as the car hastened to Croke Park, he could not believe his good fortune to be playing in the theatre of his dreams. Not only did P. O'Boyle take his place on the side but, as it turned out, he was the star of the show as the Wee County put in a terrific performance to defeat the Lilywhites.

Incidentally, Kevin had stitches inserted in his neck from a procedure in Armagh the previous Wednesday. When he went for the first ball that day he burst the stitches but did not feel the pain! Playing there overcame all normal obstacles. After the game, he was feted with another good meal and was back in the college for the end of night study at nine o'clock. His pals and friends were amazed when the full story emerged on his return. Walking down the college recreation corridor the next evening, one of the priests stopped him and, knowingly, asked would he be any relation of P. O'Boyle who had played in Croke Park the previous day! Kevin just smiled and continued to chat animatedly with his friends.

When the semi-final of the Leinster minor championship came around that summer and Kevin was on holidays P. O'Boyle was, unsurprisingly, dropped from the Louth team and was replaced by one Kevin Beahan. Again, he was the outstanding performer as Louth cruised into a Leinster final encounter with Westmeath. Here, they were up against a well-drilled team, superbly marshalled by future Galway All-Ireland winner and midfielder extraordinaire, Frank Eivers who lived in the midlands county at that stage.

Still, that did not deter Louth and Beahan from playing brilliantly to emerge as Leinster Champions on a 3-9 to 2-5 scoreline. Kevin was on top of the world. They were now due to play the Connacht champions. However, there were a series of objections and counter objections in the west re the results of games and the eligibility of players so that the All-Ireland semi-final between the two provincial winners did not take place until October.

Such was the controversy in Connacht that Louth's eventual opponents, Roscommon had actually been originally beaten by Galway in the Connacht final before the latter were disqualified. Referring to the subsequent loss of a winning momentum from a Louth perspective, Kevin recalled how other misfortune visited them that summer.

"We had a great team but the prolonged delay did nothing for us. One of our players was killed in a car accident in the interim. Two of our star players were not available as they had entered religious life at the beginning of September. Patsy McDonnell went to Maynooth and Phil Hearty joined the Brothers.

"In addition, the main Roscommon pitch on which the match was to be played was flooded and, at the eleventh hour, a field full of hay ricks was decided as the venue. The hay was only removed on the morning of the game. As the summer momentum and incentive had become lost, we did not play well. Roscommon won the game and indeed went on to win the All-Ireland final itself. It was a pity because I still feel, if events had run smoothly, we had a good chance of winning the title."

Kevin Beahan became nationally recognised as one of Louth's best-ever footballers and top scorer, his career culminating when he starred for the Louth team who beat Cork in the 1957 All Ireland SF final by 1-9 to 1-7. He died on July 24, 2022 aged 89. It was All Ireland final day!

Seamus McRory is a native of Derry but has lived and worked in Longford for a number of decades. A retired primary school principal, he and his wife Olive are the parents of Diarmuid and the late Mairéad. Seamus is a keen GAA follower and has written a number of books including 'The Voice From the Sideline' (1997), 'James McCartan, The King Of Down Football' (2010), 'The Dove Of Peace' (2013) and 'Born To Lead' (2019).

'He wouldn't see a foul in a henhouse'

Frustrated Sligo fan's judgement of the ref after the 2002 Connacht final

From Bangers To All-Ireland Tickets, Forgotten 'Gates' And Lost Playing Status

Vincent Cryan

The GAA world I was born into in 1935 was much different to the one that the youth play in today.

Even when I had graduated to playing senior football in the 1950s, there was a predominance by teams to 'import' players from other counties. Why not? After all, there was no television and there were few photos of intercounty stars. So even the finest of players could play as 'bangers' right through the height of the season without any fear of being caught.

And there was another reason which I will come back to at the end of this little story about my own team Keash from near Ballymote, playing in the Sligo Co. junior final against Coolera from the Strandhill area.

I had played the earlier rounds with the club even though by that time I had gone to work in Athlone where I became very friendly with many good footballers, including the Westmeath defender Henry Cuffe and Rogie Martin, who was a great corner forward for both Granard and Longford.

Now there was never any point in getting to a final if you didn't have the ambition to go on and win it. With that in mind, the mentors of Keash approached me to see if I could get a few good players down for the day to bolster our chances of success.

I mentioned the two names who I thought would be of interest in helping out and I was told that in the event of the lads agreeing to travel that the club would pay for the hire of a car to ferry them up and down for the final.

Henry, who has since gone to his eternal reward, was first to sign up and I didn't need to do much persuading for Rogie to also jump on board.

I arranged for the car and the three of us drove down in plenty of time for the game. I lined out at fullback with Cuffe beside me and Martin playing at right half forward.

I knew we were home and hosed after 15 minutes as the three balls that came Rogie's way he tapped over the bar as nonchalantly as if he was out for a Sunday afternoon walk.

We ended up winning well with neither Henry nor myself being over-extended thanks to the strength of the team. In fact, the most pressure I came under was when walking off the field at the end of the match was confronted by three fellas standing at the gate who were supporting the other team.

"How many effing clubs do you play for?" one of them asked in an aggressive tone. I decided discretion was the better form of valour and kept going with my head down and said nothing.

Naturally we celebrated well into the night before returning to Athlone for work the next day. My abiding memory of our sing-song was Cuffe's rendition of the song of 'Fraulein' which he sang in German. It brought the house down.

The next time I saw my fellow travellers togged out was when Westmeath and Longford played in a league game shortly afterwards with Cuffe at left corner back for Westmeath marking Martin at right corner forward.

As they went for the first ball down their wing, I shouted "C'mon Keash" and both of them fell around the place laughing.

Which brings me back to the other reason that teams got away with having players from other counties playing for them.

Sometime after winning the county final, I got to know a fellow from Coolera called Eddie Scanlon who worked in the ESB. Naturally, most of our chats were about football. One night he was talking about that particular final and he started to give out to me about bringing down Henry and Rogie to play for Keash.

Then as a funny afterthought he added: "Sure we couldn't complain even though we knew your pair of boys were illegal as we had more than a few ourselves who were imported to play."

* * *

Before going to work in Athlone, I had won a Longford junior championship with Granard. I arrived in Moate one Sunday to play for Athlone and was picked to play full-back in a junior football match.

As we were warming up in front of the far goal, I noticed a number of officials from both clubs conferring around the halfway line before the Athlone chairman walked up to our group and beckoned to me to come away from the group.

"Seemingly because you won as a junior in Longford, you transfer as a senior player rather than a junior one into Westmeath so you can't play in this match or both you and the club will be suspended," he informed me.

As it happened, the Athlone senior team was playing after the junior match so he softened my disappointment by assuring me that I should leave my togs on as I'd be starting in that game.

After the first game was over, I went out with the seniors but in the warm-up one of our players and myself went running after the ball in an effort to get possession. Our legs hit off each other and I immediately felt something go in my knee. It was my cartilage and for a second time that day I was ruled out of a game I was scheduled to play in. Of course, I was annoyed at how unlucky I was that day but luckily the knee came right and I was able to play for years before retiring.

One of the funniest stories I ever heard in the GAA was not about a game but an All-Ireland ticket. While I was working in Tralee in Kerry, I got to know many people but I had a special spot in my heart for one.

This man was as decent and honest as the day was long and would always try to help you if he could. In the lead up to the 1968 final between Kerry and Down, he asked me if I intended going to the game. I said I'd love to but I didn't have a ticket or didn't have a way of getting one.

He said off the cuff: "Don't worry about that, we'll get you a ticket alright."

And he did.

I came into work the next day and he presented me with a Hogan Stand ticket.

I had the Monday off after the All Ireland final, a match I greatly enjoyed as a neutral so when I went in on Tuesday and asked him how he had got on.

He had a whimsical look on his face and after a few seconds he said: "A strange thing happened on the way into Croke Park when I handed in my ticket. The lad on the turnstile looked at it and then at me as if I had two heads and said: "Sure that's a ticket for last year's All Ireland."

My friend had a habit of wearing two waistcoats and after giving me his own ticket must have assumed he had another in the Hogan Stand for himself.

Obviously, he gave me his real ticket without examining either of them too closely.

Faced with failing to get in to support his beloved Kingdom, he went out onto Jones' Rd and within a minute, a person he knew had told him not to worry and put a Hogan Stand ticket into his paw.

* * *

During my time in Castlebar, I played for a year and a half with the Mitchells. While there I became best pals with Johnny Feeney as we worked and played together.

He told me the story of a Connacht final in the mid-sixties which was hosted at the local grounds. Shortly before the match, one of the Connacht officials knocked on the door and asked Mrs Feeney for the loan of a table.

"Certainly," she said, and after directing them into the sitting-room, she cleaned the top of the table and they carried it over to the stadium.

Later that evening after the match, the officials knocked on Feeneys door, gave back the table and thanked her for her kindness in loaning it to them.

She directed them to put it back where they had found it and thought nothing more of until a few weeks later the family were hosting a Church 'stations' in the house.

The table was pulled out to act as an altar and as she was cleaning it again, she opened the drawer to find £200 strapped up in notes – a sum which would translate into about €5,000 in today's money.

The mother straight away went to Johnny Mulvey, who was secretary of the county board for over 20 years, and handed the money over to him. Neither Johnny, her son, nor herself ever heard another word as to why the money wasn't missed at the time.

One thing for sure though, even if they knew it wouldn't be missed, Mrs Feeney would return it as that was her honest way of doing things.

Vincent Cryan is a native of Ballinafad, Co Sligo and played for the Roscommon Vocational Schools which won the All-Ireland title in 1953) and with Sligo minors for two years. Married to Florrie, they have a family of four. Vincent is a former drapery shop and dress-hire centre owner who worked as a manager for many years in different parts of the country, including Longford, Westmeath, Kerry, Mayo, Cavan, Monaghan and eventually settled over 52 years ago in Portarlington, Co Laois. Vincent, now 87, still loves to talk football, particularly with the old Gaels like former Offaly star, John Smith, about olden times.

'*Colin Corkery on the 45 lets go with the right boot. It's over the bar. This man shouldn't be playing football. He's made an almost Lazarus-like recovery from a heart condition. Lazarus was a great man but he couldn't kick points like Colin Corkery*'

Micheál Ó Muircheartaigh

The Match I Refereed Without A Watch

Eamon Moules

I bet you never heard of a match being refereed by anyone without a watch. It all took place one wonderful sporting Sunday more than 65 years ago, and no one was any the wiser of it.

As a young referee I was told by a former member of the Leinster Council: "Ned, never forget that one of the greatest rules is the rule of common sense." This stuck with me. I would say that common sense prevailed on this occasion and I got through by applying it.

There was one Sunday in the mid-fifties that I will never forget. It was the semi-final of the An Tóstal Medal tournament in Wicklow. Unluckily, I was asked to take charge. Two of the finest teams in the county were in opposition. From An Tóchar, the highest village in the county, came the big men, wearing red jerseys and willing to stop everything in sight if it was in the way of the title. From Kilcoole came the men with doughty football ability, men who were able to mix it and ask questions afterwards. Standing in the middle of these fine teams was me. The smallest man on the pitch. Intent only on keeping the peace.

I have one great rule about timing matches. I always start a match, whether it is an All-Ireland or a local club game at 5:30 on my watch. I know then that when the minute hand and the hour hand are in a straight line, it is half-time. For 12 years it worked wonderfully well for me.

At this time, I possessed a wrist watch of which I was extremely proud. It had never lost a second in all my years in football and I relied upon it to do the vital job of time keeping. There was about 10 minutes to go to half-time and An Tóchar conceded a 50. I naturally swung around to be in the place where the ball was going to be placed, and the defender drove out the ball to me. I put down my hand but the minute I stopped the ball, I got the surprise of my life.

I heard a whirring noise like a quiet alarm clock and looked down to find the two hands of my prize wristwatch chasing each other around the dial.

"Damn it," I said to myself as I awarded the 50. What would I do? This never happened before. Would I stop the match and ask for a watch from the side-lines? Could I trust those earnest supporters to give me a watch that was accurate? Could I trust anyone? The game was a needle affair.

"Keep cool," I said to myself. I did my best. I succeeded. It was a chance in a lifetime, and I won. I would not like young referees to take such a chance, however.

The 50 was taken. No one passed any remarks. No one knew anything about it except me. By heavens did I sweat! I kept the game going and for once overlooked another piece of advice that was given to me. "Forget about everything but the match. Stuff your ears with cotton wool."

This time I didn't. I listened as shrewdly as I could to the sounds from the animated touchline. I waited until I heard those famous words: "Has your watch stopped, ref!?" Little did they know. "Are you going by old time, ref?"

Still, I kept the ball moving, all the while looking at my broken time piece as if it was moving like the clock at the Ballast office. I don't know what made me do it but suddenly I decided to blow for half-time. As I did, I waited for complaints of: "Hey ref, you have two minutes to play."

Those shouts never came.

I thanked the man above and said a silent prayer that the next time I would have a watch that could withstand the rigours of football at full force.

Worse was to follow. The crowd came on to the field to offer advice and assurance, but I slinked away to the umpires. "My watch is broken, give me yours," I said to the umpire. He had none. Trouble. The other man had only a pocket watch. I grabbed it gratefully, saying this will do. Little did I know.

After the usual 10-minute interval, I lined up the sides again with the big pocket watch in hand. It was awkward but it kept the time. I naturally swung it around to 5:30 again but you may not believe this, when I pulled up the winder to move them to 5:30, I forgot to push it down again. You can imagine what I said to myself when I looked at the watch some time later to find that those hands were still serenely pointing to the same time. 5:30.

I nearly died. Now it was really too late to do anything. The match was extremely close and there was nothing I could do about it.

I kept the game going, wondering as I lost loads of sweat fretting over the outcome. Adding to my worries was the fact that the chairman of the district, Mr. Bart Fitzsimmons, from whose district the two clubs came, had issued a warning to one of the sides asking them to control their supporters. Now you can only imagine how I felt.

So, for that second half I opened my ears and depended on the unofficial timekeepers on the side-lines. I waited again for the: "Hey ref, it's time", "hey ref, the match is over" before I decided to blow for full time. For 60 shattering seconds I waited for the crowd to scream, but they didn't. I couldn't believe my ears. My unworkable watch had worked. I had won. I never heaved such a sigh of relief in my life.

That long blast of the whistle must have brought relief to many of the winning side's supporters. I cannot even attempt to tell you of the relief it brought to me. Not until this telling do people know that I refereed the game without a watch. It is a bad habit, don't ever attempt to do it.

Eamon 'Fitch' Moules, who died in November 2021 at the age of 97, was a former top-class referee who took charge of several major games including the 1962 and '63 All Ireland football finals. A native of Annacurra, the Aughrim resident was also a dominant figure in the Wicklow circuit where he refereed 12 county senior football finals, not including replays. This article was written by him for a Wicklow publication.

Fermanagh Woman Lays Down Law

Liam Keane

"What's this I hear, you're running a Gaelic team, Liam?" The strong Fermanagh accent accentuated by the well-trained and experienced teacher's voice made me shudder to a standstill.

A delightful young teacher, many years my junior, the intonation of her voice meant I didn't know if I was being told off or being questioned with the authority of the local constabulary.

"You never told me. I didn't know you were running a Gaelic football team." Now Marie was heading straight for me.

I stood still to be questioned some more, with no time to answer or 'defend' myself.

A 'Plastic Paddy', setting up a Gaelic football team in the suburbs of London at an all-girls Catholic school. I could tell this Irish lady wanted to be part of the game being played out on the Sportsfield of St Philomena's.

"If I had known, I would have got my tutor group involved," Marie added.

This second-generation Irish boy mumbled before telling her that training was taking place each Thursday after school. "I'll be there." With that she walked away. Great, I no longer needed to find a member of staff to accompany me to the All-Britain competition. I was thankful for that as I would not have had the courage to tell this Fermanagh woman if I had invited somebody else!

Liam Keane is a teacher who is married to Kirstie with whom he has two boys, Jack and Dylan. Liam runs the Gaelic football team at St Philomena's in Surrey.

Bill Hodgins – A Legend Struck Down In His Prime

Davy Donohoe

On September 23, 1893, Peter Hodgins, a coal porter from Clarendon Street, Dublin, married Mary Scully of Brideswell, Gorey, Co. Wexford. They had one daughter, Jane who died in 1899 at only a year old, and two sons – Bill who was born on December 29, 1894 and Michael born in 1896.

Bill exchanged the poverty of inner-city Dublin for the equally poverty-stricken north Co Wexford at the turn of the twentieth century when he came to live with his aunts and uncle Paddy Scully in Brideswell. He was enrolled in the local Ballyellis National School on May 6, 1901.

Tales of his athleticism even while at primary school are part of local lore. He was an expert long jumper, and skilled in hurling and football.

While there were two football teams formed in the parish within the first decade of the founding of the GAA, there is no record, oral or written, of organised Gaelic games in the first decade of the new century. This changed when in 1914, the teenage Hodgins, a dynamic figure both on and off the field of play, was instrumental in the formation of the Brideswell hurling and football clubs.

The nucleus of the football team comprised Hodgins' neighbours and four of his cousins. The club contested county football semi-finals or finals every year between 1915 and 1921, winning the junior football championship of 1918. The hurlers were Gorey district winners in 1916.

Hodgins' exploits attracted the notice of the local press when in September, 1915 a correspondent wrote: "...Mention of training reminds me of a tale I heard on the field at Enniscorthy on Sunday as we were watching the wonderful play of the youth Willie Hodgins all the way from under the Wicklow Mountains.

"Born in Dublin, he came to live with his uncle at Brideswell. He took to the country like a fiddler to Strauss. The lad was a born athlete. As for choice he preferred to run a distance rather than walk it. On Sunday it seems he ran before the cars conveying the team to Gorey, arriving long before the horse-drawn vehicles. Willie Hodgins will yet do great things for Wexford both on the hurling as well as the football fields."

Hodgins was soon recognised at senior county level when he became part of the great Wexford four-in-a-row football team, winning All-Ireland senior medals in 1917 and 1918.

On Sunday June 13, 1920 he incurred a leg injury while playing for Wexford against Kildare in the first round of the Leinster football championship in Croke Park. Despite his protests, he was brought to Jervis Street Hospital. In hindsight, as interpreted in his local area, his reluctance to receive medical attention may have had to do with his involvement with the North Wexford Battalion of the IRA.

He was still in hospital on Thursday, June 24 when a neighbour and fellow patient sent word to Brideswell that Bill would be home at the weekend. Understandably, the Scully household was overjoyed with the news of his recovery and the imminent return of Hodgins to give much-needed help on their 16-acre holding.

On Friday Bill's Uncle Paddy arrived home in a distraught state from his work in the fields, insisting that his sisters "get a mass said for the lad". This premonition led to their worst fears being realised when news came through that Bill Hodgins was dead. The indestructible youth lay in a morgue in his native city.

Following his untimely demise, the rumour mill went into overdrive. Food poisoning, the wrong injection, why was there no house wake? Conspiracy theorists suggested that he had been smuggled out of his hospital bed to take part in an IRA sortie at Clonroche, south of Enniscorthy, in which he was fatally injured.

At a time of national unrest and heightened tensions in north Wexford owing to the assassination of RIC District Inspector, Percival Lea Wilson, on June 15 in Gorey, such theories possibly received exaggerated currency locally. Whatever the truth of the matter, the official cause of death recorded on Hodgins' death certificate was "malignant scarlatina", occasionally a fatal illness in the pre-antibiotic era.

Within a few years of Hodgins' death, the Brideswell club folded. His passing created a void both as player and administrator which those left behind were unable to fill. He was buried in Deansgrange Cemetery.

Ode To Bill Hodgins

He sleeps, the great Bill Hodgins, where the Liffey meets the sea.
But his legend still lives on in the foothills of Sliabh Bhuí.
Your great heart lies stilled near the place where you were born,
Your spirit roams through Brideswell, awaiting resurrection morn!

Dave Donohoe is a Wexford man who has always had an interest in sport. His other passion is local history, and he has compiled a number of local journals over the past 20 years. He is presently working on Volume 5. He met his Galway-born spouse Mary through their mutual participation in amateur drama. Having recently bought a campervan, their intention now is to become known as the old man and woman of the roads.

'It beggars belief that people who consider themselves supporters of a team would castigate members of that team, the management and the county committee in a crude and, in some cases, personal fashion. Nobody sets out to play badly, nobody sets out to lose an All-Ireland, but it happens. Supporters, who are members of GAA clubs, who attend club games, and who know the commitment and sacrifice the players make, understand this. Unfortunately, it is a point that seems to have escaped far too many people in the last week'

GAA President Larry McCarthy revisits a theme last year which he raised earlier at his inauguration

Goalkeeping In Our Family Through Generations

Sean O'Sullivan

My dad, Tom O'Sullivan, was born in 1925 in Carrigane, Asdee, Co. Kerry. He often recounted stories as a young boy watching Kerry greats Jack Moriarty and later Jack Walsh kicking football at the field near Craughdarrig Cross. Also, listening to the wireless through the window of a neighbour's house during an All-Ireland final and shouting for one of his boyhood heroes, Danno Keeffe.

After the Second World War ended, my dad emigrated to London to seek work. It was there, in 1947, he got involved with the newly formed GAA club called St. Josephs. Having initially played outfield he converted to the goalkeeping position and went on to win league and London intermediate championships in that first year. Due to work and family commitments, his playing career was cut short. In 1950, he married Nell, the love of his life, and they went on to have six children. They spent over 60 years together, having moved back to Ireland and settled in Ballylongford, Co. Kerry.

Fast forward to the 1970s and continuing the footballing stór. Three of his sons, Michael, Tommy and Seàn, played for the local club. It was Seán who was cornerback for the U-14 team that won NK league and championship, who then converted to become a goalkeeper at St Michael's College, Listowel, under the guidance of coaches Johnny Flaherty and John Molyneaux, and played the rest of his career in this position.

In the 1990s, Tom's grandson Ciarán Woods played underage football as a corner forward. However, as a minor he too converted to goalkeeping and played for a number of years with the club before emigrating to Sydney.

In the noughties, another of Tom's grandchildren, Shane O'Sullivan, played wing forward on underage teams until, at U-16, he was converted to goalkeeping by his coach (his dad, Seán, who always knew from the time they kicked ball in their back lawn that he was a 'keeper').

Shane still plays for the Ballylongford seniors and his grandfather, Tom, got to see him play on many occasions. Last year, the goalkeeping legacy continued as Tom's great grandson Ronan Woods, having played all his juvenile football as a forward, converted to the goalkeeping role for his club Ballyhooly, in Co. Cork.

So, the goalkeeper legacy of Tom O'Sullivan continues almost 100 years from his birth and this piece is dedicated to the late and great man (1925- 2015).

Sean O'Sullivan is a native of Ballylongford, Co. Kerry. He works as an environmental technologist in Limerick and is a lifelong member and activist in the Ballylongford GAA club.

A Tale Of Two Penalties
In The 'Gut Your Man' Era

Tom Hunt

There was a wildness about the GAA in the 1940s with law and order frequently collapsing as players, released from the constraints of everyday living, lost all sense of discipline on the field of play.

Football in Westmeath was no exception and what the great poet Patrick Kavanagh referred to as 'Gut Your Man' types of games were frequent.

The county chairman was generally the one faced with the task of cleaning up the mess arising from these incident-filled occasions.

In 1944 and 1945, the chairman of the Westmeath Co. committee, Dan Leavy, had to confront two such challenges arising from the awarding of penalty kicks in matches involving the Mullingar Football Club.

Brother Thomas Wilfred Hogan was the architect of a remarkable revival of the fortunes of the GAA when he arrived in Mullingar in 1942. Hogan hit the town like a tornado and his impact revolutionised the GAA in Mullingar for a brief period.

A native of Grangemockler, County Tipperary, his brother Michael (Mick) was shot by British forces in Croke Park on Bloody Sunday, 21 November 1920. Brother Hogan's impact was such that in 1944, the Mullingar Club contested both the senior hurling and football finals, winning the hurling and losing the football in the most controversial of circumstances.

The senior football final played on August 27, 1944, between Mullingar and Kinnegad was a novel one and for the first time in 40 years featured a Mullingar team. Despite the atrocious weather conditions, a huge crowd attended Cusack Park. Hidden behind the final score of 3-7 to 2-8 in favour of Kinnegad is one of the most controversial county finals in the history of Westmeath GAA.

The outcome hinged on a dramatic last-minute penalty kick which was driven wide by Mullingar's Thomas Lynch. The penalty was almost certainly the first awarded in a Westmeath final.

Lynch was totally exonerated for the miss by 'An Fear Faire' who wrote the Mullingar club's newspaper notes. He explained that 'no blame whatever is attached to the player taking the kick' as "at least one of the Kinnegad players actually attempted to obstruct the ball in such a fashion that it would be a physical impossibility to score."

This is a reference to a Kinnegad player placing his foot on the ball before the kick was taken and pushed it into the mud. It is also part of GAA folklore that sods were thrown at Lynch as he took the kick but there is no contemporary mention of such a happening. It was claimed in the subsequent objection that two Kinnegad players charged Lynch as he attempted to take the kick and "at least eight Kinnegad players crowded round the place kicker."

The referee failed totally to implement the rules which required that all players, except the goalkeeper and the kicker, remained outside the 21-yard-line.

Anger poured from the Westmeath Examiner match report written from the Mullingar perspective by 'An Fear Faire.' As Mullingar attacked in the final stages several melees occurred around the Kinnegad goal. The loss through injury of Johnny Lyng in the second half was a crucial factor in the Mullingar club's defeat.

'An Fear Faire' was convinced that injuries to Mullingar players were "due to the settled policy of three or four of the Kinnegad players." It was made clear in the column that the Mullingar Club planned to object to the match result: "The wanton and deliberate attacks on Johnny Lyng and Andrew Duncan were too obvious to be overlooked. We must protect our young players; we must ensure that sportsmanship is upheld."

Tribute was also paid to the "sportsmanship of 11 of the Kinnegad players." The column concluded with a veiled suggestion that unsportsmanlike behaviour was not confined to the Kinnegad players. After congratulating the Mullingar supporters for their loyalty, it was suggested that greater discipline was required "to prevent ugly, uncalled for and unwanted scenes."

In his column a week later 'An Fear Faire' suggested that "all the over-enthusiasm both on and off the field in the last quarter" was inspired by the gambling associated with the match and the "fear of losing the bets which looked at the time not the easy money they may have been before the game."

Andrew McCarthy, in a letter to the Westmeath Examiner, provided a Kinnegad perspective on the events and tellingly asked 'An Fear Faire': "To explain the fact that the crowd was orderly during the first half of the match when Mullingar was playing better football than Kinnegad, and was not only disorderly but pugnacious when Kinnegad appeared to be winning the match?"

The subsequent county board meeting held on September 8, 1944 revealed what lay behind the request for improved discipline amongst the Mullingar supporters when the county chairman, Dan Leavy addressed the issue. Leavy explained that the heavy rain during the course of the game was "probably responsible for the conduct of several spectators who encroached on the playing pitch."

The Mullingar objection reportedly inspired an "edifying debate seldom equalled for dignity, sportsmanship, or eloquence even in the Dáil" that continued for over three hours and concluded just before midnight. The key objection was based on the breach of rules associated with the infamous penalty kick.

Brother Hogan explained that several of the Kinnegad players refused to stand outside the 21-yard-line as they should have done according to rule and surrounded Thomas Lynch who took the kick. Two Kinnegad players actually charged him as he was kicking the ball. The referee, in his evidence, explained that the penalty was awarded following consultation with the umpires.

The Kinnegad players initially refused to leave the goal. Several players from both clubs were grouped around the kicker as he was about to take the kick but "he did not see anyone impeding Thomas Lynch in any way."

This evidence was crucial but the referee admitted when questioned by Brother Hogan that some of the Kinnegad players were only two or three yards away from Lynch as he kicked the ball; the rule was not observed as there was a tense atmosphere at the time and he found it difficult to get the players as far as the 14-yard-line.

He allowed matters to stand as he was anxious to get the match finished.

Hogan argued that as the rule was not observed, the Mullingar objection should be upheld. However, the referee was certain that he had seen no player impede Thomas Lynch and this was the crucial piece of evidence. Dan Leavy ruled that the championship final be awarded to Kinnegad and recommended that his decision be appealed to the Leinster Council.

In his subsequent Westmeath Examiner column, 'An Fear Faire' congratulated Kinnegad on the victory and unreservedly withdrew his remarks on certain Kinnegad players.

This was the last important game that involved Brother Hogan as within 12 months he had passed away in a Dublin nursing home. His loss to the Mullingar and Westmeath GAA was inestimable.

History was repeated in 1945 when Mullingar's senior championship campaign ended in bizarre fashion with another controversial penalty incident central to the game's outcome. The local 'derby' championship match between the Mullingar club and The Mental Hospital Club played in Cusack Park on July 22, 1945 was an ugly, brutal affair punctuated by acts of violence and thuggery that were abnormal even for the standards of the day.

The Mullingar team held a two-point lead entering the final quarter when law and order completely broke down and in the words of 'An Fear Faire': "The remaining quarter of an hour was one long succession of fouls, over vigorous tackling and brawls. Both sides may take their share of the blame, although roughness on the part of some of the local lads was most apparent towards the end".

It all kicked off when in the language of the report "a Mullingar player was badly tackled and took the count." In the chaos of the final quarter, the Mental Hospital scored four points and were two points ahead with time almost up.

There was one final incident. In a last desperate attempt to salvage the game, Andy Duncan raced through the Hospital defence and was hauled to the ground inside the square. A penalty kick was awarded but the Mental Hospital defenders refused to leave the goal whereupon the referee abandoned the game with the Mental Hospital leading by 1-8 to 2-3.

The official in his report fleshed out the gory details of the match which from a Mullingar Club perspective did not make pretty reading. All went well up to 10 minutes into the second half, according to the referee's report.

The referee reported: "What happened after that was a disgrace to the GAA and I had to warn a Mullingar player for striking a Mental Hospital player At this stage spectators encroached the pitch – mostly Mullingar supporters.

"With the assistance of the guards I got the game re-started. When awarding a free to a Mental Hospital player, another Mullingar player approached me and threatened that if Mullingar did not win, I would not leave the pitch alive. Then when a Mental Hospital player was in a position to score a goal, another Mullingar supporter rushed on to the field and pulled him down. I then had to warn a Mullingar player for striking a Mental Hospital player. Playing overtime, I awarded a penalty to Mullingar. Six Mental Hospital players refused to leave the goal. I had no alternative but to blow the whistle and award the match to Mullingar.

"While this was happening, spectators were crowding around the goal shouting. The Mental Hospital players may not have understood or heard my decision."

At the subsequent Co Board meeting Thomas Lynch of the Mullingar club admitted to losing his head and "entering the pitch with his togs under his arm" where "he went for the ball with Wade but did not go for the man. If such were his intentions, he would hardly go out with togs under his arm." The Mental Hospital's claim that the players did not hear the referee's instructions to leave the goalline quickly fell apart. Vincent Gillick of Mullingar pointed out that he distinctly heard the referee inform a Mental Hospital player that they had two minutes to leave the goal and the player then "ran in and tried to get the rest out."

The referee confirmed this version of events but again came to the rescue of the Mental Hospital club when he stated that he did not give the hospital players "time to consider what their refusal would involve."

The Hospital club's delegation also claimed the match, arguing that it was clear from the referee's report "that they could safely conclude that Mullingar played a rough game and according to rule such a team, even though winning a match, could be disqualified."

The Mullingar club's case was simple and clear cut. According to rule, when a player or team leaves the field or refuses to continue, the referee was entitled to award the game to the opposition. Unfortunately for the Mullingar club the mood of the delegates favoured a replay and the issue concluded when Chairman Dan Leavy ordered a replay which was easily won by the Mental Hospital Club.

A case of two penalties awarded to them yet on both occasions, Mullingar emerged as losers.

Tom Hunt is a native of Clonea, Co Waterford but has spent over four decades in Westmeath. He played for Waterford and was a Munster panellist in football in the seventies and eighties. He also won a Sigerson Cup medal with UCD in 1973. A teacher by profession, he is a former quiz champion, author of a number of books and is still a leading member of the Mullingar Shamrocks GAA club and is the current Westmeath delegate to the Central Council of the GAA.

Dilemma With Our
Own Giant Haystacks

Mark McGaugh

Ifaced an awful conundrum that late September day in 1959. Would I go to the match or stay and finish forking the hay onto the reek to my committed farming brother Eamon?

He and I had planned to get the hay saved in the haggard the first fine day that came our way. At that same time, my club Carras had made great progress in the South Mayo minor championship and had an important mid-week challenge game where the mentors would finalise the team to play in the final some 10 days later.

Unfortunately, it had rained constantly over the previous days – as it can only in the West – thus disrupting my grand plans. I was the only member of our family interested in football. My older brother Tom was a keen cyclist but Eamon had (as Patrick Kavanagh might have said) the smell of the soil in his nostrils. I knew there was no way he would see any importance in playing this game. I was also sure he wouldn't lend me his bicycle which I needed to travel the nine miles to the game.

The sun rose early and spectacularly on the day of the game and I was already excited about the prospect of playing. We made great progress in bringing in the hay, which was in good condition, and I felt we could clear the two-acre field of hay in plenty of time before heading off for the game. While working, my mind would drift to thoughts of my new boots and of holding on to the number 12 shirt with a good display.

By early afternoon my mind was made up; I would make a quick and unexplained exit from the haggard. I knew Eamon had his own plans if we finished the hay early, as there was a field of turnips waiting to be pulled and snagged. His view was that if we used the couple of hours before the sun went down that evening, it would create a great head start for the following day's work.

The night before I had hidden my gear in the barn just under the Raleigh bicycle. The key part of my 'escape to football' plan was to get Eamon up on the reek when I was about to depart. We'd taken turns all day with one pitching the hay and then going up the ladder onto the reek to walk it and keep it 'square' so that it would be made properly.

In my plan it was important to have Eamon up on the reek. I'd forked half of the last cart of hay when I downed tools and said I needed a drink of water.

My failure to return within a few minutes coincided with the arrival of my younger sister Margaret. She gave him the news that I had left for a football match on his bike. Apparently he was livid... but what could he do?

As it came to pass, we won our game. I played well enough to ensure my name was on the 12 shirt, and returned home later that night. The reek of hay was topped off and made secure, and like many a hard and tough football match, the forgiveness between two brothers was soon sorted.

The incident was soon forgotten but the story was retold many times in later years in family folklore when I returned from England on holidays. However, there was a further twist to the story when in 2009 a celebration was held by the famous Garrymore club in honour of the winning Carras team who 50 years earlier in 1959 had won not alone the South Mayo final but also the Mayo County Minor final.

Sadly, by then a number of the panel had passed to their eternal reward. During the celebrations I was presented with my county medal... 50 years later. To my amazement and a little embarrassment Peadar Hughes, who was a lifelong dedicated supporter of the GAA, told the story of my abdicating my farming responsibility in hay making in favour of attending the football match.

In my mind this story and countless others are the fundamental building blocks of what the founding fathers of the Gaelic Athletic Associations had in mind when they embarked on the formation of one of the greatest amateur organisations in the world.

Mark McGaugh is a native of Shrule, Co Mayo but has lived in England since emigrating there in 1960. Married with three grown-up children, he was a successful entrepreneur and businessman for 40 years before retiring to write his memoir, 'Gold In Them There Tills.'

Two Names In The Game

Michael O'Dowd

It's rare and very unlikely to happen again but seldom can a Celtic Cross be assigned to a name before a final is even played with a certainty that the right man will receive his medallion after the game.

The year 1954 was an exception, though. That year's All-Ireland final was contested by Kerry and Meath and the above-mentioned possibility, certainly, could have taken place because in this battle of the titans, two men of the same name, from the same parish, played against each other on that September day.

Playing at midfield for Kerry was Tom Moriarty from Castlegregory and he was one of three brothers who played for three different counties. Tom himself played for Cork in 1952 and won a league medal and his brother Michael played for Kerry, also in the 50s.

Unfortunately, the Tom Moriarty playing for Kerry didn't win his Celtic Cross but Tom Moriarty from Castlegregory in Kerry did.

Let me explain! Back in the 1930s, Tom Moriarty relocated from Castlegregory to county Meath and was full forward on the victorious Royal team in that final of '54. He won a railway cup medal in '56 with Leinster and then transferred back to Kerry and won a Munster junior medal with Kerry and played with the legion club in Killarney. The Tom Moriarty who played only for Kerry was regarded as one of the greats and passed away in 2002.

Michael O'Dowd is from Cloghane and runs O'Connor's Bar and Guesthouse on the Northside of the Dingle peninsula. He emigrated in 1986 to New York and won a junior medal with St. Brendan's. Michael married Elizabeth Cheryl Lopez in New York and they moved back to Kerry in 1995 to run the family business but sadly Elizabeth passed away in 2018.

Excuse Me Ref,
But You're Wrong

Peter Gordon

In 1956 the noted Leitrim Gaelic footballer, Willie McKiernan, returned to his native Aughavas after a sojourn in the USA. When in New York he played with the Leitrim/New York team. He also acquainted himself with hurling.

At that time the Leitrim hurling championship was a duopoly as Carrick-on-Shannon and Manorhamilton had been the only teams entering the competition. Hurling had been played in Leitrim for hundreds of years due to its having been promoted by the landlords of the big estates. The boys around Mohill played hurling from an early age. At the time helmets were not worn and one of our group, Des Clyde, spent two weeks in hospital after receiving a bang of a hurley on the side of his head.

Willie proceeded to organise a panel of players to challenge Carrick-On-Shannon who were the champions. Most of these players were from Cloone, to name but a few – Paddy Solon, John Charlie Bohan, John Joe Donahue, Charlie Mitchell and the Doherty brothers – Patsy, Michael and Martin. There were two players from Mohill, Eddie Courtney and myself. Willie McKiernan also featured. The remaining players on the team were members of An Garda Síochána stationed in Dromod. With the passage of time I cannot recall their names. Once the panel was organised, Willie informed the county secretary, Tommy O'Riordan, that he had a team to challenge Carrick. Tommy, a native of Limerick, was delighted with the challenge, as a big part of his life was spreading the good news of hurling. We called the team Aughavas as it was through the good offices of Willie we got the loan of the Aughavas jerseys.

Arrangements were made for the match to be held in the Park in Mohill – now called the Philly McGuinness Park. The contest was played at a frenetic pace so we were really glad to get the breather at half time. The selectors made a change for the second half – our goalkeeper Eddie Courtney was transferred to the forwards and I replaced him to attend to the goalkeeping duties. Although I had never played in goals before then, Carrick did not score a goal in the second half. This had less to do with my goalkeeping skills, if I had had any, but rather testament to the great defending by our backs.

As the referee blew the full time whistle he declared the result a draw. Enter stage left John Maguire, the Anglo-Celt Gaelic Games reporter. John told the referee he was mistaken, and that Aughavas had won by one point. John had logged every score and scorer and showed the referee his notes. The referee had forgotten to log one of our points.

We were then declared the winners – the first and last time Aughavas appeared in the records as Leitrim Hurling Champions. From that team three players featured in the St Finbarr's Hurling Teams of 1964-1970.

The Finbarr's team was mostly composed of players from Mohill although Cloone supplied four of the team. The three players from that Aughavas team for St Finbarr's team which won five championships in the 1960s were Paddy Solon, Patsy Doherty and myself. I like to think that the exploits of the Aughavas team sowed the seeds for the revival of hurling in South Leitrim.

Peter Gordon is a retired businessman and father of five grown up children. A proud Leitrim man, he has lived in Dublin for many years. His hobbies include gardening, walking and supporting his native county's GAA teams.

Eamon Coleman's Unique Contribution To County Final Days

Seamus McRory

Over the years, in every county in Ireland, county final day has been universally celebrated as a very special and all-embracing occasion when the supporters of rival teams – sometimes bordering on the fanatical in their intensity and application – contribute immensely to the parochial concept of the pride of the family and parish through the medium of Gaelic Games.

Seamlessly blended with this gathering of tribal, almost warlike support, has been tremendous feats of exhilarating play from some of the greatest players who have adorned our games. However, one of the most fascinating contributions by any player that I have ever come across and most emphatically the most unique, was made by one of Derry's greatest sons – the one and only Eamon Coleman.

He first arrived on the senior adult playing scene at the tender age of 14 in 1962. Watching his native Ballymaguigan train for the county final against the then local parish rivals, Castledawson, really captivated the young boy as he, uninvited, joined the training sessions under the tutelage of arguably Derry's best–ever player – and Ballymaguigan captain Jim McKeever. So impressed was Jim with Eamon's natural ability and unbridled enthusiasm that he immediately asked him to join the panel for County final day.

Such was the level of commitment and the high degree of skill shown by the youngster that he was selected as a sub for the county final. During the course of that drawn game he made his initial competitive appearance. In the replay the young Coleman came on at half-time and gave a five-star performance, scoring 1-1 in the process, and thus won his first senior championship medal. He was surely one of the youngest players ever to do so, in Derry or any other county.

"As a young boy you watched intently
When your boyhood hero majestically fetched
The ball beneath a Lough Shore skyline;
Eagerly hoping for the call
To enter the fray on those far-off summer days.
Seeing your exciting exuberance and consummate skill which belied your
Tender fourteen years – the icon duly responded.
Scoring a goal and a point, to claim
Your first County medal, was the catalyst
For a life-time of footballing fame
And a yearning desire for national success."

Like hundreds of others in County Derry, I had the privilege of knowing and liking Eamon Coleman for over 40 years. I vividly recall during my student days playing for my native Lissan club against Eamon and Ballymaguigan in 1967.

One anecdote stands out from that game. Eamon obtained possession of the ball and, as was his custom, he tried to sidestep me as I attempted to dispossess him. Unfortunately for both of us, he tripped on a rush bush and literally fell across my feet. The referee, a future prominent County Board official, shouted at me.

"If you do that again McRory I will send you straight to the line!" As I protested my innocence, Eamon looked up at me with that characteristic, impish smile of his.

"Seamus I always knew you were a bit of a rascal. Would you ever lift me up from this bed of Lissan rushes?"

I duly obliged. The referee looked suspiciously at both of us as Eamon and I proceeded to talk about Derry's chances in that year's Ulster Senior Football Championship clash the following week against Down. That was the game that the late Eamon made his Senior Championship debut at the age of 19 for Derry. Obviously, there was no managerial embargo on County players playing club football just a week prior to representing their County in the Ulster Senior Championship in those days!

Having already won an All-Ireland Minor medal with Derry in 1965 his career as a player was to see the boy prodigy develop and experience success at the highest level. In 1967 he was a member of the Derry Under-21 side which won the Ulster U21 championship. Eamon went on to win another Ulster U-21 championship the following year when Derry also won their first national title in that grade when they defeated Offaly in the 1968 All Ireland U21 final. Though he won an Ulster Senior Championship in 1970 he never achieved the ultimate prize of all. He consistently encountered the collective frustration of a very talented Senior County team that earned the dubious distinction of never doing justice to themselves on the big occasions, especially in Croke Park. Nevertheless, despite periodic spells of emigration to seek work in England, Eamon never lost his love of home and returned frequently to Ireland. By 1981 he had transferred his club allegiance to neighbouring Ballinderry where he linked up again with his fellow All-Ireland Minor and U-21 winning colleague, coach extraordinaire Adrian McGuckin.

Indeed, that particular year will always loom vividly in the imagination when we recall the times and exploits of one of the most colourful characters ever to grace our County. True he will always be fondly and justifiably remembered for his part in managing Derry to their first and only – so far – Senior All-Ireland title in 1993. But to really appreciate the totality of the man and his innate love of Gaelic football, regardless of the normal protocol of GAA rules and regulations, one must reminisce how he enlivened the County final, in two Counties, in the same year!

I believe I may be the only person in Ireland to witness at first hand the sheer uniqueness and dare I say humorous audacity of what he actually did. First of all, l I went to the 1981 Derry final between Ballinderry and Banagher. There in the forward line was Eamon who proceeded to tantalise and tease the opposing defenders with his enterprising play. Yours truly, now an exile in Longford, met a Westmeath friend, Tommy Lowry, the following Wednesday. As Tommy and his three brothers were on their club team, St Malachy's of Castletown-Geoghegan, in the Westmeath final the following Sunday, I went along to see them play their opponents, Athlone. Athlone were spearheaded by Des Dolan father of the recently retired and one of Westmeath's greatest ever players, Dessie junior. During that year Des's house-guest at this time was our Eamon who, having found employment in the Midlands, duly purchased Dessie the younger's first football as a Christmas present later that year!

As I closely watched the game, my attention gradually switched from following St Malachy's to scrutinising the distinctive dummies, sidesteps, pace and accuracy of an undoubted talismanic forward who deftly scored three points in quick succession for Athlone. Before the end, I was in no doubt as to the exact identity of my favourite player on the field. Even though I had not been speaking to Eamon since that time, 14 years earlier on a playing field in Lissan's Waterside, I knew that I had to renew acquaintances! So, at the end of the match, which Athlone lost narrowly, I went onto the field and congratulated Eamon on his magnificent performance. Though never referring to the time we last had met or indeed who I was, he looked up at me with that knowing and unforgettable look.

"Sure, it was easy playing here. There were no rushes to contend with!"

In what must be unprecedented, even before and certainly since, Eamon Coleman had played in two different county finals, in two counties, in two different provinces, all within seven days of each other!

I wonder what the GAA's present regulatory body, the CCCC, would have done if it had existed in its present format in those days!

Bray 'Wanderers' Unmasked In Rebel County

Aodh Ó Broin

Illegal players were very much a part of the scene in the first half of the 1900s and maybe a decade or two after that as well. The lack of transport and communication between one place and another meant that GAA folk knew little about the people in the next parish and nothing whatsoever about people at some distance. This led to clubs chancing their arm with what was referred to as "bangers", "ringers" or "imports."

It is well known that Bray Emmets played a major part in the winning of the 1902 All Ireland football championship for Dublin (played in 1904) and that they also contributed in no small part to Wicklow's Junior All Ireland win in 1936 but very few are aware that some members of the same club were prominent in helping Dunmanway to win a Cork Junior football title.

One summer evening in the 1930s, as I was on my way from St. Peter's School in Little Bray, I was approached by a young Corkman who invited me to play a match in Cork the following Sunday. He was very surprised that I should comment on the illegality of the proposed visit to the 'Rebel County.' Nevertheless, I was unable to accept his invitation as I was already scheduled to visit home that weekend.

I learned subsequently that he had succeeded in securing three or four of Bray's finest players for the match in question. This endeavour completely slipped my mind until I met one of the Bray lads and asked him if he had actually made the journey down to Cork. "Is it possible," he asked, "that you did not hear of the Cork venture?"

Immediately he regaled me with how he and his other travelling companions had fared on their many journeys to Cork. He even quoted from accounts of the matches as they appeared in the local press.

He pointed out that they had assumed new names as 'guest players'- names, indeed that they had found difficult to discard on their return to ordinary GAA life in their hometown. There was a glowing account of the final and of the enthusiastic scenes which took place when the match ended in victory. Needless to say, the team was feted that night and our Bray Emmets friends received special mention.

All the Bray-based lads involved in this clandestine activity had to work late on Saturday nights which meant they rose early on the Sabbath to make their way to Dunmanway. On their way to Mass each Sunday in the local parish, they noticed a collection in progress which was receiving a generous response. They afterwards learned that the collection was used to defray the running expenses of the club.

Later in the year, the lads from Bray were invited to the presentation of the medals at a céilí and dinner in Dunmanway. They were all presented with their Cork championship medals. Through their victory in the junior championship Dunmanway were promoted to the intermediate ranks. The so-called 'guest-players' made the journey for the first round of the intermediate championship and were about to take their place when they noticed two members of their own Wicklow Co Board on the sideline.

The jig was up! A hastily convened meeting with club officials there and then decided that they should remain out of sight. There was consternation in the Dunmanway camp as they frantically tried to fill the vacant places.

The Bray-Dunmanway saga had ended – or had it? Three weeks later the Cork club were asked to supply three players for a county trial match. Who was chosen? Three of Bray's finest players.

They were not to be had, however, with the club letting the message filter back that the three players had emigrated. Well in a sense they had ... but only back to Bray.

The late Aodh Ó Broin is a former president of the GAA and former long-time chairman of Wicklow Co Board. A teacher by profession, he was part of the Bray Emmets side that won back-to-back senior titles in 1934 and 1935 before he relocated to his native area to teach in Rathcoyle School. He joined up with the Rathdangan Club who won the 1936 Wicklow senior title, beating the holders and his former team in the semi-final.

Good Enough For Mayo
And Four-Goal McGee

Willie McGee

The 1967 U-21 All Ireland football championship final between Mayo and Kerry ended in a draw 2-10 each in Croke Park on September 24, and the replay was fixed for Ballinasloe on Sunday, October 8.

The Mayo team had three seminarians in their first 15 in the drawn game who were barred from togging out for the replay as they were in the seminary and on retreat. Their names were JJ Cribben, Ballyhaunis, Mickey Lally, Ballintubber, both deceased and PJ Golden of Killala.

They were replaced by three Claremorris members with Noel McDonnell coming in for Golden while James Smyth replaced Cribben and Des Griffith got a start instead of Lally. This meant I had two new teammates in the full-forward line with me.

The weather was very poor on the day as I travelled down to Ballinasloe from Dublin. I wasn't looking forward to the game because of the conditions. However, the greasy conditions did me a favour early in the game. I dived to make contact with the greasy ball as it landed near the goal and managed to punch it into the net.

I availed of the conditions again shortly afterwards to meet a dropping ball first time and drove it low into the net. The next goal came as I flicked another high ball past the goalkeeper.

The weather got better as the day went on and midway through the second half I moved out to catch a high ball. I was about 30 yards out and when I turned, I hit the ball as hard as I could and it landed in the top corner of the net. I can remember that one quite well as I was extremely pleased with the finished product.

There was naturally great excitement with the victory as we won easily by 4-9 to 1-7. Coming off the pitch, the first person I met was my father. He gave me a great hug. I could not understand why he was crying as he was neither the hugging nor the sentimental type. I suppose if my son scored four goals in an All-Ireland final I too would be tearful and I would hug the daylights out of him.

That night I was working as a garda back on duty at the Pearse St station in Dublin when I decided to go over to the Irish Press offices on Burgh Quay, less than two minutes away. It was one o'clock in the morning and I knew the country editions of the newspaper would be printed by that stage. I wanted to see what kind of report there was on the match.

To my surprise and delight the main back page heading read: 'Four-goal McGee The Hero'. What gave me more pleasure was that my father was an avid Irish Press reader and I knew he would have been delighted and proud to see that heading.

Even though that event was well over 50 years ago I have not shaken off the moniker that the heading spawned – 'Four-Goal McGee.'

Over the years the number of people I meet who were at the match were getting fewer and fewer but coincidentally last year (2020) while attending two separate funeral services, I first met a Sligo man who was in Ballinasloe that day. Shortly after while sympathising with the brother of the deceased in Leixlip, he informed me that not only was he there that day but was one of the umpires officiating at the match.

Willie McGee is a native of Newport and a former Mayo footballer. A retired Garda Detective Superintendent, he is married to Elizabeth with four grown up children, David, Sandra, Brendan and Ailish. He is currently writing a book detailing his time in the Garda Siochana's fraud division and also as head of fraud with Axa Insurance called 'A lifetime In The Shadow Of Fraud.'

That Split Second When
The Breaker Takes Over

Maitiu Maddock

Fine summer days were few and far between and this Sunday morning in July promised to be one of the few. It was not yet Mass time, the excitement of the imminent occasion had woken me early. There was time for a morning walk as the world was waking up. The Saltee Islands looked peaceful as I crossed to the back of the pier and watched the seagulls feeding at the edge of the surf where the incoming tide dislodged the mounds of seaweed deposited some days previously.

The ways of nature intrigue me, to see the sea, now calm and quiet, giving life to those beautiful creatures – the same sea, which when its mighty energy is released, crashes and seethes and will consume everything weaker than itself. I have watched the huge breakers crash on the shore, exploding its merciless energy, clawing and reaching to increase its territory and I have wondered how the Architect of our environment, using textures and levels, contains this mass of pounding liquid – surely something we should all study more closely. The bell for Mass brought me back to the purpose of this brightening day.

The trip to Dublin, as the county takes to the capital, is colourful, the holiday atmosphere typified by the hundreds of picnics in the Glen of the Downs, flags and hats in purple and gold unifying all in a common adventure.

The streams of cars seem endless as the city is approached; a parking space is sought and at last the walk to Croke Park with teeming humanity stepping ever urgently – some with flags and hats of black and amber, is undertaken. Access is gained to the stadium, a programme is secured and I make my way to a vantage point with a heartbeat faster than normal.

The minor match has just finished, the lads played great hurling but I am becoming detached from other happenings, as my mind concentrates on the two teams as they march behind the Artane Band. People are shouting and waving flags. Amhrán na bhFiann rings out over Dublin city. I am oblivious to the world around as the referee throws in the sliotar and the Leinster Final is on.

The game is a cliff-hanger in the true tradition. People sit on the edge of their seats, the build-up of tension unbearable. A long ball is struck towards the Kilkenny square, the red-haired giant leaps, his powerful arm reaches skywards amidst a forest of hurlers, the speeding sliotar is grasped nimbly in the huge hand as defenders beat fresh air, tens of thousands feel the ripple of excitement – the breaker approaches the shore – then the full forward descends, the powerful legs contact the green sod, turning their owner goalwards, the mighty swing, ash connects with leather, the multitude gulp in air as they rise – the breaker arches and begins to descend – the net shudders in a great convulsion, hosts expel verbal energy simultaneously – the breaker crashes on the shore. I sit back in my seat, mentally exhausted, emotionally exhilarated. Am I approaching the limits of sanity? But the Creator fixed those boundaries also.

Can others than the Celt equate the games they play with the speed of wind, the crashing of sea, the soaring of the spirit more recognised in the peace and serenity of the monastery?

I return home refreshed with my treasures locked safely in my memory.

The timeless sea is coming in as if for the first time...

The late Maitiú Ó Madóig (Matthew Maddock) was a native of Kilmore Quay, Co. Wexford and worked for OPW for 45 years. Married to Ina, they had two daughters, one son, four grandsons and one granddaughter. An avid Wexford supporter all his life, he was on the Wexford Development Committee and was also a former chairman of Kilmore GAA Club.

A 'Pádraig Pearse' Pose
For All-Star Photograph

John Connolly

It was the year of the first All-Stars in hurling and football and I had been lucky enough to be selected at midfield on the team.

At the time I was working for McInerney Builders and we had a team in the 'inter-firms' competition which was very popular then.

We played a team from Kilkenny in the All-Ireland semi-final of the competition, they were a creamery team, I think the forerunner to Avonmore and as you'd expect, there was no quarter given in that game.

There was no mandatory headgear protection that time and it was common enough to ship a facial injury. I ended the encounter with a black right eye and I also had a cut on the cheek which necessitated five or six stitches afterwards.

They were only war wounds and none of us ever complained about them when they happened.

When I got home later that evening, my mother appeared overly concerned and I thought she was worried about the way my features had been rearranged.

No, that was not the reason. Instead, she explained a photographer working for the All-Ireland sponsors, Carrolls, had called to take my photograph for the All-Star posters that would be produced for the 1971 team. It is a feature of these awards that every player has his picture taken by a professional in his own county colours so that the posters look really well.

"He won't be able to take my photo the way I am," I said as I pointed to the black eye and stitches.

However, the following day the man called to our house, just as he had told my mother he would. I thought he was wasting his time but obviously he was under instruction to get my photo and he wasn't going to go back empty-handed.

And that's where he had the idea of photographing me in a Pádraig Pearse-like profile. In fairness he did a great job and as you can see from the photo elsewhere in this book, I was the only one out of sync with all the others, hurlers and footballers, who were all shot face on while I am shot from my left side with one-and-a-half eyes and one cheek visible.

John Connolly is the eldest of the famous Connolly hurling dynasty and won an All-Ireland medal with Galway in 1980 as full-forward. He is also the holder of a National Hurling League Medal and won a Railway Cup medal with Connacht also in 1980. Following his retirement, he became involved in team management and served as coach and selector with the Galway senior team, while he also managed the Castlegar senior team.

The Siege Of Bedlam Became A Tale In Song And Story

Dónal Ó Gallachóir

It is hard to imagine a small rural GAA club in North West Donegal creating major headlines in 1931 but that is exactly where the Cloughaneely club found itself in the autumn of that year.

The headlines arose from the club's commitment to facilitate the newly formed Gweedore team by travelling to the latter's venue to play a challenge match. Like most GAA clubs, the Cloughaneely club derives its title from the name of the parish, which was anglicised from the ancient Gaelic name of Cloich Cheann Fhaola. The parish has two vibrant villages, that of Falcarragh and Gortahork, which are both kernel to this story.

The central figure in the incident was a Paddy McCarthy, the scion of a local business family in Falcarragh and who was a hackney owner in his own right. Paddy was also the secretary of the GAA club and therefore had the responsibility of arranging transport for the team to travel to the match which was to be played on August 23, 1931. Taking his role seriously he contacted the Derry-based offices of the Londonderry and Lough Swilly Railway Company and arranged that a bus would be in Falcarragh at the given date and time to transport the teams and supporters.

The group numbering about 40 was assembled in Falcarragh waiting for the bus, but the appointed time came and went but no sign of the organised transport. As it was well known locally that the bus driver – Phil McBride – stayed in lodgings in the village of Bedlam on the outskirts of Gortahork where he also parked his bus. Paddy McCarthy went off to Gortahork in his green super six hackney car to seek out the bus driver McBride.

On arrival at Bedlam, it was apparent to McCarthy that a problem existed as "his bus and driver" was there alright but aboard was a group of teachers and guests from Colaiste Uladh (Irish college founded in 1906 associated with Pádraig Pearse, Roger Casement and Joseph Mary Plunkett) about to travel to Downings to attend a Garden Fete and afternoon dance.

Paddy McCarthy was not going to tolerate this carry-on when he had booked the self-same bus to bring his team to Gweedore. As some urgent action was required, he duly placed his car across the road at Bedlam and defied God and man to drive the bus to Downings.

The bus driver, Phil McBride was in a dilemma. His only orders were to drive the bus to Downings. He had heard nothing about conveying a football team. The arguments started, and continued for the day. The gardai were called. Garda Fox arrived from Falcarragh but McCarthy refused to budge although he did move his car to allow other vehicles to pass. When Garda Thornton replaced Garda Fox at 7pm, he persuaded McCarthy to move his vehicle but that was of little significance then, as it was too late in the day to either play football in Gweedore or to dine and wine in Downings.

No, doubt, Paddy McCarthy felt quite justified in his protestations as the event became a real cause célebre. The story might have been forgotten soon afterwards except for a number of things. Firstly a number of photographs were taken of the scene showing McCarthy's car, the Lough Swilly Bus and the gathering of people.

Secondly, one of the ladies present, supposedly a Miss Templeton, penned a monologue concerning the episode, entitled The Siege of Bedlam or as others called it McCarthy's Fort. This reference to McCarthy's Fort is an acknowledgement of a famous eviction incident that occurred nearby on January 2, 1889 at a house since referred to as Dún an Dalaigh (O'Donnell's Fort). Finally, the prosecution of McCarthy gave the story greater prominence as shown by its coverage in a non-Donegal paper, The Strabane Chronicle.

I researched this story years ago when I had intended compiling the history of my native club, Cloich Cheann Fhaola in the Donegal Gaeltacht. Indeed, I discussed the story with some of the individuals/players involved on the day, including my own father and uncle.

Seemingly, when there was no sign of either McCarthy or the bus arriving in Falcarragh, a member of the team, Jackie McDonald who had a motorbike, went to Gortahork to ascertain what had occurred. Jackie, son of the local doctor, duly reported back re the stand-off at Bedlam bridge. He later became a member of the Irish Army and had attained the rank of colonel on retirement.

It was ironic that the incident happened at the appropriately named Bedlam which is in reality a sub-townland of Keeldrum and approximately 1km from Gortahork.

Dónal Ó Gallachóir is a native of Falcarragh, C. Donegal. A retired Garda he lives in Breaffy, Co Mayo with his wife Marian with whom he has five children Aislinn, Oisín, Síofra, Eibhlín and Ríona. Donal's GAA involvement consisted of playing most of his club football with Cloughaneely in Donegal whom he represented at U-21 level. He is a past chairman, secretary and PRO of Breaffy GAA club as well as being Oifigeach na Gaeilge with Mayo GAA.

Jackie's Unique Voting Role In Electing GAA Presidents

Jackie Napier

Bray native Jackie Napier holds the unique distinction of being the only one to have helped vote two Wicklow Presidents into power.

In 1961, as a 20-year-old, he was elected Wicklow delegate to attend Congress which was held that year in Dublin's Gresham Hotel. On that occasion, Aodh Ó Broin (Hugh Byrne) became the first representative from the Garden County to take up the high office at Croke Park.

Thirty-two years later at the 1993 GAA Congress in the Burlington Hotel in Dublin, Jack Boothman defeated Joe McDonagh and others to become president-elect with Jackie's Wicklow vote helping him to win the day.

Boothman, a veterinary surgeon by profession, then served in the top role from 1994-1997 and became the first Church of Ireland member to do so.

Jackie Napier is a native of Bray and long-term President of Bray Emmets. He has represented Wicklow as a former member of both the Central Council and the Leinster Council.

Sporting Battle That Changed A Club's History... And Geography

Sean Keogh

Let it be said from the outset that the people of Rathoe – a small rural village and townland in the centre of Carlow – take no solace from the above 'battle' following a game on Sunday, August 15, 1926.

This 'battle' description was derived from a serious pitch invasion and row that took place near the end of the Carlow senior football championship final.

The game between Graiguecullen and Milford. Graiguecullen played in Laois in the early days of their existence, but affiliated to the Carlow championship of 1905. Part of their club is in Laois and part in Carlow with the famed River Barrow River flowing peacefully between the two counties. They were almost unbeatable year after year.

The legendary Barney Hennessy was one of their great stars and was playing at some level into his sixties. Many teams tried, but failed, to lower their colours over the years. In 1926 Milford, now defunct, enlisted players from at least three other clubs which they could do at that time. The amalgamation worked very well and they made their way to the final and who else but Graigue were waiting for them?

Most reports of the game say it was keenly contested but fair. However Fr. John Lawlor, the county chairman who was at the game, stated that Graigue played in a disorderly manner from the start. Near the end of the game Milford was leading by three points when Graigue launched an all-out attack.

A high ball was kicked in towards the opposing goal. Rexie McDonald (full-back for Milford) fielded the ball but it was knocked from his grasp by John McDarby (full forward for Graigue). As the ball hopped on the ground Rexie booted it up the field with force but in doing so he connected with McDarby (The Mallet) who fell to the ground injured.

Let it be said that both McDarby and McDonald said afterwards that it was a complete accident. The Graigue spectators and supporters didn't see it that way and rushed on to the playing area, with the Milford spectators and supporters in hot pursuit. Appeals for order by the Co Chairman Fr. Lawlor's fell on deaf ears. It is said that he broke two umbrellas but all to no avail. There are many different accounts of punches and kicks and even timber stakes on the ditch being used in the fracas. Nearly 100 years on, it's hard to know how accurate these stories are but it was a serious incident.

One account which seems to hold water is that Rexie McDonald was being so badly beaten on the ground that his girlfriend, later to become his wife, threw her body over him for protection. It is strongly believed that his life was in danger at this point.

Barney Hennessy was not in Rathoe that day due to the death of his father; and many people believed that he was so influential in Graigue that he would have been able to quell the row at an early stage.

Following on from this row there were a series of meetings and investigations by Carlow Co. Board. Graigue were suspended for two years. The verdict to suspend Graigue was on a vote of 13-5. Graiguecullen appealed the decision to Leinster Council, but the Carlow ruling was upheld by 13-2.

However, the Leinster chairman at that time Bob O'Keeffe, a Kilkenny man teaching and living in Laois, said: "If Graiguecullen wished to return to Laois and the Laois board accepted them, the Council might see fit to lift the suspension before the two years expired."

The Graiguecullen players voted overwhelmingly in favour of playing in Laois. It is not certain how many voted to serve the suspension and remain in Carlow but it is presumed that some of the players from the Carlow section of the parish may have been in favour of staying in their own county.

Without serving any suspension then, Graiguecullen returned to

Laois and went on to win the 1927 Laois Championship and dominate in the thirties and forties. Surprisingly their last senior title was in 1965.

So, at the end of the day 'Carlow-Graigue' as they were known at the time served no suspension. Many believed they were a huge loss to Carlow and possibly cost the county All-Ireland titles in the forties. Imagine if the 'Boy Wonder' Tommy Murphy had been on board in 1944 when Carlow won their only Leinster title they surely would have had a much greater chance of winning the Sam Maguire.

'Cutchie' Haughney, Mickey Byrne, Mick and Andy Fennell, Dinny Byrne and Willie Brennan to name but a few were others who gave sterling service to Laois in later years. Rexie McDonald believed that after Graigue left the county that other clubs emerged and were successful giving some outstanding players to the county teams.

It was certainly a master stroke by Bob O'Keeffe to recommend that Graiguecullen seek permission to affiliate in Laois, the county where he resided and was close to his heart. Though born in Mooncoin in Kilkenny, he came to Laois to teach and played hurling for Borris-in-Ossory and the Laois county team.

With the passage of time the event is slowly fading in to history. While all incidents on and off the field were unsavoury it was what occurred afterwards in different places and to property that was a big concern. Relationships were strained for many years between people on each side of the Barrow but fortunately that has now all changed.

A pitch invasion can be serious and lead to injury. For the record there were many serious injuries received in that melee by people that were never reported) as well as generating ill-will among neighbours.

There is a man in our area whose late father was in attendance as a young lad of 12 at that time.

Like the game, all was going well for him until the fracas erupted. The youngster was in the middle of the action watching every blow that was struck so he could tell his friends about it the next day in school.

As it turned out, he had more to tell them than he bargained for.

In his enthusiasm, he got a bit too close to the action between two 'insurgents' and when one of them missed his opponent with an almighty swing, he connected with the young lad and turned him upside down.

As soon as he was able to get back to his feet, he staggered for home and as he did so, he heard someone shout: "You'd hit a chap would you?" He didn't wait to see whose arm would be raised in victory in that particular head-to-head. Apart from a throbbing headache and a black eye, he was none the worse for his ordeal. Indeed, he dined out on that day's misfortune with a smile on his face for many years afterwards.

Ironically, in a field quite close to the site of original 'The Battle of Rathoe' some 50 years later, a referee's report on a local derby game said there had been a 'pitch invasion'. When a delegate from one of the teams was asked at a disciplinary hearing by the chairman as to what had happened, he replied: "Look here my good man, I often saw more commotion at the ringing of a pig." That delegate definitely was not in Rathoe in 1926.

Sean Kehoe is a Carlow native who has been involved with the GAA all his life. Married to Mary, they have two grown up daughters and a son. A retired store manager, his hobbies include travelling and writing poetry.

Getting On Like A House On Fire At Straid

Rose Kelly

By the late 1980s, things were getting very quiet around our house in Straid. Most of us had already left home, or were making plans to do so. Our mother, Helen Farren, who had spent many years amidst the non-stop activity that comes with eight children, was facing into a quiet and restful old age. And dreading every minute of it.

At least, that was what her reaction to the news that Urris GAA had bought Crampsey's Field would seem to suggest.

Crampsey's Field is directly behind our house and I can still remember her excitement when I was home one weekend as she told me about the new owners.

"There's life coming to Straid! Now we'll waken up!" she said gleefully.

"Are you sure you don't mind?" I asked her, "You won't miss your privacy?"

"Damned apt!" she replied. And so began our mother's long and amicable relationship with Urris GAA.

"I never had any misgivings," she told me. "I was looking forward to it from the very beginning. I think they started having games in the field around 1988 or 1989 but they were about for a while before that.

They must have spent some time getting the pitch ready. I remember them coming and putting in poles. There were a lot of people coming and going and they'd all stop for a chat on the way past. John Friel, Eddie McLaughlin (Collier), John McDaid, John-Joe Cleary were all committee members.

"I enjoyed the craic, and so did Laurence [our father]. They were all regular visitors to the house and after a while we passed no remarks on them. On warm days, if we were sitting out on the summer seat, there would nearly always be someone passing by who would stop and sit a while.

"Once the games started, it was very lively. The crowds that would be parked all over for some of the matches! And during the week, the wanes would be playing matches, and training. After a while, they started running summer camps for the wanes. I used to love to hear all the shouting and laughing from the pitch. It would do your heart good. Over the 23 years that we were neighbours with the GAA, there would have been hundreds of children about and we never, ever had a minute's trouble with any of them. They were so well-behaved.

"Damien Tam was a groundsman or caretaker at the beginning. His wife worked in Centra. A really lovely, quiet man. Eddie Collier was groundsman for a while as well, before he moved on to other work. He was another really friendly man. I am the same age as Eddie's mother, Sadie, and we had that connection. Eddie often took Sadie in for a wee céilí when he would be going to committee meetings. Sadie would 'céilí' with me until the meeting was over and we would chat about old times. We would have some laugh, telling all the old yarns. Only someone who grew up with you would believe the way things used to be!

"And all along there was Jimmy Kelly, my adopted son! Aw, my God, we had some craic with Jimmy over the years. He was full of devilment. The blackguarding that went on when Jimmy was around..."

I can certainly vouch for the level of blackguarding. On more occasions that I can count, as I walked in from my car, the sound of raucous laughter coming from our kitchen would meet me. More often than not, Jimmy would be in the kitchen, either telling my father that he knew nothing about plumbing, or cars, or football, or telling my mother she wasn't doing a very good job of keeping house.

When I remind my mother of this, she laughs heartily again.

"Aw, it used to be a scream! There was nothing sacred! He heard me saying it myself often, so he knew I wouldn't take offence. I was always saying to him: 'You may take me as you find me, Jimmy, because I was never a housekeeper!' When I left Straid, Jimmy said he would be up to see me soon, and he'd know he was in the right house if there was a pile of dishes in the sink.

He could never resist the opportunity for a bit of craic. One day he shouted out to me from the car park that I'd better take my washing in from the line, because Urris had a big important match that day, and he didn't want certain articles on my washing line distracting them from their game.

"We were one big happy family. I was included in all the activities in the clubhouse. Every year, they would have a Mass for deceased members of the club. It was a lovely homely gathering. Fr. Charlie Logue would say the Mass in the old clubhouse and all the neighbours would gather around for tea and scones afterwards. Sadie Collier would be there, and Kathleen Friel. Jimmy's mother, Susan, would be there, and Frances Cleary, Catherine Kelly and Rose Kelly. I used to thoroughly enjoy the evening.

"All the Urris women were great bakers and anything that was left over, I'd get to take home in a wee doggy bag. And of course, Jimmy couldn't let me away with that. He'd be slagging me off: 'Aw aye, it's not your immortal soul you're worried about at all, it's your belly!'

"But at the back of it all, Jimmy Kelly is one of the kindest-hearted people you could ever meet. He probably wouldn't like me saying that. I remember one wild windy day I was sitting out the back as the crowd was gathering for a match, just observing all the activity. The wind was blowing from Baluba and the next thing I see Jimmy coming towards me with a very sheepish look on his face.

Says he: 'Helen, you're going to think me wild cheeky, telling you what to do in your own backyard, but I'd be afraid the ball would hit you in the face and break your glasses. You might be better off going inside.'

Poor Jimmy! He hated to tell me, but that just shows the kindness of the man, that he couldn't take the risk of me getting a whack of the ball.

"He looked out for me in so many ways. If he was about the pitch at all, and he saw me putting my snout round the door in bad weather, the next thing I'd hear would be, 'Where are you going? Do you want a lift?'"

All of us were very aware of how well the members of Urris GAA cared for and respected my parents while they were neighbours in Straid. I remember once hearing the story of how news of our chimney fire travelled in and out the road between Urris and Straid like wildfire. Seemingly, two members of Urris GAA drove past our house in a hurry to get somewhere else. As they passed, they noticed sparks coming out of our chimney.

Unable to stop, they phoned Jimmy Kelly in Urris, who phoned his brother, who was at The Cross. Jimmy then phoned my mother, who was in the house on her own, to tell her that her chimney was on fire, but that help was on the way. She was still on the phone when Jimmy's brother and another man arrived in her kitchen. Crisis averted. You couldn't get safety measures like that in the most expensive gated communities in LA.

I'll let my mother have the last word. "For 23 years, Urris GAA were our neighbours in Straid, and I am so happy and content now to think back on all the good times. There was never a cross word in all that time. Nothing but fun and friendship. I can meet any one of them now, and enjoy reliving all those happy memories. That is a fantastic feeling."

Rose Kelly is a Donegal native and has been involved with Urris GAA since 1993. A keen music fan and devotee of Bruce Springsteen, she also has a great interest in local history. She researched, edited and compiled the club's history 'From Humble Beginnings To Crampsey Park', which was launched by former GAA President John Horan to coincide with the club's golden jubilees in 2019.

Some Memories Are Hazy But This One Could Be 'Golden'

Brian McCabe

Some of my earliest memories are of football matches or going to football matches with my late father.

Like most of his generation of Cavan men, Gaelic football was a huge part of his life. He had seen the great Cavan teams of the 1930s, 40s and 50s and had watched them in 10 All-Ireland finals, bringing Sam Maguire to the Breffni County on five occasions.

As I grew up in the 60s, Cavan was still winning Ulster titles and Sunday afternoons would invariably find my father hunched by the radio listening to Michael O'Hehir's commentary.

Dad had a high regard for the great team of the 1940s with household names such as John Joe O'Reilly, Simon Deignan, PJ Duke, Joe Stafford, Tony Tighe and the incomparable Mick Higgins.

He could recall whole passages of play from some of these finals but his favourite was remembering the win in the Polo Grounds, New York, in 1947.

My father would describe the ebb and flow of that epic encounter – Kerry's whirlwind start, Cavan's plucky come back, and their dogged determination to rest the trophy in that transatlantic city. It was only as the years passed, and I grew a bit older, that I realised that my father, who had never been abroad in his life, could not possibly have been in New York on that history-making day. How then could he describe the match-winning moves in such vivid detail? The power of imagination?

Well, my father is long gone (Lord rest him) but I still thought of him every time I attended a Cavan match in the long frustrating years since then. I must admit that I shed a tear or two for him in 1997 when Cavan resumed their 'rightful' place as Ulster champions – even if Kerry were to do us in the semi-final that year.

My uncle died 'at a good age' in 2011. One of my many sad tasks afterwards was to clear out his house, with all sorts of family papers, memorabilia and, of course, albums of old photographs.

Imagine my surprise when, amongst the more usual family pictures, I came across an old sepia photo of a little girl, holding a (clearly American) pendant proclaiming 'Kerry v Cavan' and with an old football at her feet. Then, at the bottom of the old cardboard box, I spotted it – damp and musty, and with some pages decaying – but, unmistakably, an actual programme for the match itself (cost 50 cent).

Was it possible that someone from our family had, after all, attended that most famous of All-Ireland finals over seventy years ago?

There was no name on the programme but, on the back of the photograph, was written 'Susie Golden.'

I knew (again from my father's stories) that, like most Irish families, we had cousins in America and although contact has been lost over the years, I seem to recall that they were called Golden. Looking back now, I am pretty sure that one of those cousins must have attended the match and this would have accounted for the programme (probably sent home to Cavan as a family souvenir) and my father's vivid descriptions of the details of the match.

Young Susie looks to be about six or seven in the photograph, so it is possible that she is still alive today. Who knows, maybe if she sees this piece (or someone draws it to her attention) maybe she could contact us to let us know how she felt, being photographed with the ball and pendant all those years ago, and if she knew what a historic event was being commemorated?

As a boy, I could almost see myself with him in New York on that sunny September Sunday, as PJ Duke gathered a loose ball, passed it to 'The Gunner' Brady, onto Tony Tighe and then to Mick Higgins, who drove it to the bottom left-hand corner of the Kerry net.

Brian McCabe is a Cavan native now living in Kildare and is a retired civil servant. He writes regularly for various history and archaeology journals, and contributed a chapter on the history of Cavan GAA (entitled 'The Road to the Star-spangled Final') for 'Cavan: History and Society', published in 2014.

Irishtown Hero Helped Dubs Back To Top Table

Finbarr Dolan

Dublin had not contested a final since 1958...a full five years. Rumblings among supporters were that this was not acceptable for a county that had brought swerve and swagger to our national game. Heffo was drafted in as a selector which kick started his managerial career. The mantra was that Dublin should be eating at the top table again so plans were put in place to restore pride back to the city.

St Vincent's and Clanna Gael were dominating club football, so both teams were watched regularly to see what they could contribute to the campaign. In those days, the average age of county players was 25 plus. However, one player aged 19 from Clanna Gael caught the eye.

Gerry Davey was an athlete of great fitness with the speed of a gazelle and a keen eye for goal. He was the son of Eugene (Sligo) and Ellie (Clare), not hotbeds of football and to this day neither county have won the Sam Maguire.

Gerry was the second eldest of six children born in an 11-year time span, the first boy in the family of four boys and two girls. His early GAA influences were Ted Cooling, schoolmaster Star of the Sea, then onto Westland Row CBS where Br Hickey and Br Treacy nurtured Gerry's talent to the extent that Br Hickey predicted he would play for Dublin.

The question was – could Gerry cut the mustard with the Foley brothers, John Timmons, Des Ferguson and Mick Kissane?

At 19, he had massive competition from older players to get a starting spot in the campaign. Gerry grasped his chance in the league. The championship saw Dublin brush aside Meath, Kildare and Laois in Leinster before beating Down on the way to the final.

Gerry playing his part when called upon as starter or sub demonstrated a physical and mental toughness way beyond his years. The tension mounted throughout the other 31 counties as Dublin once again brought style, charisma, pride and passion both on and off the field of play.

The team was announced at training the week before the final and it was no surprise that Gerry, the Irishtown hero, was selected at number 12. A week of almost sleepless nights in the Davey household by everybody but Gerry followed. He took his elevation to hero status in his community in his stride and shouldered his responsibility like Eugene and Ellie had taught him.

The morning of the final, Gerry didn't break tradition and travelled alone on the No. 3 bus to the city, walking the remaining distance. There were no group pre-match meals in those days. The crowds in their thousands flocked to Croke Park by bike, bus, horse and foot. The ferry crossing the Liffey from southside to northside had extra boats in use due to the demand and many from Gerry's surrounding parishes availed of the ferryman.

A crowd of 87,106 thronged Croke Park for the final, the third biggest ever attendance on record. Two of Gerry's brothers, Brendan and Eugene (Jnr), paid through the turnstiles at the Canal End, the home of Dublin southside fans for years. Gerry's parents and the rest of the family, Nuala, Veronica and Paddy, took their seats in the Ard Comhairle (a premonition of victory in their blood).

The scene was set, the cauldron of noise as the players paraded could be heard far and near. The match was a tight and tense affair played in a sporting manner, as play switched from end to end. Half-time saw Galway leading by 0-6 to 0-4.

In the changing room there were no stats men, no physios, no clipboards, no TVs for reruns. However, there was a group of Dubs who knew that the city was calling, the desire to bring Sam back to its rightful place was the focus.

Every player in the 23-man squad knew that they had 30 minutes to show they would not be found wanting. Although still a teenager, this was Gerry's opportunity to live the dream, to play his part, to deliver on the biggest stage both as an individual and as a team member. Gerry was playing for himself, his team, his club, his parish, his city and he was not going to let his family down.

The Davey name would play a huge part in Dublin GAA in the years ahead and this was his stage to kickstart the tradition as his brothers Eugene and Paddy also became leading lights through the decades, both playing, managing and administration within Dublin GAA.

The players took their positions for the second half and what came next was a moment never to be forgotten. Dublin attacked into the Hill and worked the ball forward to our Irishtown hero who scored the only goal of the game to turn the tide in Dublin's favour 1-9 to 0-10.

Gerry recalls the noise from the stands and terraces after the goal and then his teammates fighting tooth and nail for the rest of the game. The referee, the late Eamon Moules (Wicklow), blew the final whistle and the rest became a blur.

Every player was hoisted onto shoulders and carried to the Hogan Stand for the presentation to captain Des Foley by President de Valera. The holy grail was reached, the pain since '58 ebbed away, pride was restored to every man, woman and child in the city. A trip to Glendalough was the reward to the squad on the Monday, schools were visited over the following weeks as a motivation for future generations with a special hurrah every time our Irishtown hero was introduced.

Finbarr Dolan is a native of Dolphins Barn, Dublin and is a retired banker. Married to Madeleine, they have two sons Barry and Ciaran and five grandchildren. He credits the brothers at Synge St CBS for giving him his love of the GAA.

Dog Gone Football Match

Paul Holland

Even in the home of football, local matches can involve more blood and hair flying than exquisite playing skills. Truly, it can be said that Kerry's All-Ireland titles, many of them close-run affairs, were won on the "playing fields of Eton" in Ireland's southwest.

Once upon a Sunday, a local lad destined to be a civil servant in the Department of Education headed down to the pitch. He had been selected on the team to play a neighbouring parish. The loyal family dog followed him and settled down on the sideline as the game commenced.

Our local lad wasn't above a bit of off-the-ball gamesmanship, which involved inappropriate comments, as well as tripping, pulling, holding and dragging down his opponent who was only trying to play football. The inevitable happened and the opponent took a swing at him – he went down.

The dog, not appreciating the context and only seeing that its master had been attacked, raced in from the sideline and bit the much-maligned visiting player. Civil war ensued, order being restored only when players from both teams, and the dog, received their marching orders.

"Dog sent off in football match" was the headline in the local sports column. From the ridiculous to the sublime – only in Kerry!

An Fathach Ar Mo Ghua

Pat Finn

Uair amháin, thóg duine ar leith páirt lárnach i mo shaol agus gan aon smaoineamh eile, d'athraigh sé mo shaol ó bhun. Níl ach captaen amháin ar an turas speisialta seo agus tá moladh mór tuillte aige, an fear láidir, ar leith , Terry Monahan. Bhí mé cáilithe mar mhúinteoir i 1971. Bhí caoga trí páiste i ranga a trí. Ní haon áibhéil sin, bhí caoga is a trí cloigeann faoi mo chúram.

Bhí sé an-dúshlánach agus bhí mé mí-fhoighneach. Lá amháin, dúirt mé leis an bpríomhoide, Paddy Haslem, 'níl ag teastáil uaim ach míorúilt sa chruachás seo. Tá an rang ró-phlódaithe.'

Ní fada uainn an mhíorúilt! Bhí mo sheomra ranga ina phraiseach ach tar éis thrí sheachtainí, tháinig an mhíorúilt chugam. Ar an 21ú Meán Fómhair 1971, chuaigh mé chomh fada leis a theach in Éadan Mór. Dúirt Terry liom go bheinn i mo bhainisteoir ar an bhfoireann peile faoi 11, dá chlub ionúin, Naomh Monica.

Gan mhoill, ghlac mé lena thairiscint fear tréitheach sin, an fear a dúirt, 'Déanfaidh tú mar a déarfaidh mise leat, tá súil agam go mbeidh sé go maith duit!' Níor cheistigh mé é agus bhí an ceart agam. Pé rud a deireadh nó nach ndeireadh faoin fear sin, ní gnáth-fhear é. Bhí cáil air mar gheall ar an méid a chur sé isteach i ngach rud. Is minic a chuirfeadh sé do do smaoineamh thú, 'Cen fáth nár smaoinigh mé air seo?'

Bhí an turas tosaithe. Fuair mé ticéad maireachtála ó Terry. Leis an bhfoireann CLG nua, bhí go leor ar bun agam. D'éirigh thar barr leis. Bhí gaois ag Terry, súile i gcúl a chinn. Ní raibh aon duine rómhór le íde ó Terry a sheachaint. Mar shampla: bhuaigh Oileán na hÉireann orainn i gcluiche iontach gairid. Rinne ár mbuachaillí cúpla botún nádúrtha ach bhí fearg an domhain orm. Uair amháin, a rinne mé an rírá seo, geallaim duit. Chinntigh Terry é! Thug sé le fios dom, go neamhbhalbh, in ainneoin mo ratha leis na buachaillí, racht poiblí eile agus beidh mo phort le Naomh Monica seinnte go luath. Ní dhearna mé an botún céanna arís.

Thuig Terry an tábhacht a bhain le moladh a thabhairt ó am go ham agus é tuillte agat. Gach Satharn, tar éis an chluiche, fhrioch a bhean chéile álainn, Patty, stéig dom. Bhain Terry, Patty agus a gceathrar páistí, Michael, Carol, Brian agus Patricia, taitneamh as a ndinnéar agus bhí an-chraic againn ag an mbord. Teach lán le cineáltas a bhí ann.

Le linn blianta go leor ag bainistiú, (táim i séasúr 51 anois), bhí Terry i gcónaí tacúil agus bhí mé faoi a chosaint ó mhaíomh éadála áitiúil. Bhí Terry ina feighlí tailte i staid oifigiúil Baile Átha Cliath, Páirc Parnell, agus bhí sé ar muin na muice nuair a bhuamar an Craobhchomórtas Sóisearach i 1987 agus i 1989 nuair bhíomar sa chluiche ceannas idirmheánach. Bhí bród an domhain air agus ba bhreá liom an nóiméad a fuair mé an creathadh láimhe ag deireadh an chluiche agus chuala mé na focail speisialta ón Terry- "Is réalt thú, Pat!' An oíche a bhuamar an Craobhchomórtas Sóisearach, chan Terry Molly Malone i dteach tábhairne, darbh ainm, the Concorde, in Éadan Mór.

Bhí aithne air ar mo chlann agus thug sé cuairt ar mo mháthair in Inis go minic. Thóg sé coinnle di i gcónaí mar ba dhéantóir coinnle é agus d'oibrigh sé i Rathborns, An Port Thoir. D'fhreastail sé ar shochraid mo mháthar agus m'athar, rud a bhí ríthábhachtach dom. Bhí taom croí ag Terry i 1993 nuair a bhí sé ag breáthú ar chluiche i bPáirc an Crócaigh agus cailleadh é. Bhí mé croíbhriste. Mar a deir an t-amhrán, 'I cried me a river'. D'oscail ár gclubtheach, smaoineamh a bhí ag Terry, tar éis a bháis. Tá portráid dó ar an mballa sa chlubtheach, bhí sé ann ón dtús. Bhí tú i láthair na mórgachta nuair a bhí tú le Terry.

Bhí tionchar láidir ag Terry orm, an fear iontach seo. Téaim chuig a uaigh go minic agus bím ag smaoineamh 'rugadh é mar dhuine maith, tógadh é mar fhear iontach agus d'fhág sé oidhreacht mhór.

Terry Monahan: Go raibh maith agat as na laethanta geala!

Rugadh Pat Finn (Pádraig Finn) i gContae an Chláir. Múinteoir náisiúnta a bhí ann ó 1971 go 2008. Anois is treoraí turais é do 'Collins Day Tours' agus 'Dublin Bay Cruises'. Tá sé pósta do Colette le triúr leanaí, Fiona, Barry agus Aisling. Bainisteoir peile agus iománaíochta le Club Naomh Moncha i mBaile Átha Cliath ar feadh caoga haon bliain ó 1971 go dti an am seo.

All-Ireland Loss As Mayo Become World Champions

Michael Larkin

Like baseball's World Series in the USA, it could only happen in America when an Irish team – in this case Mayo – assumed the mantle of World Gaelic Football Champions way back in 1932, the year they lost the All-Ireland final to Kerry.

The Anglo-Irish Trade War, or the 'Economic War', between Ireland and Britain throughout the 1930s resulted in much hardship and poverty amongst families and communities across Ireland.

While America was slowly recovering from the Great Depression of 1929, thousands of young Irishmen and women who saw few opportunities in a predominantly rural Ireland followed their 'American dream' by emigrating there.

Most of the Irish who emigrated were employed as construction and railroad workers, firefighters and policemen, though plenty also achieved great success and wealth in business, political life, sport, education, banking and commerce.

Bill O'Dwyer, born in Bohola, Co. Mayo in 1890 was one of the many Irish who prospered in the 'New World' at the time. Despite having a hugely successful legal practice and becoming New York's 100th Mayor in 1946, similar to many of his fellow Irish Americans, his love for Ireland and especially his native county of Mayo grew stronger with each passing year.

Immensely proud of the phenomenal success of another Irish American also from Bohola – the multi Olympic-winning medallist Martin Sheridan, who unfortunately became a victim of the 1918 Spanish 'flu pandemic – O'Dwyer demonstrated his true passion for the green and red when he became the chief benefactor for the Mayo senior football team's 'American Tour' in 1932.

From the previous year and onwards until the Mayo team departed from Southampton for New York in April 1932 on the SS New York liner, this historic trip generated massive publicity on both sides of the Atlantic.

Members of the Mayo team were eagerly sought out to deliver handwritten letters, holy water, rosary beads and other reminders of home to sons, daughters and siblings who had carved out new lives for themselves in faraway America.

In fact, huge crowds lined the New York docksides on May 7 to greet the team on its arrival. Throughout their tour, they were treated like royalty, meeting and being introduced to many leading personalities from that time.

For Mayo's first game against New York, former world heavyweight boxing champion 'Gentleman Jim' Corbett threw in the ball. Boston, New Jersey and Rhode Island also warmly welcomed the Mayo team.

However, it was in Philadelphia that Mayo were crowned 'World Gaelic Football Champions', following their two-game series against a team drawn from within the entire state of Pennsylvania. Mick Mulderrig, captain of the victorious Mayo team, was presented with the magnificent Pennsylvania Cup amidst scenes of great fanfare and excitement.

Following their return home to Mayo, the team was enthusiastically greeted at railway stations, GAA clubs and towns throughout the county with the Pennsylvania Cup taking pride of place at each event. Despite losing the All-Ireland final, the team was on an upward curve, winning several National League titles, culminating in the winning of Mayo's first All-Ireland title in 1936. Amidst the glory of NFL titles and a first All-Ireland win, memories of the Pennsylvania Cup faded into the background, its exact whereabouts unknown...until it 'appeared' once again in Mayo after a lapse of 84 years.

Its prolonged hibernation had not occurred in Mayo, or on the island of Ireland, but across the Irish sea in London. Bohola native and Cricklewood resident, Pat McNicholas, born in the same year as Mayo won their first All-Ireland title followed the fortunes, and misfortunes, of the Mayo senior football team throughout his lifetime. He was also a good friend of extended members of the Mulderrig family over the years.

During the course of conversation with Ballyheane, Co. Mayo, native Michael Larkin, Pat proudly, yet almost apologetically, stated that the Pennsylvania Cup is "in my cupboard" and my wish is "to display it somewhere to give it the prominence it deserves."

This conversation set in train a sequence of events which I co-ordinated in collaboration with Mayo Co. Council and Mayo GAA County Board. It culminated in a special and symbolic ceremony with the historic trophy being presented to the Cathaoirleach of Mayo Co. Council, Cllr. Al Mcdonnell in Áras an Chontae, Castlebar.

Despite the difficulties and economic hardships facing families in 1930s Ireland, this once sparkling silver cup, along with the Gaelic Athletic Association then and now, shone a beacon of hope and brought immense joy and happiness to loved ones at home and abroad.

For the first time since 1932 when the cup was proudly held aloft at receptions throughout the length and breadth of Mayo and further afield, this magnificent vessel was once again back 'home' in Mayo.

Michael Larkin is a native of Co. Mayo. He is an alumni member of the Mayo Mental Health School of Nursing and also holds a diploma in healthcare management from the Institute of Public Administration. A member of the Federation of Local History Societies, he has travelled extensively throughout the USA and has written articles for a number of Irish and Irish American historical and cultural publications. He is actively involved in supporting many local and national voluntary organisations, including his local Ballintubber GAA Club.

Objection Over Circus Performer

One of the strangest objections ever to come before a Monaghan Co. Board meeting was heard at the March 1930 meeting.

Lough Egish objected to Latton being awarded the 1929 junior football championship title on the grounds that they had included a 'circus performer' who was, at that time, starring with a travelling show on a visit to Ballybay.

The Lough Egish case was put by their delegate P. McCluskey and the objections was upheld. The 'circus performer' was in fact a rugby player who had never played Gaelic football before in his life.

Hurling And Football
'Dirty Words' In Our House

Eileen Ludlow

The words 'hurling' and 'football' were dirty words in the house where I grew up. Maybe it was for that reason that my grandmother took me to live with her, as she decided that my mother, her daughter-in-law, didn't know how to rear me properly.

I was now surrounded in a house of adults; by my grandmother, her son and daughter, my uncle and aunt. My aunt was very rigid in her ideas and was convinced that GAA games were played by lazy good-for-nothings who kicked or hurled a ball around a field watched by equally lazy good-for-nothing spectators.

I was about 15 when I felt the draw of this forbidden activity. I have no clear memory of my first encounter as a spectator but I do know I was hooked from day one.

My uncle Jim, my mother's brother, was a staunch GAA man. He had been among a group who got the local Éire Óg club up and running again after a barren patch in the 30s and 40s.

Uncle Jim was my ticket to freedom and the transport to the Cork county matches. Hard to picture it today but up to nine of us would pile into the black VW Beetle and head for Limerick or Thurles or the then Cork Athletic grounds on the banks of the Lee.

These outings were the highlight of the summer but before I got out of the house, there was the battle about the Sunday dinner. This dinner cooked by my aunt was a movable feast, it could be any time from after 9.30am Mass to before the milking in the evening. My aunt deemed it a personal insult if I missed Sunday dinner.

This led to the silent treatment being handed out to me for most of the following week by my aunt. I would be dying to talk about the match and that caused her to put the shutters up even more. Then I was off again next Sunday!

If Cork were not playing, there were club games so almost every

Sunday was spoken for and the battle of the dinner went on. I was pushing boundaries and enjoying it.

Uncle Jim's VW must have been able to expand to hold all of us. There were no seat belts or airbags but, sure, we were packed in like sardines and there was no room for movement. Uncle Jim rarely did more than 40mph and once we hit the traffic jams on the narrow roads of the 60s, it was more like 20 mph. We did not have a care in the world as we sat wedged in the backseat, sporting our paper red and white hats which would fall apart and allow the dye to colour our faces if it was raining.

My strongest memory is of Limerick. We always set out after 9:30am Mass to get there. A few sandwiches wrapped in a brown paper bag and a flask of tea packed into the small boot at the front of the VW, and we were on our way. Uncle Jim and Johnny Brady, who usually travelled with him, and Auntie Maura were all experts on the team and not only the Cork team but the opposition as well.

We, the younger passengers, were educated about the teams of the day – all we had to do was listen. As we made our way to Limerick, we never contemplated the possibility of being beaten. It was all about how we would dispose of the opposition. Memories can be very selective and while I remember trudging along the Ennis Road to the game and jubilantly racing back to the car some two miles of a walk after winning the game. Then out came the flask and the brown paper bags and auntie Maura might have something good in the tin for afters. We chatted to others who were also fuelling up for the return journey.

We ate our grub and piled back into the car. If we won the game, we had no problem fitting into the tight space of the car but if we lost, there was grumbling and groaning about the limited space. It was amazing how something like the result of a game could make such a difference to the space in a car but, believe me, it made a huge difference.

Loaded up, we edged into the line of traffic, which was moving at a snail's pace out of the city. The replay then began; shot by shot, the game was dissected. Johnny, who considered himself an expert on hurling, would outline errors and point out things that would have been done differently if he were a selector. It made us wonder in the backseat why Johnny was not on the team. Uncle Jim was soft-spoken and fairly sound and would occasionally contradict Johnny in a sensible fashion, which often resulted in a string of expletives from Johnny. This never fazed Uncle Jim.

Matches in Limerick always involved a stop off in Croom. This was at a pub with Cork connections and was always packed with supporters. A drop of alcohol never passed Uncle Jim's lips but he enjoyed the banter as he drank his orange. He was never in a rush home, the cows probably knew that Cork were playing and that milking would be late that day.

Before we left Croom, we would finish off the grub and repack into the car, content if we had won and a little grumpy if we lost.

These trips were pure gold. They started my love affair with the GAA. The years rolled on and I continued to go to games, joined the local camogie club and had some great times. Hurling was my favourite and still is but I learned over the years to enjoy football as well.

Uncle Jim loved all things GAA and rarely missed a club game or a county encounter when Cork were playing. He departed this life on July 3, 1988, fittingly for him, walking out of a Cork-Kerry game, when the Rebels won in Páirc Uí Chaoimh after a close and contentious Munster football final.

No man ever left the world feeling so honoured. His beloved Cork had sent him happily on his way across the great divide...Uncle Jim, who gifted me a lifelong love of gaelic games.

Eileen Ludlow is a native of Farran, Co. Cork and has lived in Drumconrath, Co Meath for over 45 years. She is married to Peter and they have three grown-up children and five grandchildren. Her hobbies include reading, gardening, painting and writing stories from life's events.

'There are some things in life that are more important than money and the GAA is one of them'

Joe Brolly, Sunday Independent columnist and former Derry All-Ireland winning player

Farewell To The King
Of The 'One-Liners'

Pádraig Carr

Many will know Martin Griffin for being the dominant figure he was on the field of play and his determination to win. Having played with and against him, we all knew that when he made his mind up to go for a ball, then look out.

He was a giant in our eyes, both as a person and as a player. His native cunning and quick observational wit lifted our spirits so many times and left everyone with a smile. His 'one liners' or 'comebacks' were legendary and he had nick-names on so many of us on the panel. On one occasion, I remember before we travelled back from a Ballybofey training night, Martin McHugh went into the notice board to see what the team was for Sunday. Griffin told him that "he was wing half-forward and the full-forward line was Asbestos (Sylvester Maguire), Boneyard (Seamus Bonner) and Gluaistean (me)."

His leadership qualities shone through many times, but also, off the field. I remember one Tuesday night before training began in 1984, a bombshell was dropped that there would be six suspensions with immediate effect. Bainisteoir Brian McEniff and then Cathaoirleach, Micheal MacGiolla Easbuig, told us that the five players who had travelled to New York to play that previous weekend, were suspended and would not be allowed to play against Mayo on the coming Sunday.

We were all shocked, and before anyone could speak in a very silent dressing room, Big Martin spoke up and pragmatically said that he would have also gone to USA if he had been asked and so would everyone else in this dressing room. He was also the first to say that if the six were not playing, then he wasn't either and so we all agreed with him not to play. So, he concluded, if we aren't playing there is no need to train, and he led us out the room and so begun the strike.

Brian and Micheal called us back into the room and told us they were going to have to pick an alternative team if we can't come to an agreement. We were told to pick one player to represent the players that did not travel and along with Michael Lafferty our captain, who did travel, would represent the Transatlantic 6. To my surprise, Martin proposed me to represent the players. I felt honoured and accepted and so we all agreed formally to go on immediate strike.

None of the new team announced were made aware of the dispute context and there were two players from my club, Michael Gallagher and Paddy Gavigan who immediately refused to play when they realised that a strike was underway and the rest duly followed. By the Friday night after many exchanges (which is another story), the strike ended when the suspensions on the five players were lifted. The following day, which was Saturday, a very upbeat panel had a light training session, and went on to beat Mayo in Ballyshannon on that Sunday.

But the only change after training, no longer did we receive steaks and tomatoes, it was back to sandwiches.

A fitting end to a week of conflict both on and off the field, in which Martin Griffin once again had excelled.

Suaimhneas siorai Martin. Ar dheis De go raibh a h-anam uasal.

Pádraig Carr is a native of Carrick and played for Naomh Columba, Glencolmcille, Donegal and St Brendan's Chicago. He won a senior Championship in 1978, an Ulster Championship in 1983. He won the championship in Chicago 1989. He is married to Trish and they have four grown-up children, Brian, Colin, Stephen and Deirdre. His company specialises in Waterproofing concrete and repair. His twin brother Seamus is also involved with Tir Chonaill Gaels and London County Board for many years. Their father Frank was Secretary of Leitrim Co Board in 195, and Chairman of Donegal Co Board.

KNIGHT OF THE WHISTLE: Considered one of the best ever GAA referees, the late Wicklow official, Eamon Moules, recalled a scary day when time was his enemy. *See 'The Match I Refereed Without A Watch', Page 195*

LOST LEGEND: Wexford's Bill Hodgins was one of the GAA's first superstars but his life was tragically cut short at 26 years of age. *See 'Bill Hodgins – A Legend Struck Down In His Prime', Page 197*

LEITRIM LEADERS: Peter Gordon, Patsy Doherty and Paddy Solon, who helped spread the hurling gospel in Leitrim. *See 'Excuse Me Ref, But You're Wrong', Page 213*

DOUBLE DATE:
How did the late Eamon Coleman manage to play in two county finals in successive Sundays?
See 'Eamon Coleman's Unique Contribution To County Final Days', **Page 215**

PHOTO: SPORTSFILE

CLASS ACT: Galway's John Connolly (left) in a tussle for the sliotar with Offaly's Eugene Coughlan during the 1981 All-Ireland Senior Hurling Championship final at Croke Park.
PHOTO: SPORTSFILE

SPOT THE DIFFERENCE: Galway's John Connolly (above) is the only player with a 'Pádraig Pearse-like' profile in the inaugural All-Stars poster of 1971.
See 'A Pádraig Pearse Pose For All-Star Photograph', Page 225

BATTLE OF BEDLAM: A row over team transport in Donegal back in 1931 led to a strange stand-off which grabbed newspaper headlines.
See 'The Siege Of Bedlam Became A Tale In Song And Story', Page 227

INCIDENT ON GORTAHORK ROAD

CAR PREVENTS PASSAGE OF 'BUS.

TEACHERS' & FOOTBALLERS PARTIES FOR SAME VEHICLE

YOUNG MAN SUMMONED AT FALCARRAGH.

A misunderstanding regarding the engagement of a bus to convey a party of footballers and supporters from Falcarragh to Gweedore led to an exciting scene on the public road near Gortahork on a recent Sunday. The incident was described at Falcarragh Court, before Justice Walsh

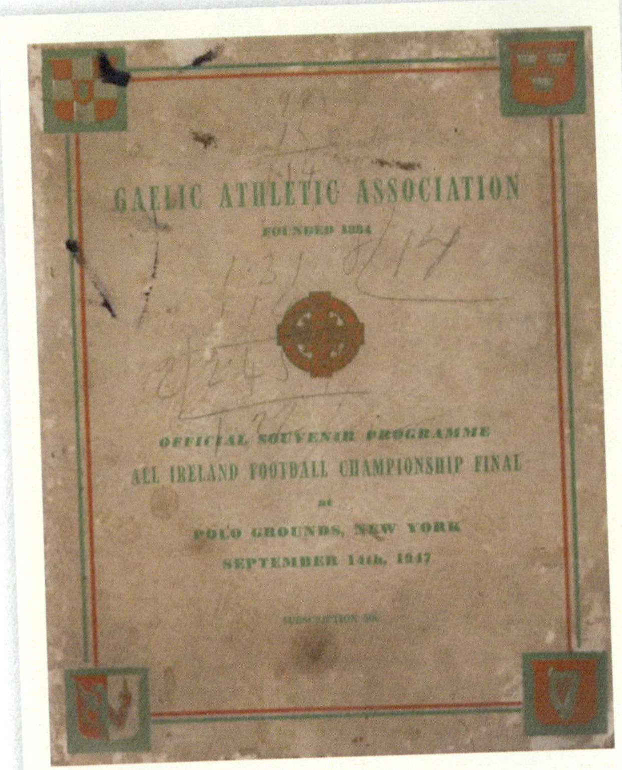

PRIZE POSSESSION: A programme from the Polo Grounds, New York, where Cavan beat Kerry in the 1947 All-Ireland final.
GOLDEN GIRL: Was Susan Golden (above) the missing link in getting the programme home to Cavan? *See 'Some Memories Are Hazy But This One Could Be 'Golden' ', Page 239*

PENN PICTURE: Former Cllr Henry Kenny, brother of former Taoiseach Enda Kenny, President of the American Conference for Irish Studies (ACIS) Professor Timothy McMahon, Caitriona Doyle, Bohola, representing Pat McNicholas, Dr. Matthew O'Brien, Pittsburgh, Prof. of History at Steubenville University, Cllr Martin McLoughlin, then Cathaoirleach of Castlebar Municipal District Council and Michael Larkin pictured outside Mayo County Library where the Pennsylvania Cup is now on display. Right: Mayo may have lost the All-Ireland that year but they were fêted in Philadelphia for their 'World' exploits in 1932. *See 'All-Ireland Loss As Mayo Become World Champions', Page 247*

DARBY'S DAY: Famous for a certain goal against Kerry 40 years ago, Seamus Darby was a matchwinner at a local level for Mary O'Connor's pub team in Edenderry. *See 'A Darby Moment Restores My Pub Team's Honour', Page 287*

PHOTO: SPORTSFILE

CÚL HURLERS: Dublin forward Ryan O'Dwyer (left) and Antrim's Maeve Kelly (right), the intermediate Player of the Year for 2021, posing with the Cultec variety of camán which has increased in popularity among players. *See 'The Longest Drive Ever To Croke Park', Page 295*

LUCKY ESCAPE:
Cork's Dave McCarthy (*back row, sixth from left*) won an All-Star for his displays in Cork's successful Sam Maguire voyage of 1973 but could have lost his gong except for a quick-thinking referee.
Back row, left to right: Donie O'Donovan, team coach, Denis Long, Ray Cummins, Jimmy Barry Murphy, John Coleman, Dave McCarthy, Declan Barron, Ned Kirby and Denis Coughlan.
Front row, left to right: Jim Barrett, Con Hartnett, Kevin Jer O'Sullivan, Billy Morgan (captain), Frank Cogan, Brian Murphy and Humphrey Kelleher.
See 'Yes, I Was A Ref Who 'Bent' The Rules – And I'm Proud Of It!', Page 323
PHOTO: SPORTSFILE

A MAN APART: Legendary Wicklow GAA man Peter Keogh, then in his eighties, walks across his beloved county grounds in Aughrim before a league match in 2014. *See 'Banner Man Got Us Going', Page 348*

PHOTO: SPORTSFILE

The Reservoir Dogs
Of Mullinahone

Joe Kearney

All week in the local cinema they had been showing 'Cheyenne Autumn' featuring Richard Widmark and Carroll Baker. It prompted us to imagine our mongrel bicycles were mustangs and broncos and that the dust of open prairies clung to our lips rather than that blowing from the Fair Green.

We even transformed distant Slievenamon into the foothills of the Sierras. It was in the time before the cinema burned down and we would find ourselves forced to endure the 10-mile bone-shake into Kilkenny in the back of Jacky Nolan's bus if we wished to see the pictures.

But all that was in the future, for now, all we cared about was holding on to the last days of freedom. You see, all summer long our gang had hung out together. Sure, we had bickered and battled but now at the onset of the return to school, we were united as one in our impending misery. What we needed was one last adventure before surrendering to autumn's anguish.

Sunday afternoons in Callan could be slow but All-Ireland final Sundays turned the place into something resembling a ghost-town of the Mojave, where both time and luck have run out. I think it was Spider's idea that we should go to Mullinahone.

He suggested a raiding party deep into enemy territory. For this was not just any All-Ireland hurling final, it was the grand final battle in a war that was waged far away in Croke Park. On this September Sunday in 1964, Kilkenny hurlers were facing their nemesis... Tipperary. Borderlands are dangerous places in times of war and we were within a decent sliotar-strike of the county boundary.

In early afternoon, we rounded up our cabal. There were six of us if you counted John Joe's dog. Saddling up, we whooped and hollered up Green Street and out past the cemetery in Kilbride. Hot tar bubbled below a branding-iron sun. It popped like bubble-gum under the wobble of our front tyres. The roads were empty. Each house we passed seemed to have its windows thrown open so that the singsong chant of Michael O'Hehir could escape out into the ripening yellow fields.

We crossed the bridge that marked the border into County Tipperary and we could gauge the score by the roars from cottages and farmhouses alike. The Kilkenny boys were struggling.

Hot and thirsty, we galloped into Mullinahone. If anywhere could be imagined more desolate than Callan, then this was it. A solitary cat spat defiance at John Joe's dog as we rode up and down the street. There was no one else to challenge. A sign, advertising Palm Grove ice cream, flapped a limp greeting to us but when we reigned on our mounts we found the shop shut in our faces. It resembled a scene from High Noon.

Nothing except pistol-shot cheers burst out from lace-curtained windows and ricocheted about our ears. It was all one-way traffic at Croke Park.

We were hungry, thirsty and at a loss...that was until Spider suggested that we raid the orchard in the walled garden at the back of Killahy Castle. The plan restored our spirits. Were we not a bold raiding party after all and were we not in the heart of the enemy camp?

It was decided that Spider and myself would do the deed while the rest of the gang kept watch. We circled the orchard until we spotted a rusty ladder attached to a giant water tank beside the wall. Overhanging dangles of Beauty of Bath apples that carried rosy blushes on their ripening cheeks enticed us in. Up the ladder, over the wall, we filled our pockets with red apples, green apples, hard apples. We were sorted in jig time.

But back on the sag of the ladder, disaster struck. We were circled by a pack of mixed hounds that leaped, snapped and snarled at our sandaled toes. Chucking apples only made them worse and the remainder of the gang had vamoosed.

We were finally set free by the owner who, when he learned we were from Callan, laughed, knowing that the final score in Croke Park should be punishment enough...Tipperary 5-13 points, Kilkenny 2-8.

The journey back seemed longer. Farmers hunting in cows for milking roared UP TIPP as we cycled past.

The thought that the day after represented the first day back at school had combined with the green apples to turn our stomachs sour and if that wasn't bad enough, our final summer adventure had been spoiled by the reservoir dogs of Mullinahone.

'And it looks like there's a bit of a schemozzle in the parallelogram'

One of the many euphemisms deployed by the legendary Michael O'Hehir during his commentaries on GAA matches for Radio Éireann, later RTÉ Radio

Placing A Value On The Man Who Beats The Briars

Ciaran Condren

The television advertisements show a pitch laboriously hewn out of the rock-strewn surrounds on the edge of the heaving Atlantic. It's breath-taking surrounds inspire.

However, the community field on which Liam Mellows ply their hurling trade stands with it in terms of dramatic setting. It is cradled on the side of Croghan mountain and from its height the land falls away to the east revealing a sweeping panorama pillared on the North by the chiselled remnants of Arklow Rock and on the South by Tara Hill.

In between a patchwork of carefully tended model county farms and houses seem to sweep down to the sometime blue expanse of the Irish Sea. On the rare occasions that the hurling fails to stir the soul, a therapeutic raising of the eyes to the east, to feast on the dramatic land and seascape can elevate mind and body to a higher place.

And then the clash of the ash propels one instantly back to the reality of the do or die struggle unfolding at the mere mortal level just before our eyes.

Before the towering containing nets were installed at either end of the ground, there was a real problem with the sliotars being launched into the adjoining field on one side of the ground and disappearing into a jungle like growth of heather and briars on the other.

In mitigation, the location of the pitch and the time of the evening when most games were played meant that most training sessions took place as the great ball in the sky was shedding its daytime splendour and was morphing into a reddish orangish radiator, shafting horizontal beams of distraction into the squinting eyes of the hardy souls who were attempting to play.

They had to overcome the shards of glinting light escaping from the grasp of the dying sun, setting over Croghan mountain before driving the sliotar in the direction of the goalposts on the more frequently used side of the pitch near the clubhouse.

As they raced and toiled, and fought, and whipped, and drove, and tackled, and hooked, and blocked, and wriggled and finally released the sliotar, or the man, to bear down on the stark half-painted goal with only a net attached to stop the goal bound shot, how many of them noticed the one or two figures behind the target?

They were not togged out in club gear. Not for them the latest banded hurley. Nor the soul-lifting joy of a perfect strike, or the sheer delight of a ball hitting the sweet spot and arching enticingly into the path of an onrushing teammate to be lashed with joyful abandon into the back of the net. Nor the communal gathering of the warriors when the foe had been vanquished and the prize of the cup was sloshing around the local pub to great merriment and fanfare.

No, the unnoticed silhouette with the duffle jacket closely collared against the rising chill of the evening breeze was brandishing a clapped out hurley, scarred to the point of uselessness by many a previous battle. He kept a focus on the blunderbuss of shots and the locations where the errant sliotars came to rest in the undergrowth. Then with a determination not to be bested, crafted from a younger day when it was his turn to drive the ball into the scrub, he lashed the briars and the undergrowth relentlessly until they yielded up the golden prize of the lost sliotar.

It was then transferred unceremoniously into the impatient and not always grateful hand of the waiting goalkeeper who promptly propelled it back into a new life cycle. This reincarnation, sometimes brief, would inevitably end with the unseen one at the back of the goal rummaging again to keep it alive.

And so the training evenings went. The youthful energy, the shouts, the fun, the occasional row, the frequent curse, the rare touch of the master that controlled the uncontrollable, the communal gasp of appreciation, the cross fertilisation of stories that connected the onlookers as they recharged themselves from the fountain of youth that bestrode the pitch.

And as the trainer gathered in the band for one last word, the horizontal shafts of light descending into a duskish gloom, in the background, unseen, the lads with the worn-out hurls were still beating the briars. There were still four sliotars missing and they were certain that they had disappeared into that particularly dense patch. They knew exactly where they were but they could not find them and the light was fading fast. If they were left till morning those young lads from the school would be nosing around and surely would lay their hands on them. And they would never be seen again in a Liam Mellows bag.

The team talk is over and the players are scattering to the ends of the parish and beyond.

The steady rhythm of the hurl against the briar comes to an end. The collared one, pockets stuffed with rescued sliotars, shuffles back towards the clubhouse and engages with the last of the players and onlookers. The chances of the team at the weekend are evaluated and current team issues aired. The pockets are emptied into the Mellows hurley bag and as the unpainted posts disappear into the enveloping gloom, the pitch quietly descends into its nocturnal slumber and silence reigns.

As one reflects on the scene that has just played out and continues to be played out in so many clubs of so many kinds, in so many places, it is apt to try to place a value on the man who beats the briars.

The catalyst, the unnoticed, the unseen hand, the gentle hand on the tiller that quietly moves in the fading light when the din of battle is over. Not likely to be the one battling to grasp control of the wheel of the ship when the AGM collapses into rivalling camps as the winter chill renders the pitch unplayable and the briar patch retreats back to a more benign winter cover. And yields the last of the hardest to find lost balls.

Likely to be a quiet soul with a love of the game and the club and the code that defies any kind of logical analysis.

When the sideshow of who will grace the top table for another year is just a memory, thoughts refocus on the field, on the game. Hope rises that this is to be the year.

An eternal triumph of hope over experience. New leadership

and new ideas. The sliotars once again begin to rain down into the renaissance briar patch. Each strike sharpening the skill set, paving the way to the promised land.

The figure in the duffle coat will shuffle out, the old soldier with the gnarled hurl, once again to make war on the briars, to keep the show on the road. The keeper of soul in the club.

Or do we expect too much?

Thank you, Mr Briar man.

Ciaran Condren is a farmer living in Macamores in North Wexford. He is married with two adult sons.

Our Comfort Blanket
In Life And Death

Tony Fearon

It was on the first Saturday in March 1995 that my late brother, Dr Joe Fearon's life ended, all too soon, at the age of just 35, in St Vincent's Hospital in Dublin. The last resort to defeat liver cancer, ended after an attempt to transplant this vital organ, performed by the skilled surgeon and Meath All Ireland Winner Gerry McEntee, failed due to medical circumstances.

During his short illness it was the GAA that sustained both himself and his surviving family members. From his teammates in his local Armagh club, (he was still playing when diagnosed in late 1994), Portadown Tir Na Nog visiting him in his local hospital in Armagh the evening they clinched the Armagh Division 2 trophy that year, right through to the expert care of Gerry McEntee, not only medically but pastoral-like in trying to keep spirits high, going way beyond the call of duty.

Then there was his teammates from the 1982 Queen's University Sigerson Cup winning team making regular treks to Dublin with special mention to Belfast solicitor and Fermanagh gael, Seamus Leonard, who put at our disposal a house owned by his family in Dublin, to allow us be close for our brother's final days.

The death itself saw a mass mobilisation of the GAA network, from the local club in Portadown, providing chairs for the wake and unqualified support in all directions, the phone call from the great Sean O'Neill, Queens' 1982 Sigerson winning manager, callers at the house including legendary Armagh captain from 1977, Jimmy Smyth.

At the funeral itself his coffin was draped in three GAA jerseys, Armagh (whom he had represented at all levels), Queens and his local club. The principal celebrant at the requiem mass was County Louth native, the late Fr Dominic Rafferty who had managed the local Tir Na Nog club, every single one of his Sigerson teammates from 1982 was there as well as the Gaelic games coach from his alma mater, St Patrick's College Armagh, Noel Mc Clurg, who had selected my brother on his all-star 15 from his time in charge at the College from 1965 to 1982. We were sustained by all this, not to mention a huge turnout of players and members from the local club.

A cherished memory after the burial was seeing the great Sean O'Neill approach my late Father, a humble lorry driver, who was so overcome with shyness, he couldn't speak to the Down legend.

A month after his death the local club in Portadown hosted a fund raising evening for cancer charities and the clubhouse was packed to the rafters, with entertainment provided by a rival club, Clonmore's Gerry Cunningham and his band More Power To Your Elbow.

It has been over 27 years ago, but the support from the GAA community has never waned. The club in Portadown named the Senior Player of the Year trophy in honour of my late brother and even as recently as 2018 when the local club celebrated its 75th anniversary, beautiful tributes were left on my brother's grave and those of many others in the same cemetery in Portadown. What a thoughtful tribute that was.

My story is like thousands of others in every county and indeed beyond which simply illustrates the enormous role the GAA plays at times of bereavement.

The huge comfort blanket the association throws over us all is always genuine because it is done by our own GAA neighbours who in essence are an extended family for those suffering their greatest loss. Long may this continue.

Tony Fearon is a native of Portadown, Co Armagh. A member of the local Portadown Tir Na Nog GFC, he has been an avid follower of his club and county for nearly 50 years.

Thady's Exploits Had Team Groupies In A Tizzy

Rosemary McDermott

Back in the mid-70s, a group of my friends and myself took a huge interest in the GAA. While we didn't really know much about the game, there was one big attraction for us – the players. When our search for talent at local matches failed to produce results, we shifted our interest south of the border.

Every week, dolled up in the latest fashion, we'd trowel on make-up, shiny lip gloss and thick coats of black mascara, before making our way to the match. Arriving at the pitch, we'd find the perfect spot to ensure a plum view of the action. The atmosphere was electric as the game got underway and we thoroughly enjoyed the banter between the supporters as they cheered on their team.

There was one tall, dark handsome fellow who'd caught my eye. I'd christened him Thady, after the Cork man who'd inspired the penning of the popular, traditional Irish ballad, The Bould Thady Quill.

The Thady that I admired, however, played midfield and when he came racing towards the sideline to mark his opponent, I'd smile broadly and furiously bat my eyelids. Sadly, my firm belief that this alluring tactic would net me the man of my dreams was shattered when my friend, Tilly, asked me if I'd developed a nervous twitch in my eye!

One week, the regular goalkeeper was unavailable, so the handsome Thady was asked to play in goals. As I was considering my next move to attract his attention, a drama began to unfold. Jumping up to make a save, the tall, gangly player banged his head on the crossbar and knocked himself out. As he lay on the ground, we moved over towards the top of the goalmouth. Our fear for Thady's life increased as a priest, who'd been watching the match, rushed to his aid.

"Oh no, Thady's dying," I wailed to my friends. "The priest is about to give him the last rites."

A short time later, a collective sigh of relief rippled through the crowd as a dazed Thady raised himself up on his elbows. As we stood looking on, the thought crossed my mind that if I could just get closer and gaze into his handsome face – my eyes, pools of molten emerald, would soon revive him. However, before I could make my move, the priest, a red-faced, jovial man, helped Thady to his feet and declared: "You'll be grand, lad." As Thady was led off to recuperate at the side of the field, I overheard a burly bystander proclaim to his pal: "If that boy had horns, he'd do damage."

Jealous toe-rag, I thought, especially with what I'd been reading in the local newspapers. Every week I avidly read glowing articles about Thady's future in Gaelic football. I read and re-read the reports about the brilliant and outstanding player who was bound for Croke Park. I felt sure that he would captain the county team and could imagine him holding aloft the Sam Maguire Cup on All-Ireland Sunday.

Later in the season, as we were enjoying a match, two female supporters approached us and asked if we'd like to buy tickets for an upcoming GAA fundraising social and dance. With the tickets tucked safely in our handbags, our minds were in overdrive as we wondered what we'd wear that would get us noticed by the players at this exciting event.

In the weeks that followed, we made several journeys to Strabane and Derry but failed to find the perfect outfit to wear on our very promising night out. Suddenly, Tilly had a lightbulb moment and came up with a wonderful idea. After a few trips to Harley's Drapery shop in Strabane and to our local dressmaker, we were kitted out in tops and bell bottom trousers in our beloved GAA team's colours.

When the night of the social arrived, we felt we looked irresistible as we preened and twirled in front of the mirror, before setting off to the social. The parochial hall was buzzing when we arrived and, as we settled into seats, our eyes swept around the room for a glimpse of our heartthrobs.

A short time later, the big moment came as the team, in all their glory, arrived for the supper and dance. As they mingled with the crowd, we were mightily impressed by how well they had all scrubbed up for the night. Any interest in the tea and buns that were being served took second place as we gazed down the long trestle table.

As the night wore on, the tables were cleared and the music struck up. The players danced with several girls but, much to our disappointment, they didn't even glance in our direction. I watched enviously as Thady, who was oblivious of me, waltzed a stunning blonde girl around the hall. My heart sank to my toes at the sight of the attractive pair pausing to smile broadly for a photographer.

The snapper then moved in our direction to take our photos. "He's a brilliant player," I enthused, nodding towards Thady.

"Oh, what makes you say that?" He asked with amusement, as we posed for the camera.

"I've read in the paper that he'll go down in sporting history as the man who led the county team to the All-Ireland," I replied knowledgeably.

"Ah lass," the man sighed, "You shouldn't believe all you read in the papers." Then leaning towards us, he whispered conspiratorially; "I'll let you into a secret."

My jaw dropped as he added; "Sure it's that boyo's father who writes the reports for the newspaper!"

Rosemary McDermott lives in Strabane, Co Tyrone. She is married to Sean and has four sons and three grandchildren. She is a member of The Gateway Writer's Group in Lifford and has had several short stories published.

Croke's Support A Vital Part Of GAA's Wildfire Spread

T. W. Croke

'One of the most painful, let me assure you, and, at the same time, one of the most frequently recurring reflections that, as an Irishman, I am compelled to make in connection with the present aspect of things in this country, is derived from the ugly and irritating fact that we are daily importing from England not only her manufactured goods, which we cannot help doing, since she has practically strangled our own manufacturing appliances, but, together with her fashions, her accent, her vicious literature, her music, her dances, and her manifold mannerisms, her games also and her pastimes, to the utter discredit of our own grand national sports, and to the sore humiliation, as I believe, of every genuine son and daughter of the old land.

Ball-playing, hurling, football kicking, according to Irish rules, 'casting', leaping in various ways, wrestling, handy-grips, top-pegging, leap-frog, rounders, tip-in-the-hat, and all such favourite exercises and amusements amongst men and boys, may now be said to be not only dead and buried, but in several localities to be entirely forgotten and unknown. And what have we got in their stead?

We have got such foreign and fantastic field sports as lawn-tennis, polo, croquet, cricket, and the like...very excellent, I believe, and health-giving exercises in their way, still not racy of the soil, but rather alien, on the contrary, to it, as are, indeed, for the most part the men and women who first imported and still continue to patronise them'

The of Cashel, Thomas William Croke, in a letter to GAA founder, Michael Cusack, Dec. 18, 1884.

Was It A Parish Priest's Curse That Cost Us The County Final?

Tom Lawlor

When it comes to the GAA, victory and defeat are not so much two different countries as two totally contrasting continents.

When you win, you are saluted and deified for your achievements; when you lose, everyone and everything is blamed, from the weather to the players to the referee. And in our case, following the greatest Kerry senior county hurling final I can remember in 1948 between my native parish Ballyheigue and neighbouring club, Kilmoyley, you could add two more – a priest's curse and a surfeit of pre-match imbibing.

We lived in a rural area called Booleenshare and we just trotted across the fields down to Mass...the Sunday of this county final the pews up the church were light on numbers as most of us GAA folk knelt at the back whispering our thoughts on how the game might turn out.

When Mass was over and the congregation spilled outside, the talk of the game continued with a number of older men warning us that there would be trouble in Tralee that day.

Now I was only a young lad at the time and didn't know what that remark meant but I felt safe enough as two neighbours of mine, goalie Johnny Guerin and centre forward Tommy Walsh, who both worked on the farm for my father, would be with us.

We bolted down our earlier Sunday dinner, yoked the pony to the car and travelled as fast as she could go into Tralee. When we got there, we headed straight to the stables which cost sixpence-a-day to mind and feed the horse or in our case, the pony.

The stables were just across the road from the Greyhound Bar.

From the moment we arrived in the town, we could indeed smell "the sulphur." I became more anxious because I was only five years old and wasn't sure what to expect.

The reason for all the kerfuffle that Sunday was due to the fact that Charlie Kerins, an IRA man executed during the Emergency, was brought from Dublin the previous night for reinterment in Rath Cemetery, Tralee. Coincidentally, this went on the same day and the same time as the county final was due to start.

Thousands lined the streets and marched behind the hearse... after the corpse had been kept overnight in St Johns Mortuary Church. That Sunday, Kerin's coffin was paraded around the town and every time the coffin bearers changed to allow others the honour of carrying him, volleys rang out from rifles and double-barrelled shotguns all over the place.

This slowed down the procession considerably which resulted in the game being delayed by two or three hours. It was said the county board was afraid to start the final while the procession was taking place.

As we were walking up Bothar Buí to the Austin Stacks Park, the powder from the gunshots hung heavy in the air around us. You would nearly imagine you were walking through falling snow.

It was only when the cortege had finally reached Rath graveyard that the late John Joe Sheehy, who played an important role for many years as a footballer and a hurler and was later president of the GAA in Kerry, came back into the Austin Stacks Park and informed the teams to go ahead.

However, during the hours that the final had been delayed, several players from both sides developed 'a fisherman's thirst' and went down to the local Sportsfield Bar, initially for "one" to settle the nerves but subsequently many more pints were consumed. Both teams had messenger boys operating between the pub and the outside world, relaying as best they could the likely time of the ever-changing throw in.

In the heel of the hunt, as the afternoon went on, the drinkers got the feeling that there was always time "for one more"...and they didn't vacate the hostelry until the word got back close to three hours later that it was time for them to head down to the pitch to tog off.

When asked sometime later about how much porter they had on board, one of the bar's patron's that afternoon said: "Put it this way, none of us would have passed the breathalyser test."

With the match being played in September and it coming up to quarter to five before the game began, a big part of the crowd had already departed for home as most of the people attending were involved in agriculture and would have cows to milk, pigs to feed and sows to look after.

Once the match began, it was played in a sporting manner and while the standard was maybe lower than usual, there might have been extenuating circumstances for that.

"Despite the game not reaching the heights," the Kerryman reported, "the spectators could not grumble at the lack of thrills and excitement as the two strong, well-balanced teams went headlong into their work regardless of the close tackling and hard pulling."

At the long whistle, it was our opponents Kilmoyley who came out on top in what the newspaper described as "a ding-dong battle".

Kilmoyley won on a scoreline of 5-2 to 3-6 and their supporters were overjoyed as the presentation of the cup was made to their captain.

For Ballyheigue, the post-mortem commenced on the way home and straight away it focused on the amount of time some players spent in the pub before the match. While as many Kilmoyley players had partaken in a similar bout of drinking, by winning, their antics only served to heighten the regard their supporters held them in. It is indeed true that victory spawns a thousand fathers while defeat ends up an orphan.

The more pragmatic followers of Ballyheigue accepted that on the day the team wasn't good enough but there were others who felt there were more sinister forces at play.

We had our own version of Biddy Earley's curse to Clare teams in our own parish. It originated when a parish priest took umbrage at a player having the temerity to start up a dance hall in opposition to his own parish hops.

He sought to have the individual dropped from a county final line-up and when the selectors went against him, the priest declared that as long as a member of that family played for Ballyheigue, they would never win another county final.

The gentleman of the cloth had a great capacity to dislike those who didn't acquiesce with his demands. I myself had the distinction of being cursed off the altar in 1964 for being seen in a newer dance-hall started up by the same man. I was good friends with his son who let me in the back for free on the night I was observed defying the clergyman.

I think I might have the last laugh in that particular row with the priest. He told the congregation that I wouldn't see Christmas for defying him and the church, yet here I am pushing 80 and still walking around in 2022, having long since concluded that this particular priest's curse didn't really carry much weight at all.

Tom Lawlor is a native of Ballyheigue. Married to Julianne Kenny, they have two children Rosemary, who is vice-principal of Kilmoyley National School and son Kenneth, an honour's graduate who left his role with Teagasc to become a dairy farmer. Tom is the former chairman of North Kerry Hurling Board and former Chairman of Kerry IFA.

A Ticket For Tom

Brendan O'Connor

There have been many changes in the GAA over the years but one thing that remains constant year after year is the scramble to secure tickets for the All-Ireland finals. Unfortunately for us here in the Royal County, it's been 21 years and counting since we have encountered that particular problem. Back in 1999, our footballers defeated Armagh in a thrilling semi-final to set us up for another decider against our old friends from Cork sparking off the usual search for the precious tickets. This time however the seeds of a plan to secure a pair of tickets were already germinating in my head.

A few weeks earlier I had been listening to the build-up to the hurling final on the radio while travelling to work every morning. Ian Dempsey was on 2FM at the time and Des Cahill would present the sport reports during his programme. In the week before the hurling decider, they asked the listeners to send in poems about the final and a prize of two tickets would be given to whoever was deemed to have the best poem from each county. I assumed they would do the same for the football final and already had an idea for my entry.

I started bringing my son, Tom, to games in the summer of 1996 even though he was still a few months shy of his fourth birthday. As I recall, hopes were not particularly high as we started off that campaign but Sean Boylan's new look team surprised us all and ended the year as All-Ireland champions, defeating Mayo in that famous replay. Unfortunately, having been at all the other games I could not bring Tom to the final or replay because it was impossible to get him a ticket. When 1999 came around, remembering how disappointed he was three years earlier, I was determined that he would get to go to the final. As it happened, Tom's seventh birthday, on September 25, would fall that year on the Saturday before the All-Ireland final and that gave me the inspiration to write "A Ticket for Tom" as my entry for the competition on the radio.

Having sent in my poem the previous week, you can only imagine how delighted I was when Des read it out on the Monday morning before the final. Ian Dempsey played the music of Red Sovine's tear-jerking song Teddy Bear as Des read the poem and it seemed to go down well with both of them. For the rest of the week, I listened attentively to all the entries and on Friday morning we all sat around the radio with great anticipation. When the phone rang and someone from the Breakfast Show asked whether I would be prepared to talk live with Ian and Des, it sparked wild celebrations in our house. I was declared the winner of the competition; the poem was read out again and both Tom and I got our few moments of fame speaking to Des Cahill on the radio.

Later that day, two tickets for the recently opened corporate section of the new Cusack Stand were delivered by courier to our house and we saw that the prize also included access to the new Lounge for refreshments after the game. Tom and I arrived early on the big day and took our seats high up in the Cusack stand near the Canal end. The atmosphere before the game was fantastic, looking down on the pitch as the teams paraded behind the Artane Band amid the noise and colour of the packed stadium is something we will never forget.

During the first half, we had a bird's-eye view of Evan Kelly's three points and Ollie Murphy with the goal before half-time. We had a few nervous minutes early in the second half when Trevor Giles missed a penalty but Graham Geraghty scored three excellent points and our good friend and neighbour John McDermott played his part at centre field in a famous victory for the Royals. So, thanks to Ian Dempsey, Des Cahill and 2FM, Tom received the best birthday present ever, as he got to see Graham Geraghty being presented with the Sam Maguire cup in the middle of the pitch in Croke Park.

After the presentation, we met my wife Mary and my mother, who had been sitting together in the lower stand. I guessed back then that seven-year-old Tom, unlike today's version, would have little interest in the post-match drinks, so he went home with my mother and father while Mary and I went back up to the lounge. As we were getting out of the elevator at the top of the Cusack Stand, who did we meet only Des Cahill. After I introduced myself and thanked him again for the tickets Des asked where Tom was. As soon as I began to explain that he had gone home with his grandparents Des started slagging me saying "Go on you chancer, you used your young lad to get the tickets and then you wouldn't even bring him to the game".

Brendan O'Connor is a member of Curraha GAA Club in Co. Meath where he has served as a player, selector, secretary and chairman. Married to Mary, they have four grown-up children, Robert, Tom, Aidan and Sarah. Like all his family Brendan is a fanatical Meath supporter. His other interests include reading and writing and he is a member of the Limetree Writers Group in Duleek.

'There won't be a cow milked in Clare tonight'

Marty Morrissey after Clare's 1992 Munster championship victory

'There won't be a cow milked in Finglas tonight'

Keith Barr after Erin's Isle semi-final win in the 1998 All-Ireland Club championship

Unlikely Amalgamation That Brought All-Ireland Glory To Kerry

Eamonn Brennan

The kingdom of Kerry boasts many beautiful sights, none more impressive than the Ring of Kerry. The Iveragh peninsula begins at Kells after you leave Glenbeigh behind and it stretches all the way to Sneem, about 50 kilometres further along the coast.

Cahersiveen, the town of the peninsula, was immortalised by Sigerson Clifford in 'The Boys of Barr na Sráide', as the town that climbs the mountain and looks down on the sea. For generations, the area thrived on the harvest of the sea.

In the 1920s the great shoals of mackerel stopped coming and appeared only erratically after that. The population declined and emigration increased. Seine boats, an open boat 30-feet long, were the fishing boats of the time. They were powered by 12 men and a cox. Working in pairs, they encircled the fish and caught them in a seine net. Every summer, the excitement is fever pitch as seine boat races take place all along the coast. Another popular pastime is beagle hunting but the most popular of all is Gaelic Football.

There are nine GAA clubs in South Kerry, featuring at various levels from Division 1 to Division 5 in the Kerry County League. Cahersiveen, with the largest population base, has dominated the South Kerry Championship for 100 years.

Typical of the smaller clubs in the area are St Micheal's, Derrynane and Foilmore. St Michael's and Skelligs Rangers are in the parish of Prior, one of the smallest in Kerry. Skelligs Rangers is situated around the village of Portmagee where the bridge connects to Valentia Island. St Michael's takes in the townlands of the Glen and Ballinskelligs part of the parish.

When you cross the mountain between Portmagee and the Glen, a beautiful valley sweeping down to St Finians Bay, you have divided loyalties. Some families play for Skelligs Rangers and others for St Michael's, now known as St Michael's Foilmore. You may well ask where the Foilmore connection comes from.

Foilmore takes in a small area which stretches from Kells to the outskirts of Cahersiveen. In the early 1990s, with emigration rampant, St Michael's and Foilmore were struggling to field a team at adult level. St Michael's and Foilmore are 13 miles apart, with no obvious connection.

Kerry County Board chairman Seán Kelly – later to become President of the GAA – encouraged the two clubs to amalgamate but keep their underage teams independent. The obvious amalgamation would have been with immediate neighbours Skelligs Rangers in St Michael's case and Cahersiveen in the case of Foilmore.

As a 'Cold War' often exists between neighbouring clubs, that was never going to happen. Neither club wanted to join with immediate neighbours, fearing loss of identity. Anyway, Cahersiveen and Skelligs Rangers indicated they would take a few players; the best ones, no doubt.

It wasn't the only good idea Seán Kelly had, and in this case, both clubs took his advice. The new amalgamation came into being and quickly began to make waves.

They were blessed with a passionate management duo whose friendship was forged in the building sites of London. On their return to South Kerry, the trainer James Mike O'Sullivan of St Michael's and his assistant Tom 'the Smith' O'Sullivan of Foilmore built a mighty team. Their unity and friendship avoided all selection difficulties.

Despite not being taken too seriously by other clubs in South Kerry, they won a number of South Kerry League and championship titles. They began to climb through the Kerry County League and got promoted to Division 1 of the Kerry County League. They won the Kerry Intermediate Championship and the Munster Intermediate title, in 2008.

The crowning glory came in February 2009, when they won the All-Ireland intermediate final in Croke Park. What a wonderful occasion it was, as people travelled from far and near and abroad to support their team. The most unlikely amalgamation had won the All-Ireland intermediate championship, the first team from the South Kerry Division to do so.

Eamonn Brennan is a native of St Finian's Bay, the Glen from the St Michael's /Foilmore club in SW Kerry. He is a resident of Longford town since 1981. Since his retirement from teaching, he has been involved with Longford Co. Board.

'Hurling looks a bit like a cross between lacrosse and second degree murder'

Bangor, Co. Down-born David Feherty, former Ryder Cup golfer and now golf broadcaster in the US

'I'm always suspicious of games where you're the only ones that play it'

Former Republic of Ireland Manager and England World Cup winner, Jack Charlton when asked his views on hurling

Mixed Fortunes And
A Hint Of Bribery

Michael Walsh

My Uncle John enjoyed a rare experience while playing a hurling match challenge for his club against local opposition in Tipperary. The visitors were short two players and were being hammered halfway through the second when a mentor asked for the loan of a player "to balance up the numbers and save embarrassment."

John volunteered and as an incentive was offered a new sliotar by the mentor if he got a few scores for the opposition. After bagging 4-1 for his own team, he switched jerseys and scored 2-2 for the opposition. At the final whistle the referee congratulated him on being the leading scorer on both teams, but John did not receive his reward after the match...so much for bribery, he thought.

However, a week later a man drove into his parents' farmyard in a Model-T Ford and, after introducing himself as Billie, presented John with a brand new sliotar. He then enquired if John might be interested in 'changing club colours' and playing for his team but John left him in no doubt that such bribery wouldn't work, as he was totally loyal to his club.

The year was 1937 and during this time John thought about emigrating to England. After writing to his cousin, Mick, in Liverpool, he got word back that "jobs were going" in that city, and was told "a hurler would always be welcome to join a club."

Three weeks later, with a heavy heart, my uncle left Ireland from the North Wall for England on the 'Leinster' boat; his luggage included his hurl and that brand new sliotar.

After a short time, he secured a job in Liverpool, working as a barman. A few days later, he met his cousin Mick in the Lord Nelson Hotel, who said he was "a supporter of a team called Éire Óg" and was asked to keep an eye out for hurling talent coming in on the boat from North Wall.

Over drinks, Mick asked John if he would consider lining out for them in an upcoming match. At first, he refused, saying it would be hard to get time off work (in those days, a barman got only the odd Sunday off). However, he relented when offered a ticket to the All-Ireland hurling final, telling the cousin that one of his boyhood dreams was to attend an All-Ireland Final in Croke Park.

Mick casually told him that through a contact in Dublin he received a ticket every year for the hurling final, but seldom used it himself. After a long chat, the deal was agreed.

Following a few Sunday morning training sessions with the team, John was, according to his diary, "ready to go" but fate was to deal him a cruel blow.

Travelling to the match venue at Thingwall Road in Broadgreen, he was injured when knocked off his bicycle and missed the match. While nursing a shoulder injury in hospital he was visited by Mick who assured him that the promised All-Ireland ticket would still be his one day.

John protested on the grounds that he didn't play in the match. He subsequently played a few games for the team, but before the season ended, disaster struck again: The recurrence of an old knee injury forced him to fully retire from the game.

After his retirement, John regularly met Mick for drinks in the Lord Nelson Hotel and over the years, often visited him and his family in their home. Mick was still able to get a ticket each year for the All-Ireland hurling final, but despite this being one of his dreams, John kept putting off the decision to travel.

My father enjoyed many holidays at John's house in the early 1960s, each time inviting him to make a visit to 'the family and neighbours' in Ireland but without success. Little did my uncle suspect how this trip to Ireland and fulfilment of his dream to attend an All-Ireland Final would finally come about.

In August 1966, during one such holiday, my father put pressure on John to finally visit Ireland after all those years away, but my uncle once again said he "wasn't in the humour to travel."

However, fate works in strange ways. On my father's return journey from England, he arrived accompanied by John at the Docks in Liverpool and suggested that they both go onto the boat early "for a few farewell drinks."

John readily agreed (in that era, those seeing off passengers were allowed on board for a limited period prior to departure). Time passed and in fact was soon forgotten in the midst of reminiscing about olden times until finally John decided to leave, saying that his wife would have his dinner ready.

Going up on deck after several whiskies, he saw the port of Liverpool fading rapidly into the distance. He was on his way to Ireland, whether he liked it or not.

He arrived accompanied by my father but with no luggage.

"I better ring the missus," John said. The 'missus' was a bit hard of hearing and didn't understand that her husband was no longer in England, and replied in an angry voice: "Well, your dinner is going cold here on the table."

A few days after arriving, John wrote to cousin Mick in Liverpool asking if there might be any chance of sending on that promised ticket for the All-Ireland final. The ticket arrived two weeks later and he attended the final in Croke Park on September 4, 1966, between Cork and Kilkenny, which the Rebels won on a scoreline of Cork 3-9, Kilkenny 1-10.

In a letter to my father after his return to Liverpool, John wrote in glowing terms of his satisfaction at finally attending an All-Ireland final, stating: "My dream has come true."

Quizzed numerous times if he had plotted John's return to Ireland, my father denied plying his brother with whiskey to make the journey a reality, but we all knew by the grin on his face that he had planned the trip alright.

Michael Walsh lives in Dublin and is an avid GAA fan who has spent many years stewarding at Croke Park. While a member of Trinity Writers, he contributed to publications by the group, and also had articles published in magazines such as Ireland's Own and The Far East. His interests include social dancing with wife Maura, walking, language study, reading and golf.

"The first time I brought the boys to a match they were shocked at the abuse being heaped on Seán. I kept trying to tell them it was the referee the supporters were shouting at but they said: 'Mammy, the referee isn't bald'"

Tina Boylan, wife of legendary Meath manager, Seán

A 'Darby' Moment Restores My Pub Team's Honour

Mary O'Connor

It was 1990 and pub football mania was sweeping the Faithful County. It was the latest and greatest craze in Edenderry too, when pubs were reportedly crammed during post-match celebrations and the craic was mighty.

The latest match was the daily topic of conversation as the exploits of the stalwarts from Damo's and Byrnes were discussed with vigour and enthusiasm and consequently, we saw our nightly customer numbers dwindle as the 'regulars' decided to savour the post-match buzz in other hostelries.

Our major domo, Tommy 'Snap' Ryan, decided it was time to take action. Snap was one of the town's best-known sportsmen and was always available to don a jersey when requested. He was known to have played for Edenderry, Ballyfore and Clogherinkoe at various times during the one season.

He loved to be involved in sporting activities and couldn't take another slagging from the 'boys up the town', as they sneered: 'Hey Snap! Have yis neara team in the Harbour or are yis not able to field one?'

He reckoned it was time to take positive action and suggested that we organise our own football team. He secured positive assurances for sufficient numbers of imbibers, once he guaranteed them actual selection on his team, that they would be kitted out in proper jerseys (on loan from some local street team) and, most importantly, the guarantee of free beer and a few sambos after the matches.

The team was named Connor's Cowboys and Snap assumed full control of the team selection, the organising of matches and the venues. He also successfully negotiated the provision of a minibus in the event of an away game in Rhode or The Derries. His major worry was that those who said yes would actually turn up on the day.

The first match was scheduled to be played against Damo's and it was agreed that the post-match session would take place there. The venue was the local football field. The game was described as relatively uncontroversial. However, Damo's (O'Donoghue's) won easily enough and Snap was subjected to a sustained slagging. Furthermore, his difficulties were compounded when they were drawn against Byrne's in the next round.

He knew that defeat was a foregone conclusion. We wouldn't stand a chance as Byrne's could call on most of the Edenderry squad and ours were a motley crew. It transpired that Snap's forebodings were accurate and we were subjected to a humiliating defeat.

He couldn't suffer another hammering and endure the endless sneers of 'yis are only a shower of write-offs.' He would have to take drastic action and come up with a master plan in order to salvage an already disastrous situation.

Then, one Monday afternoon, Ger McLoughlin, a barman in The Round O pub in Navan arrived. It was his day off and his first words were "Well Snap, how are the matches going?" As a litany of defeats were recalled, Ger came up with a plan. He would arrange a match between Connor's Cowboys and The Round O Raiders. It would be the craic of the century.

The following week, he announced that the Raiders were ready and willing to travel. So, plans were made for this greatest of pub matches between the Faithfuls and The Royals.

It was decided that the match would take place on April 4,1990. Preparations were immediately underway. The school field on St. Mary's Road was the chosen venue. Eddie Flynn volunteered to video the game free of charge and Seán (Bocky) Donoghue, whose voice was identical to Michael O'Hehir's, agreed to do the commentary on similar terms.

Snap sourced a set of jerseys and decided to search for some new blood to the team. This was essential if the Cowboys were to salvage their reputation by winning a game. So, he embarked on a recruitment campaign which resulted in 'bagging' Offaly's legendary footballer, Seamus Darby, who agreed to tog out if he were available on the day. This was unquestionably a coup, which would give the team's morale a much-needed boost.

Snap assumed his undisputed role of captain. However, to present a more organised appearance, local stone-mason Sam Williams was appointed manager, while George Maloney and Kevin (Shaker) Farrell were nominated as linesmen. The selection of the team was dependent on anyone who offered their services on the day. The call was out and Snap, who was persistent in his recruitment campaign, was now verging on being cautiously optimistic.

On Sunday, April 4, a coach-load of Round O players and supporters arrived from Meath, led by their manager, Ger McLoughlin. This was like the eighth wonder of the world as a coach-load had never before arrived at the Harbour. The boys from the Royal County were young and fit. They would be a formidable opposition.

We were praying that Darby would arrive as this would give the Cowboys a massive psychological boost. Snap looked anxious. His team included Joe McDonnell and Paul McLoughlin, who could be stalwarts, while Michael (Banana) Nolan had hurled and boxed for Edenderry. Sam Williams made a strong 'victory at all costs' speech. Defeat would not be tolerated and that was his ultimatum.

The teams and supporters assembled on the footpath and were led to the Tech Field by the resounding sound of 'Flynn's Men', Kit Flynn on accordion and his sons Herbie (Michael) on the bodhrán and Hog (Brendan) on the banjo. Just as they reached the field, Darby was spotted parking his car at Tommy Cullen's (Sweeny's) service station. There was a collective sigh of relief from the Cowboys and a groan from the Raiders.

The referee was Tomo Doyle and the match began. The Raiders scored a couple of points and the Cowboys responded with a point. It was largely tit-for-tat until Darby, in the full-forward position, scored a goal. This was followed by another goal by Paul McLoughlin who upended his brother, Ger, in his eagerness to get to the ball.

The icing on the Cowboys' cake was when Darby weighed in with a second green flag. The boys were jubilant and World War Two veteran Charlie Donoghue, who had lost an eye at Dunkirk, got a loan of a jersey and was on the field when Tomo blew the final whistle. The final score was Connor's Cowboys 3-2, the Round O Raiders 1-7.

As he came off the pitch, Seamus noticed Charlie down on his hands and knees near one of the goals. "What are you lookin' for Charlie?" he asked.

"I'm lookin' for me eye, Seamus," he replied.

Snap was the toast of the Harbour that night, as Flynn's Men gave it a lash in true Edenderry style. The one-point win was like winning an All-Ireland, Snap confided later, though he also revealed that he had a Plan B, if it was needed.

"What was that?" we wondered.

"Well, you can't cod Tommy Ryan and they were all slagging me up the town, so I picked Tomo as the referee."

Indeed, everyone in the town knew that Tomo was Snap's cousin. You can't beat the auld dog for the hard road.

Dr Mary O'Connor is a retired publican who lives in Edenderry, Co. Offaly. On her retirement, she commenced her legal studies and graduated with a PhD in Law from Queen's University Belfast. She has contributed a story to every rural anthology and has had articles published in Law Journals and has presented papers at Law Conferences in Ireland, the UK and Croatia as well as the World Conference on Family Law, which was held in Dublin.

The Long And Winding Road To Croker... And Back

Danny Gormley

Most people have memories of their first encounters of various happenings in their life. These can range from where they went, how they got there, who they met, the list goes on.

One particular event that often comes to my mind was my first visit to Croke Park. To GAA people, this equates to mecca for Muslims. It happened when I was at an impressionable age and this adds to the nostalgia.

The occasion was the All-Ireland final of 1961 between Down and Offaly. Down won the game (3-6 to 2-8) and it was witnessed by the largest crowd ever to attend a match in Croke Park: 90,556.

The result may not be significant today but the occasion and the journey there and back is worth recalling. It is a normal procedure today for children and young people to attend matches in Croke Park but for a 16-year-old from Fermanagh, things were a lot different in the early 60s. My parents then did not have an interest in football and it was through my older brother Harry and my uncle Packie Darcy that the love of the game was fostered.

In the late 40s and early 50s, Cavan was the team immortalised by these men but now Down were All-Ireland champions and a different type of team. They played a brand of football that was fast and attractive and they were one of the first teams to use the hand pass.

To add to these features, they had outstanding individual talents amongst their squad. Such was their charisma that it created an impression on the minds of young people like me, to such an extent that even today I still remember the lineout of the team, along with the clubs they played for. In light of this, it is easy to imagine the excitement of getting to Croke Park to see these heroes.

Not every household had a car then and a short time before, my uncle Packie acquired an Austin van with windows on the sides. He had learned the basics of driving in the absence of a driving test, and while he may have been the king of the road in his native Carrick, Co. Tyrone, his suitability to drive to Dublin was an entirely different matter. He was determined to go and assembled a cohort of passengers, the likes of which might never have graced Croke Park before or since. The words of the song 'Delaney's Donkey' comes to mind. Any neighbours who were willing to go seemed to be welcome. Having an interest in football was not a prerequisite.

The first man in the line-up was Robert Couter (Coulter was his proper name). He lived down the road in Coel and was a Protestant man, who had never been to a match in his life. The next was Jim Carroll, a neighbour of Robert and a man who had probably never seen a football. The third passenger was Frank Haughey and he couldn't see the football because at that time the crowd at each end stood up and Frank could not see over them (he was a very small man and a sympathetic supporter loaned him a small radio).

The fourth man was Jim English, a Dublin man who was working with Robert Couter in Omagh. He was equivalent to Sherpa Tenzing who accompanied Sir Edmund Hillary in climbing Mount Everest. This man knew the road to Dublin and without him we could not have gone. I was crushed in somewhere, too, with Uncle Packie driving. The first voyage of the Titanic comes to mind. I left home on the Sunday morning well before seven o'clock and cycled to Carrick. The passengers were rounded up and we were away by eight... a journey into the unknown.

We went to Mass in Omagh and then through Aughnacloy and Monaghan. I fail to remember much about the journey but with the invaluable help of our guide, we arrived in O'Connell St. and parked close to Nelson's Pillar. This was to prove a useful landmark throughout the day that followed.

We got breakfast in a restaurant nearby called The Red Rooster. It was underground with heavy glass panels in the roof which formed part of the footpath above. It's long since gone from O'Connell St. The next port of call was a pub and I was left outside to sit on the window sill. It was from here that a change in procedure took place.

Supporters were passing in droves with all their colour and pageantry and I came to the conclusion that the ground would be filled and we wouldn't get in.

Without consulting with the others inside, I headed off on my own; I wasn't going to miss my first visit to Croke Park. Now, in retrospect this was possibly an irresponsible action. There were no tickets then, so I joined the queues at the canal end. The admission then was 7/6, which sounds and looks strange today.

This could best be described as 75 per cent of fifty pence. To put it in some form of context, approximately 25 per cent of a day's wage then. How does that relate to admission charges today? Not all that different really.

When I came out onto the Canal End terrace, the scene was unbelievable.

Today, it might be described as a 'wow-factor' and for someone who had never been there before, it was difficult to comprehend.

This was the holy grail and it sent pangs of excitement through my body.

At that time, the terraces did not have seats and the crowd, on occasions of excitement, would surge forward and backwards.

This was quite dangerous even with the inclusion of surge barriers. Here I was, alone in the midst of over 90,000 strangers, and unaware of any dangers. This was Croke Park and an All-Ireland final, everything else was of secondary importance.

I don't remember much about the game itself. What I do remember were the Down players. Leo Murphy at full back could kick the ball out every time to the halfway line (the goalkeeper seldom took kick outs then).

James McCartan at centre-forward was a power-house of a man. Similar in ways to Dublin's Dermot Connolly of 2017, only bigger and stronger. Sean O'Neill to his right was a genius, (he was brilliant in later years at full-forward). To McCartan's left was Paddy Doherty, one of the greatest forwards ever to grace Croke Park. He had no equals then or since as a left-footed free-taker. Right hand side or left made no difference; penalties the same.

After the final whistle and the claustrophobia of Jones's Road, it was back to O'Connell St. to face the wrath of my uncle. Nelson's

Pillar now came into use as my landmark. The van was still there, of course, and I need not have hurried as my fellow travellers did not turn up until half seven. They said they were searching for me but there were indications to suggest that the searching was done in licensed premises where I was not the priority. Packie was cross but relieved to see me safe and well.

The road home was slow, due to the occasional 'pit stop' and I was asked to drive for part of the journey. Licence or insurance wasn't mentioned and I was delighted to be afforded the opportunity. I drove from outside Ardee to near Castleblaney. The van had a column change and an umbrella handbrake, something not seen on vehicles today. This meant that three people could sit in the front in comfort, no seat belts.

We arrived back in Drumquin and Carrick at midnight. It was a great achievement for my uncle to drive to Dublin at a time when driving to him was a novelty. As far as I remember, he left me home along with my bicycle. The bicycle was important, as I had to cycle to Ederney the next morning to get the 7.30 am bus for school in Enniskillen.

I never thought of it at the time but I am sure my mother was worried about me being on such an adventure virtually on my own. She sure was glad to see me home safe, even if it was one o'clock in the morning. It is only when you have a family of your own that you realise the significance – and source of worry – of such ventures.

Danny Gormley is a native of Ederney, Co. Fermanagh. A retired Further Education Lecturer and a 'semi-retired' farmer, he is married to Fidelma and has a daughter Una, son Donal and six grandchildren. Danny spent many years travelling the length and breadth of Ireland to various fleadhanna and set-dancing events as well as supporting his local GAA club St Joseph's Ederney and Fermanagh GAA.

The Longest 'Drive'
Ever To Croke Park

Tom Wright

The fifth tee at Birr golf club offered a commanding view of the surrounding countryside. Three men out for their weekly round of golf surveyed the surroundings. The morning sun rising over Ard Erin in the Sliabh Blooms was on their backs and left Knockshegowna overlooking the plains of Tipperary.

Northwards, the twin cooling towers of Ferbane power station cast a lazy plume over the vast boglands. Ahead west lay Banagher on the Shannon. A celestial scene, but more important business intervened.

They lowered their gaze to focus on the fifth green over 500 yards distant. The honour of hitting first lay with Tony McTague, Offaly football legend and no mean golfer. He propelled the ball way down the middle of the fairway.

"Can you beat that?" Tom Wright (me) roguishly challenged the third member of the group. An old golfing ploy to incite the other to over extend and make a mess of the shot; a kind of harmless sledging.

"Can I take a run at it?" John Grehan answered smoothly, recognising the gee up.

"Aye, like a line ball, over the bar," I remarked. "Eoin Kelly does it no bother".

"I was in Thurles the day John Fenton scored a goal off the ground from midfield," Tony interjected.

"Yes, and I remember a Clare man, Moroney, when I was a minor," John added.

"Golfers are hitting the ball miles further, the courses are getting too short," I said.

"It must be them new shafts," Tony surmised.

Thus began a discussion on modern sporting equipment. The question was posed. Why not modern hurleys too?

The seed of the idea for Cúltec hurleys was sown. Myself and John experimented with different types of timber, laminates and production techniques before deciding to research the synthetic possibilities.

Both of us had experience of hurling and coaching. John had been a dual player with Offaly and is still involved in coaching with Naomh Ciaran ladies. An engineer widely experienced in modern materials and processes. The right man in the right place.

At the time, I had just retired from teaching engineering at Ferbane Vocational School. For a number of years, project work that entailed research, evaluation and production was part of the Leaving Cert engineering exam. This experience, time to spare and patience practised over 40 years of teaching lively teens possibly complemented John's talents.

Over a number of years, samples were produced and tested, scrapped and remade until finally a prototype judged good enough to go to market was produced.

Cultec Limited was registered in 2006. John made contact with Steven Lee (Lee Ming Hsien), a Taiwan national, who owned a factory producing a range of sporting goods from synthetic materials.

To overcome language difficulties and let him see the game first hand, we invited him and two colleagues to Ireland for a weekend. The Kilkenny senior semi-finals were on that Sunday, so we took them to Nowlan Park. After a fast and exciting first half, I turned to Steven to get his reaction.

"There's no one dead," Steven gasped incredulously. But he grasped the essence of the game during the remainder of the afternoon, having recovered from his initial astonishment.

During this time, we had a number of meetings with officials in Croke Park. Guidance from Pat Daly, head of games administration, was especially helpful.

"We cannot approve anything that will upset the integrity of the game," Pat clearly directed.

Our challenge then was to replicate the optimum ash hurley.

At this crucial juncture, Paudie Butler, the then national hurling coaching co-ordinator was approached. A hurling visionary, an inspirational figure, not only for us but also for the overall game.

The GAA correspondent in the Examiner referred to him as "the apostle of hurling". He inspired our mission statement: "Give every young person in Ireland the opportunity to own a reliable hurley."

The brief was clear now, we were on the road, but, oh my, the road was rocky. Offaly Local Enterprise Company provided guidance through business obstacles and Athlone IT shared expert technical information and also validated the tests required by Croke Park. A serious roadblock emerged when they informed us there were two important tests they were unable to complete: the length of the puck and the comparative breaking resistance of the Cultec.

"What will we do now?" I just scratched my head. "We'll have to think of something," John offered...the classic answer to all problems.

John and his good friend, the late Paddy Curran, were interested in duck shooting around the Shannon and also took part in clay pigeon shoots. Paddy actually made clay traps, devices for slinging up clay discs at speed to act as targets. He ingeniously adapted the slinging arm to grip a hurley and strike a sliotar off a tee. That was that problem solved.

From the engineering class, Tom was acquainted with the Izod Test, a means of finding the impact strength of materials by dropping a known weight from increased heights until the material fractures.

This test was set up in Jimmy Egan's barn in the townland of Coole near Ferbane. John is Jimmy's son-in-law and lives nearby. As an aside, the townland Coole and the colloquial name 'tec' for my school was behind the name Cultec.

Dr. Mark Atterbury of the materials research department of Athlone IT came out to Coole and conducted the required tests. The college then issued a comprehensive report which, with our shining new prototypes, I took to Croke Park to meet Pat Daly and Ned Quinn of Kilkenny. Ned was then chairman of the Hurling Development Committee. They scrutinised the camán closely and tentatively by tapping a sliotar on it.

"Could you see it used down there in Croke Park?" Ned enquired from his vantage point of their office in the Cusack stand. I assured him I could.

The inimitable Pat asked: "Would bits fly in a clash?"

As we watched in amazement, he proceeded to lash the pristine prototype against the concrete steps of the Hogan stand. I rushed towards him shouting "stop, stop, I need it to show to others." But Pat was satisfied, nothing flew! Another crucial test passed.

The GAA granted official approval to Cultec. The patent for the project was registered and incidentally had to be relied on a few years ago. Diarmuid Horan of St. Rynaghs was the first county player to use it in a senior hurling championship match between Offaly versus Kilkenny in 2008.

Unfortunately for Offaly, his work took him to America. He continues to use the Cultec and returns annually to his club for the championship. Although injured, he came off the bench to get the winning scores for St. Rynaghs in the 2019 final.

We are constantly researching and tweaking to improve performance. A major and expensive change related to the size of the bas. Hurling Equipment rule 4.5 in the Official Guide then and now states;

"The bas of a hurley at its widest point shall not be more than 13cm."

John's son Gerry who was in college at the time pointed out, "that bas is way too small, they're all using big ones now".

Had we met a legal checkpoint?

At an Offaly versus Kilkenny U-21 game in Tullamore, Richie Hogan broke his hurley and threw away the pieces. John directed Gerry: "Run over there and pick that up". The size and shape of the big style of bas was examined and the decision was made to take the chance the rule would not be applied. New tooling was installed, formulae recalculated and the big bas Cultec was born. Journey's end was in sight.

Brian Cowen, then Taoiseach, announced the birth of the new camán at its launch in the Hogan stand.

St. Galls of Antrim played the 2008 All-Ireland intermediate hurling final in Croke Park. Six of the team used the Cultec. If that was the baptism the arrival to the hallowed ground was confirmed by David Herrity of Kilkenny in the following senior All-Ireland.

A drive that took off with a running start from Birr Golf Club reached Croke Park. The dream became a reality. It has by now seen action on that hallowed turf on final day at all levels of hurling and camogie. Through continuing research and development, the Cultec has further improved in performance and safety. The latest hurley 'Elite' is now available.

It has recently assumed maybe a more vital role in our national game. The onset of ash dieback is unfortunately threatening the stock of ash in Ireland and worldwide. This fungal disease is highly contagious and scientists suggest that the ash species could be entirely wiped out.

Did the panorama around the fifth tee at Birr Golf Club offer a prescient glimpse into the future?

Tom Wright is a native of Tipperary and a former hurler at all grades with the Moycarkey-Borris club. Appointed to Offaly VEC in 1962, he taught for 30 years in Ferbane where he hurled with Belmont and coached teams in hurling, football and camogie at school and club level. A lifelong GAA activist, he is married to Eileen and they have two children Fergal and Deirdre, the latter of whom has taken over the Grehan's shares and currently runs the company with her husband, John Donohoe. Tom holds a watching brief.

No Tickets? No Problem!

Nola Farrell

It was October 1988. Cork versus Meath in the replay. The Rebel County against the Royal County. My friend, Mary Anne and I, decided to go to Croke Park to see the clash of the Titans, both secure in the tribal belief that our respective county would win. On Saturday evening I called on my local family butcher to collect the promised tickets but unfortunately, the tickets never materialised.

Undaunted, we headed for Dublin on the Sunday morning but unfortunately, there was no golden ticket to be found for either of us. Instead, we charmed our way into the hallowed ground as the men on the turnstiles were enthralled by our banter over the fact that there was such a thing as friendly Meath-Cork rivalry. As sensible strategists, we waited until everyone was well in and seated, in the Hogan Stand, before we made our move. We wandered up the stand looking for some empty seats, using our match programmes as pretend tickets.

Eventually we spotted a single seat at the edge of a row, near the top, which we shared. The man beside us was most sympathetic and confided that the stewards were more interested in identifying forged tickets holders that day rather than hound those with incorrect 'bums on seats.'

As the game went on, we were less concerned about being asked to move. Meath won by a point and as my mother always put a relic of Saint Oliver on the television when they played, I believed that there was high intervention in the win.

Now, many, many years later, the enduring mystery we talk about when we meet is how two non-ticket holders got into the Hogan Stand to watch the All-Ireland final in 1988. Mary Anne and I are still friends and we have often laughed at how we gate-crashed the big day armed only with charm, personality and (of course) our good looks!

An dtarlódh a leithéid inniu? Sin í an cheist! Ní dóigh liom é.

Nola Farrell is a native of Longwood in Meath. She is a retired guidance counsellor and now lives in Gorey, Co. Wexford.

Dub Who Devoutly Supports The Kingdom

Ciarán Byrne

I am Dublin born and bred. I was born in Dolphin's Barn and grew up in Rathfarnham. My wife Patricia was born and bred in Dún Laoghaire. Technically, we are both Dubs. In my case, it's black and white. Both my parents were Dubs as were their parents before them.

Patricia's father is a proud Galwayman. Her mother comes from Glenealy, Co. Wicklow. Therein lies the root of this obsession. Incidentally, we have lived in Wicklow for over 20 years. Apples falling from trees on Patricia's side, not to mention my surname.

Patricia is a fanatical supporter of the Kingdom. She will drive to Killarney or Tralee and back in one day for a league match just to see the green and gold. Munster finals are almost an annual pilgrimage.

A member of the Kerry Supporters' Club for I don't know how long, she is a weekly player of the Kerry lotto. Annual car draw tickets are a must and don't get me started about the number of Kerry polo tops, body-warmers, jackets and jerseys. One wardrobe is taken up with Kerry items of clothing. There is a box in the attic which contains match programmes going back to the almost five-in-a-row team. The Kerryman nowadays is purchased more often than The Wicklow People.

So how did this fanaticism for all things Kerry football start? I blame the mother-in-law. As children, Patricia and her family would spend all the school holidays and most weekends in the maternal grandfather's home in Glenealy. Being a Wicklow man, her grandfather had very little to cheer about whenever it came to championship. Being from Wicklow, cheering for Dublin would be on a par with Wicklow cheering for Carlow.

Following Heffo's Army's victory over her father's Galway in 1974, it looked as if the Dubs were indeed back to stay. That September

Sunday in Glenealy was particularly depressing – not only had the Dubs won but they had beaten Galway. The following year it looked as if the Dubs were going to do a back-to-back...until Mick O'Dwyer's young guns defeated Heffo's Army. That day, Kerry got a life-long supporter.

Although I was acquainted with Patricia since the early 1980s, it was not until the late 90s that we started going out. Of course, matches in Croke Park were a must, especially whenever Kerry were playing. Parnell Park and O'Moore Park were Sunday afternoon dates in the early days. I recall the Munster final in 1997. Clare were taking on Kerry in the Gaelic Grounds. Kerry colours were worn for the week prior to the game but not to be outdone I got a Clare jersey for the game, not that it stopped the Kingdom on their way to lifting Sam later that year.

Wedding Day in 1999 could not clash with the Munster final. There was not even the slightest suggestion that Kerry would not be there. The wedding date was set a year before so it would not clash with the clash in The Park. The honeymoon had to be over in time for the final. The years between 1995 and 2011 were lean for the Dubs. Called "the Croker chokers" in the media, I witnessed five-point leads being whittled away ending in defeat again and again. In the meantime, Kerry were winning league titles, Munster titles and All-Irelands. For the long-suffering Dub at this time Armagh and Tyrone were angels in disguise, as long as they were not playing Dublin.

In 2000, we were on holidays when Kerry played Armagh in the semi-final. The game ended in a draw which resulted in a replay, for which we would be home in time. Tickets were duly acquired and we found ourselves in the unfinished Hogan Stand. The upper deck was non-existent and a section of the lower deck was open for the game. Our tickets were only a few rows back from the sideline. The teams came out onto the pitch and ran to the bench to sit for the official team photographs. Patricia had her camera with her and decided to get as close to the team as possible. She was leaning over the advertising hoarding when she was approached by a steward who seemed to be on the verge of reprimanding her.

However, she said something to him and he ended up opening

the gate and told her to line up with the photographers and as soon as she had the picture taken to go straight back to her seat. The photograph was enlarged and put into a frame. Some weeks later, she had a contact who organised for her to send the mount from the frame down to Kerry with Mike Hassett, who was a teacher in Wicklow at the time. The mount was signed by each of the panel and now the framed photograph hangs in a prominent place in our home.

Kerry always come first. Whenever holidays or events are being planned, Patricia's first sentiments are always: "When are Kerry playing?" This all came to a head for the 2000 All-Ireland final. Some months before, Patricia and I were asked by her sister to be godparents for her newborn son, to which we replied we would be delighted.

However, Patricia stipulated that the christening could not clash with the All-Ireland. Calendars were consulted and it was decided that the christening could be held any day as long as it was not Sunday, September 24, as Kerry were playing Galway in the All-Ireland final, just like this year.

The christening was set for Saturday, October 7. A precious ticket was secured for the match. The game ended in a draw 0-14 apiece. There had to be a replay...and the date was set for, yes, Saturday, October 7, the day of the christening where Patricia was to be godmother.

She has never been forgiven.

Ciarán Byrne is a retired National School teacher. He served as PRO for Cumann na mBunscol Cill Mhantáin for 13 years and PRO for Cumann na mBunscol Náisiúnta 2007-2009. He has been the kitman for the Wicklow senior footballers since 2009. Ciarán is married to Patricia, who is a voluntary steward in Croke Park. They live in Ballinaclash (near Rathdrum) with their dog Olaf and the dog they don't own they call Pepsi.

'The only acceptable recipients of money from the GAA are administrators, coaches, security, bar and catering staff, hawkers, programme sellers, pirates, general scavengers, some managers... but no players. Stalin or Fidel Castro would love the way the GAA has and is being run. Even if something is wrong, nobody questions it'

Former Meath two-time All-Ireland winner, Colm O'Rourke, who in 2022 was appointed Meath manager

Joy Of Travelling By Train To Big GAA Games

Norman Freeman

It's hard to beat the atmosphere on a train heading for the final. The carriages are full of excited talk and banter. The murmur of expectation seems to keep in time with the rhythm of the wheels over the tracks. There is always some anxious soul making their way along the carriages, seeking a spare ticket.

In reality, the halcyon days of the match excursion train are long since gone. These days, Iarnród Eireann puts on no more than half a dozen specials. Most people travel to the game by car or by bus.

Several decades ago, most went by rail. There were 20 or 30 excursion trains. Railway stations were full of crowds and of clamour. Trains packed full of eager followers left for Dublin in the small hours, arriving in the city with the dawn. They returned with their weary and bedraggled passengers near midnight and into the night.

It created a genre of storytelling about all the ups and downs of getting to and from big matches, engines breaking down, missing the last train, getting on the wrong train.

Women and men sitting round a table in some pub or hotel swapped yarns. There was an undercurrent of competition. The phrases: "I'll tell you a good one" and "You won't believe this," were often used.

On many occasions I found myself sitting round a table in a pub or lounge while fellows waited their turn, hoping to top the tale just told.

One famous for his own exploits told me that, on one occasion after an All-Ireland final, very much the worse for wear, he had scrambled into the heated carriage of a train, unseen by the guard, and curled up asleep in a quiet corner.

He had intended to get off in Templemore. Instead, he was woken up next morning by cleaning ladies wielding buckets and mops; the empty, silent carriages were in the sidings behind the station at Cork.

One raconteur told of a weary group of Clare followers staggering up to the station in Thurles after another Munster final disappointment in 1978. They were singing a grating chorus of 'Spancel Hill' as they emerged onto the platform. A tired and irritated porter held up one hand to silence them. "It's 'The Last Train to San Fernando' you should be singing – the excursion train for Ennis is gone an hour ago."

There used to be a jocular remark among Tipperary followers who attended All-Irelands in the halcyon days of Tipp hurling dominance. "Are you taking the train to Brittas?"

This referred to one famous instance, when a crowd of roistering Tipperary supporters, celebrating an All-Ireland win, tumbled into Heuston Station. They rushed on board a southbound train. Only when the train was thundering through the countryside did they discover, to their consternation, that it was a nonstop express to Cork.

They had a solution. When the flying train began to approach the woods of Brittas, just outside Thurles they crowded round a door and one of them pulled the emergency communication cord. As soon as the train slowed down, they jumped off, one after the other. The last man was nearly caught by the train guard who grabbed him by the tail of his raincoat. But this intrepid fellow wiggled his way out of the coat and went racing across the field to the sanctuary of the woods, where his pals had gathered, panting.

"Jumping off a still-moving train down onto the limestone chippings and losing your raincoat can sober you up fairly fast," he told me years later.

My own story is about an incident in Thurles station on the evening of a Munster Final in the 1980s. I was among a horde of followers, still excited by the game, milling about the platform. Then a Dublin-bound train approached. Almost before it had stopped, it was rushed by many in the mob.

The red-faced ticket inspector, cap on his head, beads of perspiration on his forehead, was nearly trampled into the floor of the carriage. He got very annoyed. He accosted one lanky middle-aged fellow and demanded to see his ticket in a loud accusatory voice. The man bristled at this; he refused to produce his ticket. The inspector threatened to put him off the train. The man still refused. The train began to move but the inspector waved out the window to the driver and it came to a halt after a few yards.

The station master was called. He came hurrying forward, settling his braided uniform cap on his head authoritatively. The two adversaries told their stories; the lanky fellow declared he would not be treated as a rail cheat while the inspector insisted on his right to ask people for their tickets. By this time there were many interested onlookers both in the carriage and on the platform.

A diplomatic solution was found. The lanky man showed his ticket to the station master, who examined it and then formally confirmed to the inspector that it was in order. As the train was waved off there was a final loud exchange between the two opponents, heard by those of us sitting nearby.

Lanky Man; "I won't allow you to take my character away."

Inspector: "No, no. It's tickets I'm after."

Dubliner Norman Freeman has published two books on hurling and two others based on his seafaring experiences. He is a regular contributor to the Irishman's Diary column in the Irish Times.

Ewe Turn Helped Halfway-House Bunclody On Its Feet

Anonymous

When local councillor Martin Kehoe (Curragh) got funding for the Vocational School in Bunclody in Co. Wexford, the park committee was forced to consider selling the land on which it was built and which, up to then, had been their playing grounds.

A decision had to be made as to who the beneficiaries of the sale would be, as both the soccer club and the GAA had an interest in it. A programme produced for a match describing it as Gaelic Park tipped the balance in favour of the GAA club. They got 80 per cent of the proceeds, with the balance going to the soccer club.

Subsequently, the GAA grounds were purchased for £22,000. The field was bought from Mrs Breen and consisted of about seven acres of reasonably flat land. It was swapped for a field on the other side of the road, owned by Dermot O'Connor.

This land required considerable development. Not everyone was in favour of the swap. Michael Mahon was chairman of the club finance committee and development committee. He convened a special meeting and presented all the advantages of the swap to the club and managed to ease the concerns of many members.

He also secured a number of state grants and to raise the balance of the money, the club bought 140 ewes. They asked locals to take one or more of the animals and give back the proceeds from the sale of the lambs for five years and then the proceeds of the sale of the ewes.

A hundred people were involved, with some agreeing to take more than one ewe. One woman took three and another man returned the price of the two lambs every year. The single ewe apparently never produced only one lamb and returned an amount far higher than what was achieved on the open market.

Mucky Business Afoot As Boot Flies Over The Bar

Betty Devenney

Every Sunday in the late 1950s, our family would gather in Granny's house to listen to the GAA match being broadcast on the wireless. I remember an elderly neighbour who never failed to call in. He was a GAA stalwart back in the day and had so many yarns to tell he could have filled the pages of a book.

He told us that himself and a half dozen die-hards used to get together a few nights a week for a pint in the local bar. The chat was all about the lack of GAA matches being played. With so many of the young people emigrating to find work, there were hardly enough players left to get a team together. The men decided to reform the club, with the aim of rectifying the situation. So, a committee was elected.

It was decided they needed to get the word out, so a notice was put up in the bar. Anyone interested in playing was to leave their name with the barman. The new committee didn't expect much of a response but a few weeks later the list was filling up with names, most of them from neighbouring parishes! This fuelled the club's enthusiasm even more. Soon after, they had organised for everyone to come to the field near the river on a specified date and time.

The following Saturday morning, an assembly of eager young hopefuls arrived. After the selectors watched them play, a team was finally decided on. The weeks of training were going well. The young team turned out to have some talented and committed players, so a 'challenge' was arranged to take place between them and a team from the neighbouring county.

Two weeks later, game on. Unfortunately, the rain wasn't taking time to come down that day but sure what harm was a bit of rain going to do? No one realised it then but the field where the match was taking place was prone to getting waterlogged.

Half an hour into the match, the players looked the worse for wear, drenched and mucky, but they struggled on. The supporters were in uproar, some calling for the game to be called off, the majority urging the match to go ahead. The majority won out and the game continued. The only way to tell which team was which, was by the goalpost the players surged towards. It was a mud bath on the pitch that day, every man was encased in wet slippery splattered togs.

The score was even, and with minutes to go a player managed to get control of the ball. Next thing it was soaring over the post just as the referee was about to blow the whistle. Everyone held their breath.

Then, on investigation, they found out it was his boot that had soared over the post like a bird. A replay was on the cards, until miraculously the ball was discovered in the back of the goal mouth. Apparently, when the young lad kicked the ball, his muddy boot had slipped off and went flying as well. Everyone just took for granted they were watching the ball flying high.

No one had noticed anything untoward, so it was grudgingly accepted it was one of those days when anything was possible. But it was the last game played on the saturated pitch.

A few nights later in the local bar, the group of GAA men met up again. As they sank their well-earned pints, they remarked it was a lucky break that the ball had found its way to the back of the goal mouth. The unanimous conclusion was that the young team had made their mark and there would be plenty more games on the cards now.

After telling us this story in Granny's house that evening, the elderly man went on to divulge the mucky business that was afoot that day. He told us that, with all the commotion, the ball caked in muck was lying unnoticed next to the goal post.

He'd spotted it and gave it a quick nudge with his heel. We gasped in amazement at his daring stunt. He justified it by telling us it was fate – the ball just slithered over the line towards the back of the net.

Betty Devenney is from Strabane Co. Tyrone. Married to Danny 50 years this year, she has four children and five grandchildren. Her hobbies are painting, gardening, and creative writing.

Beaten By A 'Fellustrum Cutter' In Glen Of Tír na nÓg

Tom Aherne

We heard a lot about hurling in the green when it was introduced by the Limerick County Board to cater for the young boys and girls in city areas in recent years.

It recalled the late 50s and early 60s for me, when hurling was played daily in Kennelly's Glen in Glensharrold in West Limerick. Each evening when the day's work was done, it was down to the glen for a game with the neighbours' children.

It was a small playing area of 45 yards by 25 yards with a cliff on one side, and the White River flowing by on the other. The goals were home-made, from the timber growing on the nearby trees to the lime used to line the playing area. It was mainly a game of backs and forwards and it was competitive and tough, due to the proximity of the participants. Despite the limitations of the surroundings, it was our Croke Park.

This was the 'peak cap' era and many went flying skywards during the hectic exchanges. There were no modern facilities available in those days and togging off was done under the ash, black-thorn and whitethorn trees. The well nearby was used for drinking water during a break in the action. A good dip in the river afterwards refreshed mind and body.

A brown leather football was secured in a newspaper offer by saving the lids of polish tins. We also had to whip up a certain amount of our own money. The shoes of the district were never shinier as the long evenings approached and the need for the football grew.

Injuries were common but a dab of iodine mercurochrome, or green Cheno Unction cream, (suitable for veterinary purposes like sore cows' udders) took care of the cuts, until the time to milk the cows arrived and then you suffered. A small flat ice-cold stone from the riverbed kept any swelling in check. No talk of health and safety, pulled hamstrings or groin strains in those days.

The surface was uneven in places with a fair coating of Fellustrum and Buachalláns (ragwort) growing within the playing area. After a few nights of keen hurling, however, it became nice and level and clear of such obstacles. The old saying 'beaten by a daisy cutter' was replaced in our area by the saying of being 'beaten by a Fellustrum cutter.' Another saying from that time was 'give it the hobnail', which was a reference to a type of a boot at the time.

The goalposts were made from ash and the crossbar from a long branch of hazel cut in nearby Connell's Glen. The cattle would often knock them down when scratching on them and repairs had to be done before we could commence playing. The goal areas were re-sodded each winter to allow time to bed in for the return to action in the early spring.

Several players had their own hurleys that had hoops and tape to protect them. A few homemade hurleys cut from the plentiful supply of ash were also in use. One hard-pulling individual, Joe Doody, had one of these and it was a fearsome-looking weapon. The other players tried everything to knock it out of action but to no avail. It was pulled on from every angle, and it was even cut part way through, but the ash stood firm and the pulling continued.

'When the ball's in the sky in the glen in July, that's Joe Doody.

When the ball's in the air, who's that man in the square, that's Joe Doody.

When the ball's in the net and the fellustrums are beat, that's Joe Doody'.

(To be sung to the air of Amoré).

One Sunday afternoon a lively match was going ahead in the glen and, following some hectic pulling in the goalmouth, Joe Doody received a nasty cut over his eye. It required first aid. He was brought up to the nearby abode for running repairs. Maggie, the woman of the house, was out visiting a neighbour, so her son Johnny Kennelly took charge of the situation. Joe was laid flat on the kitchen floor and an Odlum's flower bag was cut into strips to use as bandages.

As the blood spurted down his face and onto the floor, Johnny reached for the oil lamp and, kneeling beside Joe, pulled back the broken flesh and poured the oil into the open cut. Joe exploded with pain and rage and sprang to his feet but the bleeding stopped.

He was then bandaged up and sent home with no doctor required. In time the cut – which should have got a dozen stitches – healed but left a protruding skin mark. It never bothered Joe and he was proud of the mark and lived a long life passing 80 years before the final whistle blew.

Of all our gang, the late Joe deserves special mention. He had a huge passion for the games in the glen and was a great follower of parish teams. He became known all over Limerick and North Kerry for his vocal support and colourful comments. He put many a good free-taker off target with his urgings and he was as good as a sixteenth player.

He also had a set on referees and many the funny incidents happened – he was often removed from the field of play. He was a legendary figure at all venues and known far and wide and, despite the banter, he was respected by the opposition clubs. The skills gained in the rough and tumble in the glen and his fleetness of foot often helped him to escape from his angry pursuers when attending away matches.

The glen is silent now but the memories of some 55 years ago are still fresh in the mind. The clash of the ash and the thud of the brown leather are no more. When I visit the glen now, sure they echo back to me when the wind blows up along the calm and peaceful White River.

"Oh, where's the heart that could feel so sad,
While listening to those cheers,
That swept across the oceans wild,
To the exile's longing ears."

Tom Aherne is from Glensharrold, Carrigkerry, Co. Limerick and is the father of two grown-up daughters. A retired cabinet maker, he is a columnist with the Limerick Leader and has had articles published in several leading magazines. His hobbies include history, sport, country music and set dancing.

'There's men in that dressing-room who haven't had a pint since last Wednesday night'

The late Eugene McGee, former editor and newspaper owner and columnist, answers a journalist's question about how bady his team wanted to win on the morning of the 1982 All-Ireland final victory against Kerry

When A Bit Of Karma Is An 'Ojus Thing'

Gerry McLaughlin

For sure, a bit of karma is 'an ojus thing!' And even though our late great father Willie 'The Kid' McLaughlin wouldn't have a bull's notion of what such a title meant, for sure he always enjoyed getting even and, in a way, often achieved that through us, his sons.

In his day, Willie was a skilful Gaelic footballer, an All-Ireland medal winning actor coached by the great Tomás MacAnna, a marksman, a fisherman, a balladeer, a seanchaí and the heartbeat of a unique Donegal/Fermanagh cross-border club called Corlea, which was founded with the blessing of the Ulster Council in 1932.

Corlea was a small border townland that had its own 'Ballroom of No Chance" opened in 1932 and they fought from the hall to the crooked bridge, a distance of 100 yards, in honour of the affair according to the 12-year-old Willie.

The club held their meetings in the hall and also put on plays and were allowed to pick players from Belleek, a village about a mile from Corlea on the Fermanagh side of the border.

The club was unique but had a powerful neighbour in Aodh Ruadh, Ballyshannon, county Donegal who were not too happy about this young upstart on its doorstep.

The club progressed and had county stars like Patsy Rooney, who played for Donegal and Fermanagh, Eddie John Gonigle (Donegal), Yankee Jimmy and Yankee Tommy Gallagher (Donegal), John Doogan (Fermanagh), Jimmy Mulrone (Donegal), Kevin McCann (Fermanagh) and Paddy Gonigle (Fermanagh). Willie hit the frees and was also club secretary and treasurer at different times.

In 1946, a young Corlea team reached the Donegal SFL final but were well-beaten by a great Gaoth Dobhair team. They won a Donegal JFC title the following year before what Willie called "the pygmy amateur politicians of the GAA shafted us."

It was a three-pronged attack.

The Fermanagh County Board wanted the likes of Rooney, McCann, Doogan and Gonigle while Donegal wanted Eddie John Gonigle and the giant Yankee Gallaghers. And it also suited Aodh Ruadh, Ballyshannon and a new Mulleek/Belleek combination who went on to record a Fermanagh League and championship double.

A disgusted Willie refused to have anything to do with either club and transferred to a neighbouring junior club called Cashelard. As well as clubs, there were a few individuals, long deceased, who also benefitted in their GAA careers due to the carve-up. Willie remembered that too. He tried to save the club by suggesting that the respective county boards take the players they wanted for county duty but leave the unique small club intact.

But those who mattered said 'no' and Willie fumed in silence.

"We would have won a Donegal title but the Ballyshannon big wigs in Aodh Ruadh would not have that, it was a terrible tragedy and it ripped the heart out of the club and the townland. We looked after our players well, even buying them their boots," he recalled.

Willie single-handedly revived the club in 1951 against the odds and brought in ringers from here, there and everywhere but to add insult to injury, Ballyshannon won the Donegal SFC with many of Willie's former comrades on board.

"I brought players in but there was no work, the hall closed in 1952 and it turned into a townland of trees. That oul Corlea team would have tightened the jacket on any outfit," he would say as he nonchalantly threw back a Powers in a local pub called 'The Congo' in our townland of Cloghore.

As the eldest boy, I heard all these stories when Willie was digging spuds on the family farm in Corlea in the 1960s and 1970s. And I often wondered why he seldom attended club matches (we played football and hurling for Erne Gaels Belleek and we were from Donegal) or indeed to see Liam and myself playing for Fermanagh.

It was only when he was in his nineties and frail that he told me he was so proud of us and I found out later that he would secretly buy the Irish News to follow our hurling and later journalistic careers.

The only problem was...we were not playing for beloved Corlea, his Shangri La.

"But bejasus I am even more proud of yiz for captaining Fermanagh and the two of yiz from Donegal because we never had any borders in Corlea!"

I think it was his way of saying that it might take time but "a bit of karma was an ojus thing, alright!"

Gerry McLaughlin is a well-known journalist on the national stage who hails from Meenaleck, The Rosses in Donegal. He is married to Agnes Kelm, who is a member of a famed Fermanagh family.

My Younger Days With The GAA

Steven Roche

I grew up in a country village on the Cork-Kerry border. Football was played in our area more than hurling and we had a good junior team. I can remember going to my first game with my family in the back of a railed-in lorry with 50 people all packed close together.

Health and safety how are ya?

I started playing football for Cork at the age of seven up in Curtins Field at the back of our own House. Four wooly jumpers for goalposts and no referee.

I remember one year we played the full Munster Championship in one day. We started off in the morning by beating Waterford in the first round. Then we beat Clare in the semi-final and we were two points ahead of Kerry in the Munster Final when my mother called us for the dinner.

I enjoyed playing from the age of seven; we played and won several pretend 'Munster championships' where we had four jumpers for goalposts.

When I emigrated to Birmingham in England, I found that having played football was very important in securing a job. All the main building contractors were involved in the GAA clubs and a good footballer or hurler was always guaranteed a good job.

I played football and hurling for the Kingdom club in Birmingham for four years and won three county medals in Warwickshire. These were special times because of the amount of friends I met, who are all still very close to me to this present day.

Steve and Joan Roche were both working abroad in the sixties but met at a dance when they came home on holidays and what followed was one of life's great love stories.

'Cut The Grass' Laid Path For All Hobans

John Hoban

What's in the value of a name – particularly one like Hoban? And even more so, what's the value of a nickname – one like 'Cut the Grass'? What history does it carry and what lineage do we inherit when we share that surname?

More than I thought as it turns out. When I was old enough to travel, I found the name Tommy Hoban had gone before me. The Hoban clans are chiefs of the Kings of Connacht, of the Hy Fiachra Tribe. O'Dugan says the clans were "Binn slua nam-borb chliathach", which means "Music loving hosts of fierce engagements."

On Sundays in the 1960s, our family would go visit Westport Quay, a village all of its own with three houses there. Petie and Violet Hoban and family, the Dunnings and then to Tommy and Gertie Hoban. He was a second cousin of my father, Christy.

Visiting Tommy and Gertie's house was special. No sooner were we there than Tommy produced a few hurls and a sliotar. Out we went with him to a field near the house for a game of hurling. I knew Tommy was a great hurler and footballer in his younger days but it was still special to be coached by him.

I played football for Emmet's and Castlebar Mitchells underage but I loved hurling more than any other sport. So, even those windy showery Sundays, I felt we were in the company of hurling royalty in Tommy Hoban. I'd always feel good heading home.

Many years later I found myself playing music in a really fine pub 'The Plough and the Stars,' in San Francisco. It was owned by Sean Heaney. Later that night I met a group of exiles from Ireland, among them a man called Noel Gantley. He presented me with a sliotar, autographed by him and his friends there, Vince, Jimmy, Cormac and Kenny. Noel and Vince came from hurling backgrounds in Beagh. The club went back in history to the founding of the GAA and was connected to Michael Cusack, one of the GAA's founders.

Later that year, myself and my friend Walter visited Gantley's home in Tober, Galway. Noel's father greeted the two strangers at the door. Inside we met Mrs Gantley, a wonderful, kind, gentle woman and Fr. Paddy, Joe's brother. Both Joe and Paddy were famous hurling men, originating from Grannagh, Ardrahan.

Fr. Paddy played on the winning Railway Cup team in 1947 for Connacht. They beat Munster as the 15 Galway men brought the cup back over the Shannon for the first time. Fr. Paddy was man of the match after playing under the name P. Gardiner as a priest was not supposed to hurl.

In Cork, he hurled for Glen Rovers and they said that he even out hurled Christy Ring on occasion. Paddy and Joe played for Galway, Ardrahan and Beagh.

When they asked our names, I saw Fr. Paddy nod at Joe...once again, I learned the importance and value of a name.

"Are you, by any chance, a relation of Tommy Hoban from Westport?" Paddy asked.

When I said I was, they both smiled and they shook my hand once more. Fr. Paddy said: "Tommy Hoban came down here on his summer holidays and taught us how to hurl." High praise indeed.

I felt so proud and happy to be connected to these fine people and the great game itself through the name Hoban.

On another visit, I learned from Finbar Gantley, Noel's brother and an All-Ireland winner for Galway in the 1980 hurling final, that Tommy Hoban's nickname around Tober, Beagh, was "cut the grass," a reference to his great skill in ground hurling.

One photo on the mantelpiece of my uncle Tommy Byrne's house in McHale Road, Castlebar was very important to me. It was the Connacht football team of 1945.

Two Mayo men were on the team, Tommy Byrne in goal, an All-Ireland winner for Mayo in 1950, and Tommy Hoban corner forward. Tommy Hoban also played hurling for Connacht with 14 Galway men. These were the days when to play for your province in The Railway Cup was a major achievement. It was as important as playing for the Sam Maguire or the Liam McCarthy. Only one other

Mayo player represented Connacht in both hurling and football, Keith Higgins in the noughties.

In the 1970s, I visited Dingle, Co. Kerry to visit my sister who was working there. I played the mandolin, the guitar and sang all class of songs and tunes. One memorable night, we headed to Paddy 'Bawn' Brosnan's pub; it was the No. 1 football pub with historic pictures all over the wall. The Fear an Tí had played a star role for Kerry in teams that had won the Sam Maguire cup. When a few of the older people there heard my name, we were treated to some free drinks in memory of, and with respect to, Tommy Hoban.

The Hoban name is found in two places in Ireland mainly, Mayo and Kilkenny. The hurling blood carried in the name.

Buíochas le Dia, fair play to Tommy and all belonging to him.

John Hoban is a well-known composer, singer, musician and author from Castlebar, Co. Mayo. He is highly regarded for the unique and deeply personal nature of his music. John is currently writing his second book. His first book was called "From the Plain of The Yew Tree: The lifetime journey of a County Mayo Musician."

'The special thunder
of the island shore,
He hauled the boat in,
sheltered near a rock
And smiled to hear the
sea's defeated roar;
Breathing as though the air
were infinitely sweet,
He watched the mainland
where the hard wind struck.
The island clay felt good
beneath his feet,
A man undeceived
by victory or defeat'

**Lines written by the late, great
Kerry poet, Brendan Kennelly
about arguably the greatest ever
GAA footballer, Mick O'Connell**

Yes, I Was A Ref Who 'Bent' The Rules – And I'm Proud Of It!

Dermot Collins

When it comes to referees, seldom if ever do you hear one of that sacred breed admit to making a mistake or not following the GAA rulebook when officiating.

So straightaway, let me put my hand up and say 'mea culpa' because I knowingly bent the rules... something I have never regretted given the circumstances.

The match was a Cork County Junior Hurling quarter-final in 1973 between Clonakilty and Glen Rovers and neither team was sparing the timber in going for the ball.

This led to a huge fracas in the centre of the field after 10 minutes. In those circumstances, you have to use your judgement and I managed to restore order by warning players that I wouldn't stand for any more of that behaviour.

Just as I was restarting the game, I noticed out of the corner of my eye a Clon player running down the middle of the field and delivering a blow to one of his opponents. Inevitably, this led to another bout of fisticuffs. In the dust-up, I managed to lose track of where the player was and, in fact, I had to travel 30 or 40 yards to the sideline where he was now standing.

As I approached him, the computer inside my head told me that this was Dave McCarthy, a star of the All-Ireland winning Cork senior football team of that year. He was announced as an All-Star and the only thing that might revoke that honour was if he got sent off in a game.

This was a rule for a number of years in the All-Stars and it was only sometime later after one of the selectors, journalist Martin Breheny, resigned in protest in 1985 from the All-Stars Steering Committee at this unfair stipulation that it was finally changed in 1990.

In that time though, several top names suffered including Dermot Earley (Roscommon), Pat Fleury (Offaly), Mick Brennan (Kilkenny) and Eamon McEneaney (Monaghan), whose case was the straw that broke the camel's back for Breheny, then of the Sunday Press.

That was my dilemma as I ran across towards the normally genial Dave McCarthy because he and I, and indeed everyone else at the game, knew my decision could deprive him of a glorious individual accolade.

I said: "Dave, you know what will happen if I send you off. Of course, I should, but I'm going to book you and warn you that if you look crooked at the sliotar for the rest of the match, you'll get the line."

This was pragmatism rather than bravery but I felt a lot better about my decision in the following days when I heard that Dave had been incensed after a member of the opposition had decked his brother John in the melee... there was some mitigation in the fact that he was only standing up for his own flesh and blood!

That, I reasoned thereafter, was a case of what was good for the goose, was good for the gander, meaning that I could at least partly justify my decision. Although living in Kinsale, down the years I've bumped into Dave on occasions and he always introduces me to whoever he is with at the time as... "the man who got me my All Star."

About three years ago during one such encounter, I said casually: "You know Dave, I've never seen your All Star."

I was surprised some time later when I answered a knock on my front door in Kinsale to find that the 'Clon' man had driven all the way down to introduce me to his 1973 All Star award.

In light of the 'Breheny Ruling', and the fact that the game I refereed back in '73 ended in a draw with the Glen winning the replay, all things considered, I think I came to the right decision.

Dermot Collins is a native and resident of Kinsale, Co Cork. Married to Breeda they have four adult children and 12 grandchildren. A retiree from Eli Lilly (supervisor in safety, health, security department), he has been deeply involved in GAA at all levels as a player, administrator and referee.

Dermot Collins is a former Mayor and member Kinsale Town Council, and an ex-Chairman of Kinsale Harbour Commissioners. His hobbies outside of sport include coin and stamp collecting.

Cratloe's Historic Australian Odyssey

John Ryan

In being the first ever parish club travelling from Ireland to Australia, Cratloe GAA has written its own unique piece of history. Others will follow, but there can only be one first – like Neil Armstrong as the first man on the moon.

The germ for our Australian odyssey was probably sown two decades earlier, in 1978, when Aussie football and hurling panels toured Ireland to great acclaim, even playing Croke Park. The visitors included Cratloe native Tom McMahon and they also played Cratloe (H) and Kilmihil (F) in Clare, followed by enjoyable socials and exchange of mementoes.

Teams had certainly gone before us, mostly of a corporate nature – Aer Lingus, Army, Banks, Compromise Rules and Meath was the first county team. The Civil Service Club (Dublin) went about six years earlier. To the best of our knowledge, that club did not qualify as a parish unit. A university team from Northern Ireland may have travelled, while a Cork minor team has also been mentioned.

Most of the foregoing would have played the big ball code only, while Aer Lingus hurled in Perth. Cratloe's historic achievement lies not alone in being the first parish club to travel but also in playing hurling and football in four of the six states – in Adelaide, Melbourne, Perth and Sydney.

The trip had elements of a sporting, social and cultural nature. Between the two codes, eleven games were played with an outcome of seven victories and four losses, including two finals. The hurling game against Victoria in Kyneton commemorated 100 years of a hurling association in that area. The football match against an Adelaide /Aussie Rules side, a seven-a-side tournament in Melbourne versus St. Kevins and Padraig Pearses (f), Wolfe Tones and Garryowen (H), a 15-a-side tournament in Sydney versus Michael Cusacks (which was founded c. mid 90s by Eddie McGrath and Séamus Clancy of 1992 Banner football fame, amongst others) and Central Coast (two games) and one hurling game in Perth, featuring 13-year-old Gearoid Ryan as sub-goalie, which was the first such international game in 14 years, since Aer Lingus. To put perspective on the time, a few of the travelling party went to see the film Michael Collins which was then showing in Perth.

Some of the games were played in oppressive heat against fellow Clare and Irish players. Cratloe did feature a few guests on occasions. All the games were keenly contested with the Aussies always very anxious to win. In our final game in Sydney, Central Coast featured 11 Kilkenny players, all of whom had worn the Black and Amber in one grade or another. A memento, featuring Clare and Cratloe flags on a base of Cratloe Oak and suitably inscribed, was presented to each opposing captain by the Cratloe Captain of the day.

The trip made news on state television twice in Victoria and W.A. as well as the Irish Echo and the Western Australian newspapers, plus a number of interviews on local/Irish radio stations in Melbourne, Sydney, Perth and a late night/early morning call on Clare FM.

Irish centres in five of the major cities – Melbourne, Adelaide, Sydney, Canberra and Perth were visited. Mementoes of Clare's All-Ireland '95 victory were formally presented including a specially inscribed copy of the very limited official All-Ireland photograph (buíochas do Seamus Hayes), to each of the centres for prominent and proud display. While Brisbane was not on the itinerary, the famed photo will hang in the Irish Centre there also. We carried a bag of footballs on behalf of Pat Daly, Croke Park, for delivery to Brisbane GAA.

As far as could be observed, the Clare team photo will be the first in any of these Irish Centres. The Banner leads again! Others will almost certainly follow. Copies of the print which were supplied framed, glazed and inscribed will also hang in Kyneton Aussie Rules Club, in the Civic Offices of the Clare Valley District and in Gaelic Park, Melbourne. A personal copy was presented to Cratloe native Tom McMahon, who must shoulder some of the blame for our temporary lapse into daftness.

All the photos carried the dedication "Presented to Kindred Spirits in Australia by Cratloe G.A.A. Club, Feb. '97". It would be hard to imagine any presentation being more warmly received and appreciated in any of the centres, whether by Clare folk or by Irish people generally.

Additional mementoes of All-Ireland videos, match programmes, Clare yearbooks, All-Ireland posters and Aer Rianta maps of Ireland were all eagerly snapped up as souvenirs. Ten dozen hurleys were left behind to groups and individuals, some even autographed, as were sliotars, while t-shirts were exchanged.

Many mementoes and souvenirs were in return presented to the touring party, which have been showcased on permanent display in our Club HQ. In addition to the major cities, the Clare Valley was visited and re-twinned, wine sampled, having been received in great style by the mayor and councillors. Likewise, to Canberra the capital, where we were warmly received by the Irish ambassador, Mr. Richard O'Brien, and the Sheehan family of Sixmilebridge, having earlier done a tour of Parliament House – some house, some setting!

Memories are many, varied and personal. The eagerness of Irish and Clare people to seek us out and chat us up at every opportunity. The seemingly millions of acres of corn fields on the 4000-mile road journey from Melbourne to Adelaide. The intimidating waves of heat coming at us across the plains, when we alighted from our air-conditioned bus. The vastness of the vineyards in the Clare and Barosssa valleys and elsewhere.

The Bungaree sheep shearing shed, the lack of green fields – likely the price of an Aussie summer – galvanised roofs on most buildings, the general flatness of the country, miles upon miles of boringly straight, wide, signposted and perfect freeways and hence dangerous for long driving. The Great Coast Road drive, anything but straight. The grey lunar-like landscape, the trees, gum and eucalyptus or whatever, beaches with burning sand and strong currents/waves, thousands and thousands of acres of native trees in the Dandenong and Blue Mountains.

The length of the flight – actual flying time was 21 hours each way – plus airport stopovers. Weather for us was mostly like a very good Irish summer, rarely under 25 degrees or over 30, day or night.

Five days of substantial rain, wettest day in Sydney in five years, two days of rain in the Clare Valley, where 40 degrees was expected. We missed the extreme temperatures in various places.

Overall, three weeks of beautiful heat and boringly blue skies, with rarely a cloud in view, a lot of liquids necessary. It was a sobering experience, buying cool spring water by the bottle. Oh! for Tobar an Airgid, whose clear silver spring waters sustained generations of Cratlonians, footballers and hurlers from the nearby "Hollow" field, prior to piped supply in the 1970s.

Our trip meant an awful lot to a lot of Irish and Clare people, in particular in the various centres. We met a lot of Clare neighbours and neighbours' children. They were delighted to welcome us and some travelled long distances to do so.

Mistakes? There had to be some. Such a pioneering trip with a large group could hardly be perfect all the time. These can be ironed out for the return trip – baggage/luggage is first on the list

Despite some dire forecasts, nobody was unwell from travel, heat, playing or imbibing, nobody appeared "short", no embarrassment was experienced by either host or guest. A couple of hurling injuries were incurred, thankfully minor.

The party proved themselves great ambassadors for club, parish, county and country. Our only concern now is that we may be entertaining visiting Australians for a long time to come! We told them they would be very welcome once they came via Shannon Airport.

Was it worth it? It was a trip for pioneering, individual, young-at-heart types. It was not all easy or laid back. It made demands on everybody. Most of the travelling was boring but a great learning process. Risks were involved, it was an eye opening and mind-blowing experience. It was the trip of a lifetime, though it is possible some of the party will return at some stage for a revisit. Half the group stayed on for an extended holiday. It was a visit to the unknown. It was history in the making, and 31 locals took that giant step. It will never be the same again – like '95 for Clare. On the Club's 110 birthday, it was memorable and worth it all.

It was an odyssey of epic proportions for an average group from a typical club. Such is the beauty and unpredictability of those who populate GAA clubs. They can become legends in their own lifetime and make history simply by doing the unthinkable. From little acorns, great oaks grow.

Kindred Spirits: Thirty odd years before our continental sojourn across Aussie land in 1997, an equally ambitious challenge for the time was undertaken by the Kilmore/Rathangan GAA Club (Wexford) to America in September 1967, vividly recalled by Jim Berry in Vol 1 of GAA.Grassroots (2021).

John Ryan is a native of Cooleycasey, Sixmilebridge but has been living in neighbouring Cratloe parish since his marriage in 1968 to Kitty Mullane, a Camogie star with Truagh (Clonlara). They have six grown up children. John is a former employee of Shannon Airport (Sales and Catering/Aer Rianta) where he had a service record of nearly 48¾ years between 1958 and 2006. He has held several positions at club and county level, including chairman of Cratloe GAA Club and county board treasurer.

'Prayers, novenas, pilgrimages to Knock, climbing Croagh Patrick, you name it. Thousands of Mayo fans had carried out such trips going against type to appease the gods. They even had a priest remove a supposed curse on the team. In all of sports, has there ever been such dismal record? Imagine a team losing 10 Super Bowl finals, or 10 World Series in a row. Mayo makes the Red Sox and the Chicago Cubs look like lotto winners, not loveable losers all the way. Only for bad luck, Mayo would have no luck at all'

Editorial from US-based 'Irish Voice' newspaper, carried on Irish Central, September 2017 before their loss to Dublin in the All-Ireland final by a point

A Day Of Cuts And Bruises Doing The GAA's Bidding

Sean Nugent

When the phone call came, Tom was busily preparing for the sheep shearing which was to take place on the following day. He was a sizeable farmer and liked to have things well organised and with his jeep and trailer he had just delivered his last load of sheep into the yard where he had collected them from outlying fields. He had a beautiful May morning for the job, even though heavy showers had been forecast.

While closing the yard gate the ringing of the phone was from Mary, the local primary school teacher. She sounded agitated and, after the initial pleasantries were exchanged, Mary said: "Tom, do you remember last week I asked you for the GAA field for our Cumann Na mBunscol game?"

He remembered alright that he had taken a chance in giving Mary permission as the club secretary was the usual contact man and he had not verified that it was free with him. Instead, he assumed that, as it was so near exam time, that no post-primary school games would be on.

Mary informed him she could see two other teams arriving at the pitch and felt that it didn't augur well for her game. Tom's heart sank as he now realised he had a problem. Thinking fast he said: "I'll go down now and see if I can solve the problem."

He quickly unhitched the empty trailer from the jeep and headed down to the sports field where, sure enough, there were two teams togging out. Chatting with the teachers, he found that they had properly booked the field. No joy for him there.

His next idea was to go over to the school to Mary and ask her to postpone the game but Mary was having none of it, she said the game had to go ahead as they were running out of time. His next idea was to look for another venue. The teacher agreed once he did it quickly as arrangements had to be made with the other school.

Tom thought of a suitable venue where the contact man was a teacher. He rang the school to be told that the teacher in question had gone home for lunch. By the time he got his home number, the teacher's wife informed him that her husband was on his way back to school. Tom finally contacted the teacher and was assured that the venue was free and he would have flags and nets sorted for the game.

On receiving the good news, Mary swung into action, making arrangements with the other school and arranging transport to the venue for her own pupils. Tom even offered to drive some of the players there himself – an offer that was gladly accepted. They all wanted to travel in the jeep and Tom accommodated them by bringing one group to the game and another group home.

They arrived at the venue in good time and Tom was now happy that all was going well. As the teams ran out onto the pitch, he noticed the absence of a referee. Mary approached him saying she was supposed to provide the ref and she had no choice but to ask Tom to do it.

She handed him the school whistle and walked back to the sideline. Tom still had his wellington boots on and, to make matters worse, in his hurry out of the farm, he left his cap on the pier. The hot sun was already beginning to tingle the top of his head where the hair had receded many years ago.

He decided there was only one thing for it – blow the whistle and get the game going as quickly as possible. It became an exciting game as play swung quickly from side to side. Tom had difficulty keeping up and the wellingtons were no help. In fact, they had begun to cut his feet as the game progressed.

He was anxious not to be seen to favour his own school and this began to rebound on him, as he got stick from parents of both schools on the sideline. The game was close all through with only a point or so between the sides. Tom was hoping his school would win, of course, but it was not to be his lucky day.

The game was entering the last few minutes and his side were two points down when they made a last assault on the opposition goal. A high ball dropped in around the goalmouth area. Backs and forwards struggled to get possession but the full forward, who had a height advantage, got his hand to it and diverted it into the net.

There was huge jubilation among the local players who were now one point up. Tom noticed however that the umpire did not put up the green flag and the opposition players began to shout about a square ball. Tom was out around centrefield when the goal was scored and did not have a good view of it.

He headed in to his umpires who, to his dismay, confirmed that it was a square ball; he had no option but to disallow the goal and award a free out. It was then he got the full brunt of the criticism from the sideline and, worst of all, he was sure he heard Mary joining in the chorus.

Time was nearly up but he tacked on a few minutes hoping his side could salvage a draw. Again, his luck was out and he eventually had to blow the final whistle. With feet cut off him from the wellingtons, his head burnt to a cinder from the hot sun and his ears burning from the criticism from all sides, he vowed never to referee a game again.

There was silence in the jeep as his load headed homewards. Tom knew he was being blamed for everything, the mix-up over the venue, the refereeing, the disallowed goal and the loss of the game. He knew he would be the topic of conversation in all the children's homes that evening. He dropped off the children and headed homewards.

Retrieving his cap from the pier of the gate, his thoughts turned to the sheep and the shearing the following day.

Looking down the yard he saw to his dismay that there wasn't a ewe to be seen. Investigating he found someone had left the small gate down the yard open and the sheep had scattered all over the nearby fields. There was nothing for it but to begin the round up again. Whistling for the dog he headed out through the fields. On his way, he noticed the change in the day, clouds were beginning to gather and a heavy thundery shower loomed on the horizon.

Quickly as he could. and with the dog's assistance, he got the sheep together and headed them back to the yard. Suddenly the heavens opened and as heavy a shower as Tom had seen in a long time lashed down. Drenched to the skin, he eventually closed the gate on a yard full of sheep.

Taking off the wellingtons was a major task; they were nearly glued to his feet and carefully removing them exposed lots of broken skin in many places. Entering the house with water running out of him, he threw his cap from his now painful head onto a chair and said aloud to no one in particular: "I must be mad to have anything to do with the GAA."

Sean Nugent is a native of Kilsheelan, near Clonmel and is a former player and administrator with Kilsheelan Kilcash GAA club. He has also served as chairman of Tipperary Co Board. Retired from Eircom. He also enjoys gardening as a means of relaxation.

Total Blackout For Black And Amber Fan

Paddy O'Reilly

All-Ireland final day in the sixties didn't do a whole lot for the Sunday afternoon trade in the middle of Dublin. Back in 1969 the counties of Kilkenny and Cork met each other in the hurling decider, I had my normal level of regulars that early afternoon in The Harp Bar and a few fans who had arrived shortly after the then midday opening time.

I was more worried about getting them out as near as possible to the official 2pm closing time as I wanted to clear the place up for later before heading home to watch the game on television.

I was looking forward to having my dinner and having a chance to relax because I knew I'd have a busy night in front of me once I opened again at five o'clock with fans from both counties flocking to celebrate or drown their sorrows.

I kept hounding the stragglers to let them know I wanted them out and went downstairs to check there was no one still there. I had ushered everyone out but unknown to me, one of the Kilkenny fans came back in to use the toilet before embarking on his walk up through the city.

Having already checked below, I then had a quick look around the place before I turned off the lights, locked the door and went home. That time, there were no emergency lights unless the electricity power was off so it meant that everywhere inside the pub was pitch black.

So instead of arriving in Croke Park to shout on his black and amber heroes, this fan was locked up for the next three hours. Unusually for the time, he was a non-smoker and didn't have either a box of matches or a cigarette lighter with him.

He stumbled around in the dark looking for a way out and after hours of lonely incarceration, he stumbled on the pub's pay phone.

He dialled 999 and when the guards arrived at the front door of the Harp, by then it was close to re-opening time and they told him that I would be back in a matter of minutes.

When I unlocked the door to go in, I got a big shock to find someone on the premises and when I asked him who he was, he just said: "You locked me in."

You could see he was upset about the whole episode but what I liked about him was he blamed himself rather than me for the mix-up.

I felt a bit guilty about the outcome so I gave him something to smile about when I told him: "The good news from your point of view is Kilkenny won."

I never did find out if that made him happy or more annoyed that he had not witnessed their victory but years later I was serving one night when a man approached the bar and asked: "Do you recognise me?"

I didn't and when he told me he was the man that was locked in for the match, I welcomed him with open arms and told him he would never have to put his hand in his pocket again when having a drink on my premises.

I thought it was the least I could do to make it up to him while he felt that as time went on, he had a story to tell that was different to most others from an All-Ireland final day.

Paddy O'Reilly is a native of Cavan and before leaving for Dublin lived just outside Ballyjamesduff in Castlerahan. A publican, he was manager of the Harp Bar, a well-known landmark across from O'Connell Bridge before buying his own pub, The Roselawn Inn in Castleknock, which he still runs as a family business. Married to Pauline, he is the father of four grown up children, three boys and a girl. A life-long GAA supporter, he is a former player with Casterahan and Éire Óg, a club he helped found in Greystones Co Wicklow when domiciled there in the early sixties.

Memories Of 1966 When The West Ruled The GAA World

Pádraic McKeon

In England, 1966 will forever be remembered as the one and only time the country won the World Cup. In the USA, it was the era of anti-Vietnam sit-down on the streets of Washington and for worldwide audiences, 1966 was the year Star Trek first arrived on global television screens (and is still going strong).

In Ireland, we celebrated the 50th anniversary of the 1916 Rising but, quite forgotten by many, 1966 was also a wonderful year in the West of Ireland for Gaelic football fans, as the province recorded a 'clean sweep' of all the major national titles on offer.

For the record, 1966 saw Mayo win the All-Ireland minor title, Galway annexe the Sam Maguire and completed the three-in-a-row, while St. Jarlath's College, Tuam, won the All-Ireland college title. And there's one more title that I will come to later.

I did my Leaving Certificate in St. Jarlath's College that year and was in a position to see connections between all these victories. Obviously, I knew all the college footballers. Six of them were from Mayo. Equally, six of the Mayo minor team were Jarlath's lads. This meant that six of my fellow-students won two All-Ireland medals in the one year.

Actually, there was another: Jimmy Duggan, our college's captain and star player, also won two as he graduated to playing on the winning Galway senior team.

I can still remember the Connacht final between Mayo and Galway which was the match where he made his senior debut. The scores were level towards the end when Jimmy, who had been moved outfield, kicked a long accurate pass inside to Liam Salmon, who had momentarily worked free of the Mayo defence. He punched the ball over the bar for the winning score.

Victory for Galway but heartbreak for Mayo, and Duggan was

instrumental in it. The ironic thing was that he was born in Claremorris of Galway parents; so he could have played for Mayo but opted for Galway.

There were great matches between Mayo and Galway in those years. We had our own marvellous footballers on that fine Mayo team, such as John Morley (RIP), Joe Corcoran(RIP), Joe Langan (RIP), John Carey and others, and we went on to win Connacht titles in '67 and '69, as well as the national league title in 1970.

Added to the winners' enclosure in the West in 1966 was Roscommon, who won the Under-21 All-Ireland. Included on that team was the great Dermot Earley. Having been born in Castlebar, Dermot could also have played for Mayo but he grew up in Roscommon and, naturally enough, played for that county. But still, another one that got away! Such are the overlapping loyalties that occur in GAA communities.

As for myself, having been immersed in such personal experiences at an early age, it's no wonder it gave rise to a lifelong enjoyment and passion for Gaelic games. However, there was nothing quite like that golden year of '66, when Connacht football was king of all it surveyed.

Pádraic McKeon is a retired primary school teacher, having taught in Dublin and his native Mayo. He, with others, was instrumental in setting up Cumann na mBunscol in Mayo and is at present an active member of Castlebar Mitchels.

Lá Mór In Ard Mhacha

Brian Ború

Rugadh agus tógadh me ar leithinis Ros Goill, idir Cuan na Maol Ruaidhe agus Cuan na Long sna caogaidí. Gaeltacht a bhí sa cheantar agus tá sé mar sin go dtí an lá inniu. Cha raibh mórán saibhris fán teach s'againne nó sna tithe eile thart orainn. Cha raibh uisce reatha, leictreachas nó fiú glas ar doras an tí. Mar sin féin bhí saibhreas de chineál eile againn. Bhí ár dteanga dúchais againn, bhí muid sáite sa chultúr Gaelach, ceol, damhsa, drámaíocht, seanchas agus na cluichí Gaelacha, peil agus iománaíocht ar an mhórchuid. Ta mo sháith cuimhne agam ag siúl siar a fhad le teach Stephen Jack le éisteacht le cluichí Gaelacha ar an raidió.

Nuair a fuair me post i mBaile Átha Cliath sna seachtóidí, bhí saol eile ar fad agam ach choinnigh mé greim daingean ar an chultúr. Bhí mo mháthair lei féin sa bhaile agus dá bharr sin rinne mé iarracht gabháil go Baile na Deora ar an ordog an oiread deireadh seachtainí is a thiochfadh liom. Bhíodh sé de nós agam i gconaí fanacht sa phríomhchathair fá choinne Lá Fhéile Pádraig, lá mór na nGael, ar ndóigh. Rachainn chuig an Aifreann ar maidin agus ansin bhainfinn na bonnaí as isteach díreach go Sraid Uí Chonaill leis an pharáid a fheiceáil. Gheobhainn greim bia le hithe agus b'fhéidir deoch nó dhó, caol díreach ansin go Páirc an Chrócaigh le freastal ar chluichí mhóra an lae. Cluichí idir na Cúigí sa pheil agus san iománaíocht. Ní haon iontas ar bith gur lean mé den traidisiún sin nuair a bhog mé féin agus mo chlann ar ais go deisceart Thír Chonaill i 1980. Rachainn go dtí an pharáid i mBaile Dhún na nGall, gheobhainn greim le hithe agus rachainn chuig cluiche peile no iománaíochta áit éigin. Fan am seo bhí mé mar thiománaí bus don CIE agus bhí mé ag tiomáint go rialta ón bPort Nua go Baile Dhún na nGall.

Corr uair ba ghnáth liom bus a eagrú agus an lucht leanúna a thabhairt chuig na cluichí. Bhain Dún na nGall Craobh na hÉireann faoi 21 sa bhliain 1982 sa pheil agus d'éirigh an lucht leanúna níos mó agus níos glóraí as sin amach. Is cinnte gur bhain siad sult as an chraic i gcónaí agus an chaint ar an tsean-aimsir a bhí ag dul ar aghaidh ag na cluichí. Cha raibh siad faiteach le freagraí a chuaigh go dtí an chnámh ach cha deachaigh na freagraí níos doimhne ná sin. Cha dtáinig siad 'na bhaile riamh le searbhas ina mbéil cé acu ar bhain muid nó ar chaill muid cluiche. Bhí baicle de sheanóirí i measc an lucht leanúna a bhí breá ábalta rudaí a choinneáil ciúin dá mbeadh feidhm leis.

An Domhnach a bhí ann nuair a bhí muid ag imirt in éadan Ard Mhacha sa chéad bhabhta de chomórtas na mionúr agus na sinsear. Cha raibh iomrá ar bith ar chluichí a bheith ann tráthnóna Dé Sathairn nó tráthnóna ar bith eile ag an am sin. Shocraigh mé bus a eagrú le gabháil chuig an chluiche. Chroch mé cúpla póstaer thall is abhus, thart fán Fhearthainn, Ard an Rátha agus Inbhear. Cúig phúnt an costas a bhí ar thicéad fillte. Margadh ar dóigh a bhí ann! Bhí sé de nós agam i gcónaí stopadh taobh amuigh de theach ósta áirithe leis an chéad bhaicle den lucht leanúna a bhailiú.

Seo amach duine de na seanóirí an mhaidin úd agus dúirt liom, "Thats the first law we broke today." D'fhiafraigh mé dó caidé a bhí i gceist aige. "Drinking on the premises before opening time', a d'fhreagair sé go magúil. D'amharc mé ar m'uaireadóir, Dia ár sábháil bhí sé go díreach an deich a chlog maidin Dé Domhnaigh. Bhí an ceart ar fad ag an seanóir. Bhí na fir chríonna ag teacht amach as an teach ósta, piontaí ina gcuid lámha acu, leath-bhuidéal uisce beatha ina bpócaí agus corr fhear le ciseán beorach sa lámh eile. Chuir mé ceist ar fhear amháin, cad chuige go raibh ciseán leis. D'fhreagair sé "Its for sitting on when the bus is over full."

Tháinig scaifte maith, thart fá 25 isteach ar an bhus ag an teach ósta sin. Bhí cuid acu ar bís mar nach raibh siad in Ard Mhacha riamh roimhe. Leis an fhírinne a insint, cha raibh mé féin in Ard Mhacha riamh ach an oiread. Bhí muid ag dul go Páirc na Lúth-chleasaíochta agus cha raibh tuairim da laghad agam cá raibh sé. Pé scéal é bhí me óg agus gan faitíos agus bhí teanga i mo bhéal. Ar shiúl linn go Ard an Rátha ansin agus phioc mé suas cúigear is fiche eile ansin, Dia ár sábháil bhí an bus lán agus bhí tuilleadh le piocadh suas in Inbhear. Bhuel cha raibh mórán iomrá ar shábháltacht sna laethanta sin agus bhí an ceart ar fad ag an fhear a thug an ciseán leis.

Giorraíonn beirt bóthar agus b'fhíor an lá sin mar go raibh spin maith ar achan dhuine, iad uilig ag caint is ag ceol agus cuid acu ag ól fosta. Ar thaobh na sé chontae de bhí seicphointe ag an UDR. Bhí seo coitianta go leor mar go raibh na triobloidí faoi lán seoil. Bhí an UDR eisceachtúil mar gur de bhunú na háite an chuid ba mhó acu. Ar ndóigh cé gur gaeil a bhí iontu bhí fuath an diabhail ag an chuid ba mhó acu ar aon rud a bhí gaelach. Seo an t-am ar thug na seanóirí a luaigh mé cheanna comhairle don mhuintir óg a bheith ciúin. Sheas duine acu suas agus dúirt an fear críonna seo, "Don't give them boyos an excuse to hold us back, we want to get to the game on time.' Rinne siad amhlaidh. Tháinig duine de na saighdúirí páirt aimsire seo isteach ar an bhus, a ghunna ina lámh dheis agus deirimse leatsa de réir an amharc a bhí ina chuid súile go raibh sé réidh leis an gunna úd a úsáid. Chan fhuair sé seans mar go raibh ciúnas ar an bhus agus bhí cúrsaí faoi smacht ag an seanóir. Ar ndóigh thosaigh an chaint agus an chraic i ndiaidh don bhoc seo imeacht den bhus agus chan caint chiúin nó soineanta a bhí ann fá na saighdiúirí seo. Is scéal sin fá choinne lá eile.

Mar a dúirt mé cheanna cha raibh barúil ar bith agam cá raibh an pháirc seo ach lean mé na gluaisteáin eile le huimhir chláraithe Dhún na nGall orthu. Landáil muid slán sábháilte ag an pháirc peile thart fán haon a chlog. B'in am dinnéir do go leor daoine. Thug mé féin faoi ndeara go raibh an stáisiún seirbhíse in aice na páirce druidte agus ní dhearna mé neamhiontais ar bith dó sin. Bhíodh go leor de na gnóanna sna sé chontae druidte ar an Domhnach san am sin. Chruinnigh na daoine críonna ina mbaicle le chéile ach bhí siad faoi scread asail don dream óg. Cha raibh i bhfad go bhfaca mé na buidéil beorach agus léann dubh ag teacht amach as pócaí clé na gcótaí móra, Caidé a tchím ansin ach leath phunta cáise agus arán ag teacht amach as an phóca deas. Cha raibh iomrá ar bith ar im ach chuir siad leath den cháis agus leath den liamhás idir dhá shlis arán. Shuigh siad síos ar a sáimhín só, thóg siad slug as an bheor agus thosaigh siad ag ithe. Caithfidh go raibh goile maith acu mar dá ndeanfá sin inniu bheadh tinneas boilg ort. Chaith siad an chuid eile den arán suas san aer agus diabhail i bhfad gur chruinnigh na faoileáin le béile a bheith acusan fosta. Choinnigh siad dhá shlis arán agus an chuid eile den cháis agus liamhás le bheith acu níos moille. Chruinnigh na boic óga ina mbaicle gar go leor do na daoine críonna agus a gcomhrá féin a dheanamh acusan.

Bhí go leor de lucht leanta Ard Mhacha istigh sa pháirc agus bhí lucht leanta Dhún na nGall ag dul i méid fosta. Tháinig an dá fhoireann mhionúir amach ar an pháirc imeartha agus lig lucht leanta ón dá thaobh beic mhór ghlórmhar astu. Aon uair a rinne an moltóir cinneadh nach raibh lucht leanta Dhún na nGall sásta leis léirigh siad é go bríomhar, glórmhar agus ar ndóigh bhí an rud ceannan céanna amhlaidh faoi lucht leanta Ard Mhacha. I ngan fhios dóibh féin bhí an chraic ag éirí suimiúil go dtí go dtáinig leath ama. Thug mé faoi ndeara fear beag caol tanaí ina sheasamh in aice liom fein, shílfeá le hamharc air nach bhfuair sé greim bia riamh ina shaol. Bhí sé ciúin socair fosta sa dóigh go shílfeá nach mbeadh im ábalta léadh ina bhéal. Bhí ciúnas thart ar an pháirc ansin go dtí gur chuala muid fógra ón bhfearas fuaime. Mar a luaigh mé cheanna bhí an stáisiún seirbhíse in aice na páirce druidte agus mar sin bhí go leor de lucht leanta Dhún na nGall den bharúil go raibh sé druite ar feadh an lae agus pharcáil siad ag an stáisiún. Ach ní mar a síltear a bítear. D'fhoscail an stáisiún breosla thart fá leath uair tar éis a do a chlog, tamall beag roimh leath ama sa chluiche mionúir. Chá raibh seans da laghad ag an úinéir bocht punt a shaothrú mar go raibh na gluaisteáin páircáilte sa dóigh nach mbeadh sé ábalta na pumpaí a úsáid. Mar sin bhí fadhb agus ar ndóigh bhí sé ar mire fosta agus cé a bheadh ina dhiaidh air. De réir dealraimh chuir sé scéala chuig an pháirc Lúthchleasaíochta le cur in iúl do na daoine gur cóir na gluaisteáin a bhogadh ón stáisiún breosla. Seo an fógra ar éist muid leis ag leath ama,

"Would all those drivers who parked their cars at The Lagg Service Station please shift them."

Chuala mé stócach as Ard Mhacha ag scairteadh, "Hey, Macker shift your arse, I mean your car!" Thug stócach eile freagra air, "Mind yourself or I will shift your arse and your car." Chuala muid gáire mór ón lucht leanúna uilig. Ansin tháinig an fógra amach arís,

Bhí an sos leath ama ag druidim leis an deireadh agus ansin chuala muid an fógra arís,

"This is the last call, Would all those drivers who parked their cars at The Lagg Service Station please shift them or the army will remove them."

Bhí ciúnas iomlán ar feadh soicind nó dhó. Ansin scairt an fear beag caol tanaí a bhí ina sheasamh in aice liom amach os ard, "Tell them to shift the fucking petrol station." Chluinfeá pionna úr ag titim ar feadh leath soicind. Ansin thosaigh an gáire agus an bualadh bos, ansin scairt duine éigean eile, "Great man Timmy, you are better than the wife `cause you have all the answers for them." Le sin thosaigh an gáire glórmhar agus bualadh bos arís go dtí gur thosaigh an dara leath den chluiche mionúir.

Rugadh Brian Mac Lochlainn ar leithinis Ros Goill, áit a raibh an Ghaeilge go smior sa cheantar. Chaith sé seal sa Státseirbhís i mBaile Átha Cliath agus seal ag tiomáint leoraithe do thógálaithe ansin fosta. Tá sé ag cur faoi in Inbhear, i ndeisceart Thír Chonaill lena theaghlach, áit a mbíonnn sé ag tiomáint busanna do Bhus Éireann ó Ghleann Cholm Cille go Baile Dhún na nGall.

'...And while all that was going on, Mikey Sheehy was running up to take the kick... and suddenly Paddy dashed back towards his goal like a woman who smells a cake burning. The ball won the race and it curled inside the near post as Paddy crashed into the outside of the net and lay against it like a fireman who returned to find his own station ablaze'

Description by the late Con Houlihan in the 'Evening Press' of the moment in which the quick-thinking Kerry forward, Mikey Sheehy, caught out Dublin's goalkeeper Paddy Cullen in the 1988 All-Ireland senior football final

Belfast Haunting Of A House By Sleepover Gaels

Pat Lynch

Born in Co Cavan in 1936 on the borders of Westmeath and Longford and a stone's throw away from Meath across Lough Sheelin, I was steeped in GAA history and activity in this hotbed of Gaelic sport.

One of my earliest memories was listening to the radio broadcast on August 3, 1947, of the All-Ireland semi-final, when Cavan beat Roscommon by 2-4 to 0-6 enroute to the famous final win in the Polo Grounds, New York, while on a visit to my mother's home place in deepest Co. Longford. Aside from my elder brother David and one other, everyone in that packed kitchen supported Roscommon and I was both intimidated and hooked.

From that day on, I was to become an ultra-committed Cavan supporter, missing less than a handful of championship matches during the intervening years, right up until now. In all that time, one match stands out, mostly because of an incident that I was involved in during the weekend of the match.

I was employed as a veterinary surgeon in Baltinglass during 1962 and Cavan were going well. Having reached the Ulster final, they were due to meet Down, then the All-Ireland champions from the previous two years. The match was fixed for Casement Park, Belfast, on a bank holiday weekend in mid-summer.

I had arranged to travel with a friend and colleague and fellow Cavan man, Liam Brennan, together with a Roscommon man Des, who worked in a bank in Baltinglass, having previously worked in a branch of the same bank in Belfast. Des had assured us that when we reached Belfast he would fix us up with free accommodation in a house he shared with a number of single male and female bank and professional people while working there. We had no need to worry on that score, he assured us.

We set off from Baltinglass mid-afternoon on the Saturday and when we reached Belfast, we checked out our lodgings. Des took us to a large three-storey red-brick house in a quiet cul-de-sac off the Ormeau Road.

This was the pre-Troubles era in the North. We approached the front door where we knocked, then rang the bell but got no reply. We waited several minutes before retiring to a café Des knew. After a good meal, we returned to our house hoping our hosts would be back by then.

No such luck. Des suggested we try the back door, as sometimes a key was left under a mat out the back. We found the side door to the back was unlocked but we failed to find any key to the back door. Liam tried a window alongside the door and found that he could slide it up. We pushed him through and after discovering the key to the back door, he admitted us inside.

The kitchen was in a mess and it was obvious that a typical Friday night party had taken place the previous night. We cleaned up the place and spent the next few hours hard at work leaving the down-stairs spotless, washing everything including the floor. As none of the residents had turned up by 2am, we selected three different rooms and retired to bed for the night. Early next morning Des took us to a church nearby to attend Mass.

Afterwards we returned to the house and fried up a big break-fast. We then set about tidying up the rooms and making up the beds, most of which were unmade. Two beds which had been made up, we turned into French beds. We re-arranged the furniture in each room, moving everything around. We then took female clothes from one room and transferred them to a male room and vice versa.

Having completed our work which took some hours, we left the house in pristine condition, exiting as we had arrived, with Liam locking the back door from the inside and then squeezing through the window. Now, we were on our way to Casement Park and for all intents and purposes, it looked as if no one had stayed there.

Cavan had one of its greatest victories that day. Two goals from newcomer Jimmy Stafford led to a 3-6 to 0-5 victory over the All-Ireland champions and we celebrated afterwards with our friends on the team, before making the long drive to Baltinglass late that night.

A huge anti-climax was to follow, however, when a poor Roscommon team defeated Cavan 1-8 to 1-6 in the semi-final, which Cavan dominated but missed 12 scorable frees during the game. That year's final, which Kerry won, was deemed the worst ever played – definitely an All-Ireland we left behind.

A few months after our Belfast expedition, Des was back up in the city and called into his friends. He told us he didn't know how he managed to keep a straight face as they described their shock on discovering the phantom clean up.

Des left them none the wiser however about the fact that we had stayed there – it would have taken the fun out of it. They explained to him how they had failed to solve the mystery, though initially they blamed one another for the ruse. In fact, one occupant became so convinced that the house was haunted that he moved out altogether.

Pat Lynch is a Cavan native living in Dublin who qualified as a veterinary surgeon in 1959 following which he worked in many counties across a range of private and state bodies for over four decades. An avid GAA fan all his life, he also has a serious interest in mountaineering, tennis and horseracing.

Banner Man Got Us Going

Peter Keogh

Clare native Noel Crawley bought a farm near Kiltegan in the sixties. He was a chartered accountant by profession, a horse-breeder and dealer by choice, a footballer by passion and a larger-than-life character. He was a great player with Cooraclare, Clare and Munster. In 1969, I approached him to train the Kiltegan team. He accepted.

Crowley soon discovered he did not have the numbers to make a team. On a few occasions he played in goal himself and even had to draft in his 14-year-old son Michael to make up the numbers. It did not take him long to solve the problem. Crowley lived part-time in Dublin and part in Castlequarter and would arrive with a pair of bangers whenever we needed increased head count.

No one suspected anything until a great Clare footballer played in a Corcoran Cup match. A week later, he walked into the Kiltegan dressing-room but upon seeing no-one he knew, he stood up and said: "Sorry lads, I'm in the wrong dressing room." A reassuring hand was placed on his shoulder and a familiar accent said: "Not at all pal, stay where you are."

Thanks to him, Kiltegan won the match. Valleymount, the losers, quickly lodged an objection. In the end both sides agreed to replay the match and all was quickly forgotten. Crowley remained ensconced in the club until he sold the farm and moved to Dublin permanently... although he may not have played by the rule-book, he helped Kiltegan to get up-and-running.

The late Peter Keogh was and still is a legendary figure in Wicklow GAA circles, having served in all areas of the association, including reporting and commenting on matches until shortly before his death.

Day A Red Rebel Got Tangled Up In Blue

John Arnold

On Friday February 11th last year, I was driven in the company of three others to Charleville in North Cork – mind now I wasn't kidnapped – no, I'd gone freely and with no threats or force.

The plan was that four of us who were friends would meet for an afternoon of relaxation, chat and refreshments before going on to a further evening celebration. It was February 11, the feast of Our Lady of Lourdes and also World Day of the Sick. On that date in 1858, young Bernadette Soubirous first saw a 'vision' at Massabiele in Lourdes and as they say, the rest is history.

Then in 1992 Pope John Paul II declared the same day as a special occasion to remember all sick people throughout the world. The 'fearsome foursome' was meeting to catch up with all the news – we hadn't been to Lourdes on a pilgrimage for three years so there was much to cogitate on.

With a Mass celebrated by Bishop William Crean to follow on Friday evening in Charleville, I was anticipating a few hours of sheer bliss, good food, great company and powerful prayers. What's that they say about "the best laid plans of mice and men?"

Believe it or not on that Friday evening, I, John Anthony Mary Brendan Arnold, a proud Corkman, was initiated as a fully-fledged life-member of The Waterford GAA Supporters Club.

It was in May of 1974 that I first saw the Waterford senior hurling team in action. Cork met the Decies in the first round of the Munster championship in Walsh Park. I travelled to the match with my sister and beyond Kilmeaden encountered a 'knee-knaw, knee-knaw' and we were stopped for speeding! We barely got to the game in time.

It was the day of the broken hurley hitting the umpire and Paddy Barry, our goalie, being put off. We lost by 4-9 to 3-8; there wasn't much singing coming home that evening.

Waterford hurling went through a barren spell after that, right through the 70s and 80s. Ironically two Cork hurlers who played on that losing day in Walsh Park, Gerald and Justin McCarthy led the Decies out of the wilderness and back into the land of winning Munster titles.

Over the last 25 years, Waterford have played many great teams but as the Kilcoo football manager Mickey Moran said, "no one deserves to win an All-Ireland" but with three final appearances and class hurlers, they should have won one at least.

Being the closest 'hurling county' to us in East Cork, we've always engaged with Waterford clubs in practice and tournament games. I got involved with my club, Bride Rovers, in 1972 and can recall great, brilliant and woeful clashes with Tallow, Cappoquin, Tourin, Melleray, Shamrocks, Modeligo, Ballysaggart and, of course, Ballyduff Upper.

Three times Ballyduff (Upper) have been crowned Waterford SH champions – a great record for a small community.

The schemer, the plotter, the man who 'crowned' me in Blue and White this year hails from Ballyduff. Pad Flynn is one of those legends that colour and enrich the lives of so many people in villages and parishes all over Ireland. He played hurling and football with his native club and undoubtedly was a much better player than I ever was, which is not much of a compliment.

One Sunday coming out from Mass in Ballyduff the man in charge of the local football team met him. "Hey Pad will you bring your gear to the game this afternoon?" he asked him.

Pad hadn't played much football that year but did as requested. He played and ended up on a championship winning side. Occasionally, he joined defensive forces with his brothers Owenie and Jimmy to form a 'Thou Shalt Not Pass' full-back line.

Bride Rovers often played Ballyduff and I can recall huge crowds at Fr. Smith Cup Carnival games between us in Castlelyons. Pad Flynn was a businessman in his native place – a man who never saw anyone short and gave plenty credit. A longtime club treasurer, he was and is a true Gael. A man with great faith when I started going to Lourdes in 2007, I got to know Pad even better.

Though a proud Waterford man, because Ballyduff is close to Fermoy, Pad got involved with the Lourdes Committee there and facilitated many assisted pilgrims going to Lourdes over the years. Two others, Donie Cahill from Cloyne and Jerry Galvin, Ballingeary-born but domiciled in Fermoy for years, became great friends with Pad Flynn and myself.

In fact, we've become inseparable.

In Lourdes religion is important and faith also but I must say fun, enjoyment, craic and 'divilment' is also part and parcel of that special place. Don't worry folks, St. Bernadette was a mighty girl for playing practical jokes on others – it wasn't all sackcloth and ashes!

During the pilgrimage, the four of us stay in The Agena Hotel which has become a home from home. Often in June when we're there, the Munster championship is on and the Cork versus Waterford rivalry is at boiling point.

The other three of us in this 'Holy Foursome' are blessed to have Pad as a friend. And so it came to pass earlier this year in a hotel in a North Cork town in the presence of witnesses Daniel and Jeremiah that I had to swear an 'Oath of Allegiance' to the Waterford Hurling team.

Subsequent to that, Pad formally declared me to be an 'Honorary Waterford man.' He placed the Blue and White cap on my balding head and ordered me to wear it with pride. I was, however, allowed a dispensation when the Rebels played Waterford in May in Walsh Park and for any further head-on clashes!

John Arnold is a farmer from Bartlemy in Cork. He won All-Ireland Panel Discussion and Agricultural Communicator of The Year titles with Bartlemy Macra na Feirme. A Pioneer and lifelong GAA member, John writes a weekly column for The Echo newspaper and has written several books, including a collection of poetry and three GAA publications. An avid Gaelgeoir John is married to Mary, they have three grown up children and grandchildren.

'He was the classiest hurler I ever saw. When it came to real skill he was the [Seve] Ballesteros of hurling, he had all the shots... He had shots no one else had, he used his hands like no one else could. He saw things that the rest of us would never see. He had great understanding as well as vision. He played the game differently. He was always thinking a few shots ahead'

Babs Keating on his former teammate and Tipperary legend, Jimmy Doyle

Did The Borrisokane Dog Get All-Ireland Ticket?

Louis Brennan

Borrisokane GAA Park is now formally named Gardiner Park after the late Seamus Gardiner, a former president of the GAA and officer of the Tipperary North GAA Board and county board, in addition to being an excellent official of the local club, Borrisokane.

In olden times, the park was locally known as 'The Hurling Field'. It is located centrally in the town just yards from the main street shopping area.

The park was and is a large area and the playing ground, within the park, is surrounded by a concrete wall approximately four feet high. At the town end of the park the wall is just a few yards from the goal mouth and end line.

The park behind the goal posts at the town end was separated from the adjoining gardens by a broken stone wall usually traversed by both players and spectators. One of the gardens directly behind the goal was owned by a local business woman, Ms Mary Anne Guilfoyle RIP. Today it is owned by Pat Ryan, formerly of Milford, Borrisokane.

Because of its location and prior to the provision of high nets behind the goals, similar in many GAA pitches, the hurling balls from play or close-in frees would easily land in Mrs Guilfoyle's garden. Her plot was unused for many years and accordingly had overgrown grass, weeds and other outdoor material. That condition gave rise to difficulties in locating the ball under the thicket.

Virtually every time a ball went into the garden the local lads would commence searching ahead of the officials. If supervised, they would throw the sliotar back into play...but if not, they would hold onto it and get a 'few bob' for it from either a visiting or the local club.

It should be remembered that in those days a 'few bob' in cash was much appreciated by youngsters. It has been recalled in recent times that some of the lads would hide the ball under a stone until the local official was out of sight and then retrieve it. In any event, two local volunteers had a discussion and decided to train their dog(s) to collect the ball and bring it directly to them.

A lot of that training was done both during the week and during matches. The training related to smell, sight and ensuring that the dog was following the game, particularly conditioning the dog to revert to its trainer with the ball.

The trainers were Martin Butler and Michael (Hather) Donnelly. The dogs were trained by them and their fathers and all of them became aware of the process and the purpose of the exercise. The work of the dogs and the number of balls and sliotars returned was noticeable and the success was commented on by both local and visiting teams. The most recent recorded occasion was when Martin Butler's dog, which was called 'Shot', was so good at his work that he was recognised by all local and visiting teams.

The overall success of the process has been recorded in the history of the club and it has been reported that at a meeting of the club officers, held on August 23, 1965, the issue of the distribution of All-Ireland tickets was discussed and the following agreed on the basis of an expected allocation of eleven tickets would go to – Brud Seymour for use of his field, two tickets; Rev J Minihan, Chairman – one ticket; Noel McDonnell, Secretary – one ticket; Ger McKenna -one ticket; Senior Panel: V Duff, H Slevin and T McKenna – three tickets from a draw; Junior Panel: J Fogarty and Pat Hayes – two tickets from a draw; Committee – Pake Brennan – one ticket from a draw.

Unconfirmed rumours circulating among the older generation suggested that the dogs trained to gather the missing sliotars from Mrs Guilfoyle's garden were so good that discussions took place at the above meeting to seek an All-Ireland hurling final ticket for the pair.

There is no record of any ticket having been received and the likelihood is that if it was applied for, it was in the name of the owner or some other alert official who refrained from giving any publicity to that 'retrieving balls' aspect of club activity.

Confirmation is still awaited on this and if it arrives, a copy will go public for posterity. We are, however, satisfied that the dogs(s) were owned by Martin Buttler and Michael Hather Donnelly and that they and their families were professional in their training of the dogs. We also thank them for their support and guidance in the preparation of this report.

Much progress has been made relating to how dogs are controlled and how people are protected and in addition Mrs Guilfoyle's garden has in recent years been developed and protected from intrusion from the GAA field. All this, combined with the procurement of high nets, has led to much more successful management of high balls flying from the GAA park. It is a long time since 1965!

Louis Brennan, former Secretary/Chairman, Borrisokane GAA Club and Co-ordinator of the History of Borrisokane GAA Club to be published this year. Louis now resides with his wife Regina (nee Hough, Borrisokane) in Portlaoise. He is a retired local government official.

I Was The 'Red Star' Of Game

Tom Farrell

I had great times, bad times and some funny times while I was on the Dublin GAA refereeing circuit in the eighties and nineties.

I remember in particular one Sunday morning I was down to officiate at a Parnells' versus Na Fianna football game. I always carried two ref outfits with me – the normal black and in case I needed to change, a yellow jersey as a top. It was only when I got to the ground and was taking my bag out of the boot of my car that it dawned on me that Parnells played in black and Na Fianna's jersey was exactly the yellow hue of my alternate stripe.

What was I to do in such a situation? I searched around the boot of the car and noticed a red and white jersey in the corner. "I'm saved," I said to myself but when I lifted it out and looked at its front, I could see it was one of my son's soccer jerseys.

'Red Star, Belgrade' said the name on the front around the crest, which was a big star. He was a fan of the team which was why it was in my car in the first place. I considered my options and decided that it was better to do the soccer jersey than have fans thinking if I wore either my black or yellow tops that I was already aligning myself with one of the clubs.

As I ran out onto the field, some of the players and the handful of supporters from both sides at the game started shouting, "What's that you have on, ref?"

"Listen, I told them, this is the only alternative I have to your black and yellow stripes. Now do you want to play or not?"

They agreed but they were still smiling at the good of it as I threw in the ball. Thank God there were no mobile phones in that era or I would have been on the back of the Herald the following day. I did keep a keen eye out to make sure there was no photographer arriving late to take pictures.

Once that didn't happen, I knew there would be no adverse headlines like – "Ref The 'Red Star' Of GAA Game!"

How Knockanore Helped Youghal Win A County Final

Mike Hackett

The GAA club in Youghal was founded in the Imperial Hotel in 1891. Then following many years of endeavour - the first major trophy was won in 1955. That cup was for winning the Cork County Intermediate Hurling Championship – played in Fermoy – against Mallow. Three great sportsmen from the neighbouring parish of Knockanore in County Waterford played a big part in what was a tremendous achievement for a town club in the biggest county in Ireland. To mention firstly, the three from the West Waterford parish; Gary Moloney, Joe Moloney and Garry Griffin.

The team was: Jack Dempsey, worked at St. Raphael's Hospital and later played for Blackrock club in Cork City; Garry Moloney, from Knockanore; Liam McCarthy, publican North Main Street. Liam later had a farm at Harrowhill in Knockanore; Pad McCarthy, brother of Liam; had a grocery van on the roads of West Waterford for years; Buddy Bulman, baker, whose mother hailed from Aglish in Co. Waterford; Joe Moloney of Knockanore, a representative for Pasley's and a brother of Garry; Tommy Keane, of Cork Hill, who went to work in Limerick. Tommy died young in March 1991. Bernard Cotter, of Windmill Hill, who became a priest and served for decades in Nigeria with the S.M.A. order, also played for the Cork Seniors; Paul Curley, married a local girl (June D'Alton) having come in from Tallow Co Waterford; Johnny O'Sullivan, worked at Seafield Fabrics and played for Cork Seniors; Maurice Irwin, local tailor; Garry Griffin, the third Knockanore man, from Propogue in that parish; Joe Coyne, Tallow Street; Dan O'Sullivan, married Kitty Ryan who had lived in Tallow Town; Jimmy Cotter, Windmill Hill brother to Fr. Bernard.

Just one substitute was used; Bertie Lupton, whose father was a local Garda Sergeant. Bert came on and scored the winning goal.

Jack Leanbh O'Sullivan was Honorary President of the club.

He died in March 1986 aged 87. While the Youghal achievement in winning the Cork intermediate hurling championship was tremendous, it was with the help of a large contingent from the neighbouring Deise County.

Kickabouts, Solo Runs
And 'Leaks' On One Knee

Colm Keane

Who remembers half-time kickabouts from the old days? Nowadays, there are usually well-organised mini-matches between underage teams, who get a sympathetic round of applause as soon as the referee comes out for the start of the second half.

These civilised intermissions are a far cry from the half-time kick around in my native Curry in Sligo, back in the 1950s. No sooner would the half-time whistle sound than a motley crew of 'Gaels' would invade the pitch.

They usually comprised an eclectic mix of former players who wanted to show their neighbours that they still 'had it'. Then there was the younger crowd who wanted to show selectors and potential girlfriends on the sidelines that they were the future golden boys of Sligo football. And then you also had a few lads who wanted no further distraction than to get a few kicks of a ball on a Sunday afternoon.

Now the kickabout was no place for the fainthearted. There might be between 10 to 15 bodies around the square with a similar number out the field kicking the ball in. There was ferocious competition for every ball with no rules applying.

Pushing, shoving, dragging, tripping and sneaky knees in the back were all part and parcel of the kickabout. Sometimes injuries were accrued but this was one time people hid such knocks, as this was about pride, which meant no going down like a sack of spuds to the ground.

For years there was one man who ruled the square. We will call him John Joe. Well over six foot tall with arms longer than the 'man with long arms' in the Ballroom of Romance, he also had hands like shovels.

The only time he was beaten for the catch of the high ball was when someone interfered with his cap. John Joe would 'line out' at all these kickabouts with his Sunday suit on, bicycle clips securing the bottom of the trouser legs, crowned by the ever-present cap on the top of his head. Such was his ability to fetch the high ball he was approached to play for Curry, saying he could be a county man in no time but he refused all attempts to get him to play the more orthodox game.

Out the field meanwhile, some of the ould lads would cutely hang around for the breaking ball when someone shoved John Joe's cap over his eyes and then hit off on a flashy solo run before drop-kicking the ball over the bar. Invariably this drew loud cheers from the older supporters behind the goal. "You never lost it," they would shout at whoever had just kicked a great point on the run.

"You can't beat class," others would say, much to his delight as he returned to midfield in the hope of picking up one more ball before the two teams re-emerged for the playing of the second half.

Patrons were often aware that there might be a need for interruption in play during this kickabout period. One man, who had sojourned for years with the senior team, had a weak bladder which required him to have a leak after even the shortest of activity.

With no dressing-room or toilet facilities available back then – and the ditches a good bit away, he needed the others to help him avoid embarrassment by forming a circle.

When they did as they were told and created a human shield to the crowds all around the ground, our old timer would drop on one knee and allow the call of nature to go ahead both unseen and uninterrupted in the middle of the field.

I can tell you this first hand, for I was often on duty and asked by the man himself to "get the lads to form a circle" – and to this day, some would say it was the best contribution to the half-time kickabout.

Colm Keane won league and championships with Curry in the 60s and donned the county colours on occasion. A teacher for over four decades at Gormanston College, Co. Meath, he now lives with his wife Pauline in Skerries, Co. Dublin. They have two sons, Killian and Conal, both noted rugby players, with Killian having played for Munster and Ireland and Conal captaining the Cayman Islands rugby team.

Old Sporting Icon Speaks For The First Time

Jim Fogarty

I am 111 years old now yet I am forever young. How could I age when you all come to see me so often? My caretakers tend to me as if I was a baby. Didn't Michael Lowry among others collect and pay off all my debts for me? Then the Dublin crowd wonder why Michael is so popular in Tipperary. Have they no sense?

I've seen everything in my time, All-Ireland finals, Munster finals, Trips to Tipp! Talking about music, whilst I have nothing against Jedward, Westlife and all the other groups that the young wans like, my favourite sound is the Pecker Dunne's banjo wafting over the bridge.

Tipp county final day is my special day. My favourite team, of course, was Thurles Sarsfields of the 50s and 60s, my neighbours from down the road. My favourite player was my friend, Jimmy Doyle, who came to see me every evening without fail, accompanied by his hurl, sliotar and dog. Jimmy was following in the footsteps of former Thurles greats such as 'Bunny' Murphy, 'Whitehead' Maher, Jim Lanigan, Ger Cornally, John Maher, Nicholas Mockler, his uncle Tommy and others too numerous to mention.

From my neighbours, Moycarkey, whom I saw many times in my early days, I especially recall Phil Purcell, Paddy Ryan(Sweeper), and his brothers, Tom and John Joe Hayes, John Flanagan and Jack Bergin. When I think of Holycross, in my mind's eye I see Francis Maher, John Doyle, the Stakelums and Michael Maher. The greatest full-forward I ever saw, Martin Kennedy, was the first to be present-ed with the Dan Breen cup, when Toomevara won the county final in 1931.

Golden memories too many to recall so just a few other high-lights. Mick Roche winning his first county final with the Davins in the 60s, followed by Tadhg O'Connor's similar achievement with

Roscrea shortly after. Roscrea got so fond of me that they were here almost annually during the 60s and 70s, either minor or senior. Mind you, I haven't seen them in a good while. The legend, John Leahy, brought his friends from Kickham's village to see me twice. Toomevara couldn't stay away from me for a couple of decades.

It gets very quiet here after county final day. No lights, so I'm left in darkness. That old codger, the wind, will visit every night. He will dance like a dervish through my old stand, trying to keep me awake. If that doesn't work, he will whistle and moan at me. I am well used to his tricks and I will soon drift off. I always dream. Why wouldn't I with the memories I have. Every night I see magical feats repeated on my lush green sward. I have seen all the great hurlers. I remember them, but I also remember every player who ever visited me. Minors who never trained on, intermediates and juniors who were getting a little long in the tooth and only visited once.

Without doubt the saddest evening I can ever remember occurred in August this year when Dillon Quirke passed away during a club match on my Semple Stadium sod.

Dillon was smiling during the pre-match photo with his rival captain and referee. Just before he collapsed, he set up a goal for a colleague.

Dillon was greatly loved by everyone who knew him. Winner of an All-Ireland minor and U-21 title with Tipp and a county senior medal with Clonoulty, I'd always admired his skills, particularly his sideline cuts.

His talents were inherited as his dad, Dan, scored 3-2 for Tipp in their All-Ireland U-21 final win against Offaly in 1989. He was also related to former Clonoulty stars Declan Ryan and Andrew Fryday.

Sincere condolences to his immediate family, his relatives and his many friends. May the bed of Heaven welcome him home. Ar dheis Dé go raibh a anam dílis.

Jim Fogarty, a Tipperary native, was county librarian in Kilkenny for 28 years. He is married to Marie, a West Clare woman. Jim took early retirement to write two GAA books –'The Dan Breen Cup: Tipperary County SH finals, 1931 to 2011' and 'The Cross of Cashel: All Ireland Under 21 Hurling Finals, 1964 to 2014'.

From Up And Over To Down And Under With The Green And Gold

David Carty

I was born into a sports family in 1941. This was an era when the local Skryne Club and the Meath team were in their ascendancy. My father had played for the local club and was the winner of an intermediate championship medal in 1937. He was an avid follower of the Meath team. Our trips to Croke Park every June and July to see Meath do battle with the local Boynesiders, Louth, are memories never to be forgotten.

We lived on a farm and it gave me the freedom to practise my skills. I brought that big O'Neill's football with me every day as I drove in the cows for milking – catching, kicking and solo running. The dream that I might one day play in Croke Park was uppermost in my mind.

In our little blue Ford van, we travelled through Dunshaughlin, Clonee, Mulhuddart and Blanchardstown before meeting the heavy traffic of the big city of Dublin. There were no by-passes or motorways in those days. We were almost in sight of the famous Croke Park. We parked under the trees on the North Circular Road where we gave the touts a shilling to mind the car. Our excitement grew as we walked down the streets with thousands more. I saw the big stadium come into view and watched the flags of green and gold and red and white flutter in the breeze.

My father lifted my brother Frank and I over the stiles. We went up the steps of the big Cusack Stand. Before we got to our seats I looked out the openings in the stand and saw a beautiful green carpet like sward before my eyes. It seemed to be greener than any grass I had ever seen before.

Once the first game was over the tension began to rise, as throw in time was near. We heard the roar as the dazzling red jerseys of Louth sparkled in the sunlight as they came out from the top corner of the park. Then an almighty roar greeted the men in green and gold as they emerged down under us.

My brother Frank and I were spellbound watching our heroes parade behind the Artane Boys Band and stand to attention for the national anthem. Many times after the hay was made on our farm the front field became Croke Park. I was Paddy O'Brien and Frank was Frankie Byrne as we acted out our golden dreams. It was the long hot summer of 1949 and it would take three games before the winners were known.

We were too young to attend the semi-final or final. Meath went on to win their first All-Ireland, captained by Skryne man, Brian Smyth. The die was now cast, the expectation of meeting Louth every summer became a reality. I marvelled at these legendary foot-ballers on the green sward of Croke Park, many of whom I became good friends with in later years. They included Paddy and Mícheál O'Brien from Scalestown just a stone's throw from my home, Peter McDermott (the man in the cap), Brian Smyth, Paddy Meegan and many more.

From those heady days of the forties and early fifties time rolled on. My commitment to Gaelic football grew and grew. Then one day the call came to play for the Meath senior team. The match was the Player Cup run by the Erin's Isle Club in Finglas. I was handed a jersey by one of my idols, Peter McDermott. On checking the back of the jersey, the number 10 flashed before my eyes. I could hardly believe it. I was playing against Louth. The day was made perfect by getting onto the score board and winning the match. It was made extra special by having both my parents attend the match.

The following Sunday, Meath were fixed to play Galway in the Gaelic Weekly Tournament final in Croke Park. I received a Co Board card from the secretary to say I was on the panel and was was select-ed again at right half-forward. It sent shock waves through me as now I was going to play in Croke Park for Meath. My boyhood dream was about to be and I was about to walk out on the hallowed turf.

That Sunday I was walking into the dressing-rooms at the back of the Cusack Stand which was almost the same area where I had walked with my Mum and Dad to watch those great games of the early fifties. I almost wished I was that little boy again, going up to the stand to watch and not entering the dressing rooms to play. I had to remove those thoughts from my head. This was my childhood dream and now I had the opportunity to act it out.

I laced up my boots with trembling fingers and then it was time to take to the field in my green and gold jersey. The Artane Boys Band were playing their marching tunes while the sizeable crowd roared. We kicked around before throw-in, the lovely white ball skimmed along the turf. As it came to me it felt like an elusive lump of jelly.

Once the game started, my nerves disappeared. Three times I kicked points as the game ended in a draw. My opponent was that wonderful footballer Martin Newell. I was happy as Larry and enjoyed our meal in Barry's Hotel afterwards. My colleagues on the pitch included Peter Darby, Pat (Red) Collier and John Nallen, formerly of Mayo.

I remained on the Meath panel for the followwing eight years. There were many days in the sun and there were many dark days too. Meath won three Leinster titles in that time and I had the honour of captaining the winning team in 1966. The great Galway side of that era, captained by Enda Colleran, took the laurels from our grasp in that year's All-Ireland final. Meath rose from the ashes in '67 to claim the Sam Maguire, beating Cork in the final. I was disappointed not to be on the first 15 but delighted to be on the panel and collect an All-Ireland medal.

It was late October when the Australian Rules team toured Ireland. They wanted to play the best, the All-Ireland Champions and Meath accepted the challenge. The Australian's normally played their game with an oval ball so it was a shock when they beat Meath 3-16 to 1-10 with a round ball... and afterwards invited Meath to Australia in the Spring.

The invitation was accepted by Fr. Pat Tully, chairman of the Meath Co Board. Most people were sceptical about the tour ever taking place. It took the determination and never say die spirit of the man in the cap, Peter McDermott and his cohorts who made it become a reality. In March 1968 the Meath team flew out from Dublin Airport. We were flying into the history books. We won all five games, enjoyed the boiling sunshine and made many new friends.

I feel very lucky to have lived my dream and played for Meath in Croke Park all those years ago. Who knows, maybe one of my grandsons will be lucky enough to do the same in years to come.

Biggest Fife & Drum Band In Europe

Barrie Henriques

Fadó, fadó, many towns in rural Ireland prided themselves in the fact that they could present a band of varying musical tones, to celebrate and proclaim some event in their own place or elsewhere where a musical presentation was required.

Many towns 'rocked' to the skirl of bagpipes. Many would say that most bagpipes should be played with a sharp knife. Brass Bands headed up celebrations in the more affluent locations. And then we had the 'poor man's orchestra of fife and drum bands'.

These bands were least expensive to tog out. Some could even make their own fifes with hollowed ash, and sure the drums came in every size and tone. Some were made of goat skin with an ash rim, while others used a dried pig skin for their creations.

Notwithstanding, my story concerns my own club, John Lockes GAA Callan, a match between my club and famed Mooncoin, on a Sunday in a neutral venue at Mullinavat, in the summer of 1957. A huge crowd was expected by the host venue and they were not disappointed. It was said that the entire population of the Barony of South Kilkenny scrunched into the Mullinavat venue.

Story has it that the road from Callan to Mullinavat was a slow-motion crawl for the entire journey of 12 miles – there were no kilometres that time. With little motorised transportation available, the Raleigh, Rudge and Brooks were wheel to wheel over the 12 miles.

There were plenty of girls' bikes too on the road. Many a gallant suitor used the occasion to start a relationship that concluded in front of the high altar of his local parish church with the offer of carriage on the back carrier or the bar of a good bike. It wasn't the most sophisticated form of gallantry, but as the man said, "any kind of an ass will do in a soft bog as long as the turf gets to the hearth".

Most bikes of the time were kitted out with a tool bag that carried a wrench, and a spanner for fear of punctures. They also carried a pump riveted between two lugs placed on the frame of the bike. All pumps were the same black colour.

Forgive me for using the abbreviated bicycle as nobody I knew ever called it anything but a bike. The team travelled on Tom Nolan's charabanc (bus), forever known as Nowlan's Bus. Also, on the bus with the team was the Callan Fife & Drum band.

Some quarter of a mile from the ground, the band alighted and formed up in three rows of eight fife players plus a triangle player, two kettle-drum players and Danny Shea, the big drum player. When 'the gate' was apportioned between the Callan, Mullinavat and Mooncoin officials, the figures bore no comparison to the bonanza expected by all parties, given that the venue was "jammers". Accusations of all form of nefarious practices were fired every which way. Everybody accused everybody else. All the gatemen were questioned.

No obvious credible explanation was proffered until one of the gate men piped up: "Sure half the crowd got in for nothing with the Callan band. We were wasting our time trying to distinguish between fifes and bicycle pumps. Some lads got a box in the mouth when they tried to stop a lad with a pump to his mouth. Jazus, it surely was the biggest fife and drum band in Europe," he declared.

How Counties Claimed
Their Colours

Tomás Ó Duinn

The news that the Tipperary hurlers are to wear a redesigned jersey - though the familiar blue and gold colours will remain unchanged - focuses attention on the whole matter of GAA county colours, and how they came to be devised. The origin of some county colours is lost in the mist of years, but the history of many others have been well authenticated. Research reveals some interesting information.

Take the red jerseys of the Corkmen, for example. County colours became standardised in 1913 when Cork wore saffron and blue jerseys with a large C in front. In a raid in 1919 by British troops on the county board rooms in Cook Street, the county jerseys were taken.

For the Munster senior hurling championship that year against Waterford, the Cork county board used the jerseys of the St Finbarr's Total Abstinence Hall team, which had merged with St Finbarr's the previous year. The jerseys were a dark red colour, almost maroon. This was the first time Cork wore red jerseys and they have retained the colours since that time.

Early in 1913, a special meeting was held of the Dublin county GAA board at which it was decided to adopt as county colours a light blue jersey with white breast-shields bearing the city arms, namely Three Castles, and white knicks. In 1974, it became necessary to change the knicks to navy blue for television purposes.

Kilkenny wore black and amber jerseys in their first All-Ireland final appearance in 1893. They had been bought from the Thomas Larkin Football Club, which had gone out of existence.

Kilkenny wore black and amber in the 1905 final when they beat Cork in a replay. According to my friend and colleague Peter Holohan, the retired chief reporter of the Kilkenny People, who knows more about Kilkenny hurling than any man living, there were many disputes about colours in the early years of the century, in which Mooncoin and Tullaroan figured. The disputes ended in November 1911 when the then chairman of Kilkenny County Council, John F. Drennan, presented a set of black and amber jerseys to the county board.

The origin of the Wexford colours, purple and yellow, can be traced to the patronage of hurling teams by the great landlord or land-propertied families of the 17th and 18th centuries such as the Colcloughs of Tintern Abbey, the Carews of Castleboro and the Devereuxes of Carrigmannon. According to my friend the Wexford historian Nicky Furlong, tradition has it that in the James I period, Colclough brought a team of hurlers to Cornwall where another landlord had a team.

Wagers were reported to have been heavy. The Wexford men wore yellow sashes around their waists and James I was reputed to have been at the game and to have expressed his admiration for the "yellow bellies". The name remained. In modern times, the first Wexford jersey was yellow from breast to waist and purple from breast to shoulders. In these colours Wexford won one hurling All-Ireland (1910) and four football All-Irelands in a row (1915, 1916, 1917 and 1918).

In former times, Armagh, who now wear orange colours with white trim, played in black and amber stripes. In 1926 Armagh played Dublin in an All-Ireland semi-final and wore jerseys in the present colours, said to have been knitted by nuns in Omeath.

Kildare's first jerseys are said to have been made from the white flour bags of Odlum mills. Hence, perhaps, the all-white county jerseys worn today.

Arguably, the green and red Mayo jersey and the red, green and yellow colours of Carlow are the most fetching colours of all. One of the most celebrated clubs of all in Mayo in the early days of the GAA was Tower Hill, which had for its motto "The Green Above the Red". In the 1880s, Dick Walsh, the county secretary, summoned a meeting in Castlebar to decide on county colours. After a long debate, one delegate stood up and announced: "Well that's settled, the Mayo colours are red and green".

Dick Walsh rejoined: "Not so. The Mayo colours are the green above the red. God forbid that Mayo should ever have red above the green."

Carlow wore the colours of the county champions until 1910. Then, that year, a set of jerseys in green with red and yellow hoops were presented to the county team, and these, with some variations, have remained the colours since.

There are those who, with considerable justification, will argue that the demarcation lines of most Irish counties were drawn in an uncaring manner by English surveyors. However true that be, the counties as constructed are likely to remain and, however ironic, county GAA games and colours appear destined to copper-fasten that fact.

'I never imagined it, I don't know how you'd describe it but it's been a fantastic time in my life. I don't hail from a massive GAA house'

Cork dual star Rena Buckley after winning her 18th All-Ireland medal at Croke Park

Pride And Loyalty
Walk Hand-In-Hand

Declan P Gowran

It seemed odd to me that Pádraig, a Galwayman should tog out in the county colours of Mayo. He was wearing a green jersey, red shorts and green socks as he stood on the pitch. Volunteer linesmen and umpires from each club were taking up their positions. They waited expectantly for the referee to throw in the ball. That Sunday, Pádraig, as goalkeeper, sported a peaked cap to cut the slant of the early spring sun out of his aquamarine eyes.

As the whistle blew, Pádraig started hopping about like a shocked frog. He grimaced; his teeth gleaming through his four-o-clock shadow. He prowled the faded, mucky goal line like a big cat, following the play with acid intent, every catch and bounce, every kick and the flight of the ball. The opposition half-forward whacked the ball goalwards in a perfect arc over the heads of the ineffective defenders. Pádraig leaped too in a desperate effort to try and grab the ball as it dipped, but could only fingertip it over the crossbar for an unpreventable point. It was better than three, I figured. Pádraig stamped back to earth, gouging stud marks in the mud, then somehow lost his balance and fell down on his backside with a thud.

I giggled then clapped unconvincingly. Pádraig swung an indignant kick at an upright. He stormed through the net-less goalposts to take his kick-out as the ref scribbled the score in his notebook. A wheeze and a whack and the leather spun through the bright afternoon air into the huddle of converging players. Enmeshed, they jumped and turned in mid-air like performing sea lions, grappling for possession.

I had endured a gruelling interview in Groomes Hotel on Cavendish Row to qualify for a three-month stint at a local school in the Connemara Gaeltacht. My Uncle Paul, a teacher and gaeilgeoir, thought it would greatly improve my fluent mastering of our first language. I was in sixth year in Synge Street CBS Primary School and was much supported by those with influence in my life to convince me to 'have a bash' and 'go for it'. I considered myself passable at Irish; but as a boy, I was naturally reserved. I probably did need a prod to get on that Galway train after the Christmas holidays in January 1962, to head west and take the special coach to my host's dwelling just outside Spiddal. Being instructed to alight, my first sense was one of disappointment: I thought at the very least I would get to see The Twelve Bens as I had a fascination with mountains when I was 12.

Pádraig drove me to the match against Headford in his yellow Volkswagen Beetle. The team changed into their football gear under a tree by the side of the pitch. The rudiments of a spanking new clubhouse had yet to be constructed. Pádraig's number one fan had chosen not to come with us: "I prefer playing at home", she explained to me cryptically. She often called to his house, perching herself on the high chair and preening her honeyed hair like an exotic alabaster bird before addressing me in her smouldering peat accent: "Don't you think we'd make a great team", she would demur, referring to Pádraig: "like a good match made in heaven?"

"Maybe so", I would equivocate: "but I wouldn't know anything about that."

Mrs Thornton, Bean an Tí, was a widow. She had a rounded figure with a strong creamy face and grey hair. She reminded me of Peggotty from that film of David Copperfield with her pleated dress and apron. After the welcoming of a mug of tea and a homemade warm currant bun, Mrs Thornton showed me to my bedroom. The room was small and compact, situated just off the upstairs at the side of the house. The view from the pokey window looked down into the yard of the Toy Factory, where Pádraig worked shifts. It was a state sponsored enterprise that made plastic items like trucks, boats, rubber ducks and the like that were moulded with multi-coloured plastic injection machines. Pádraig gave me a guided tour of the premises after I had settled in, and a souvenir boat to keep and bring home from a number of discards.

Pádraig was the only other member of the household: any other siblings or kin had obviously emigrated or gone their own ways.

Sometimes relations would call: one in particular arrived with his shotgun and went off shooting ducks from the pier at Spiddal. He brought home a brace for our dinner which he plucked and dressed before Mrs Thornton cooked it. Her food was solid and nourishing. Surprisingly, I enjoyed her turnips, a vegetable that I had disliked at home. Such vegetables were cultivated in small stone walled plots and fertilised from the seaweed collected from the rocky shore of Galway Bay opposite Black Head in Clare, where the basking sharks breached. I noticed the prataí were grown in flat beds of earth, unlike the drills used in Baltinglass. A pure cold spring of water slaked Pádraig's thirst as he prepared those beds for the new season's crop in the run up to St. Patrick's Day.

I guessed that was why Pádraig was so burly. He muscled two brawny Headford attackers out of his path as he caught a dangerous dropping ball and thumped it clear. The match was fiercely tough but fair. Each player was like Cuchulainn of old, imbued with the spirit of sporting combat. Pride was at stake: the pride in their abilities, the pride of their club and supporters, the pride of their parish. They would fight to the final whistle to keep the flame of victory alive and never flinch. Come what may; the elation of winning or the disappointment of defeat, these were reverse sides of the same coin. The rival fans up there in the stands could sense it. The players could sense it, too; the fanatical cheering that drove them on. Though the spectators were mainly mentors on that playing field in Headford, it seemed the teams were playing unwittingly for an imagined crowd and the result they craved. It surprised me to learn that some of Pádraig's teammates travelled a great distance to participate in their current campaign, displaying their loyalty to the cause.

Pádraig brought me to the national league match between Galway and Dublin in Pearse Stadium, Salthill. The venue was only open five years and the benches in the stand had barely smoothed. The Jackeens were utterly dominant that day, what with the gladiators they fielded like Micky Whelan, performing out of their skins. I was both thrilled and deflated. Every time the Blues scored I had to stifle a shout of glee for fear of offending Pádraig. Because he was beside me, I felt a sympathetic affinity for the Tribesmen. It was a clash of divided loyalties. Dublin won 6-7 to 1-4. In mitigation, the maroons had the nucleus of a great team to come with the likes of John Keenan in the lineout. Mendacity never mattered to these warriors, just the love of the code.

Synge Street's playing fields were located over Dolphin's Barn Bridge on the Grand Canal off the lower Crumlin Road. There, the boys tried out and trained in their blue and white hoops. I turned out early, too, to have my footballing prowess assessed. I was enthusiastic but unskilled, lacking the nous and guile of the naturals, so I never featured competitively. I did like to be involved. Once I persuaded my father to transport some equipment there for the school. The crew loaded two crossbars and four uprights onto the roof-rack of his green Bedford van, strapped them down, red flags fluttering fore and aft. We seesawed over the Barn Bridge and took a wide sweep through the gates to the grounds. The posts were erected using ropes and poles as hoists and slotted into perpendicular positions. The crossbars were clamped onto them then. Hey presto!

At halftime in Headford, the players stretched out to rest on the grass, discussing tactics and changes. Slices of oranges were distributed to moisten their mouths and provide a citrus boost. Some players preferred the bitter wedge of lemon, but all drank water to wash it down before resuming the joust.

Both teams were evenly matched. The advantage swung back and forth till Spiddal went two points ahead, nearing the end of the game. In the last few minutes, the Headford goalie made an almighty kick-out, to pressurise his opponents. One of his midfielders rose like a swan, fielded the ball with a swoop, wheeled and took off like a whippet. He soloed effortlessly and sped towards goal, dodging the despairing tackles of the defenders with his dummies and twists. He dashed almost to the edge of the square with a menacing gait and steely determination. Then he let fly.

The ball shot from his boot like a bolt aimed on target for Pádraig's goal. It spun towards the far post where he crouched, ably positioned to save it. Suddenly his full back intercepted with a good intentioned block that only served to deflect its flight path. The ball was now headed to the other post where I stood mesmerised by the finesse of the movement. In a split second. it would be in the goal, most likely in off the post. Pádraig's team would now surely lose. But I could stop the ball's progress if I intervened. Instantly an ethical dilemma unfolded. Should I save it or let it go in?

Declan P Gowran is a retired driver and tour guide with Dublin Bus. Married with four children and two grandchildren, he enjoys gardening and writing as hobbies.

'You say to me that there is more to life than hurling but if you want to carry on like a fella who is not an intercounty hurler, well then there will be more to life than hurling. Lots more. But there won't be hurling. That's the reality of it'

Legendary Kilkenny Manager Brian Cody reflects on completing the four-in-a-row in 2009

'Kilkenny, we'll see your four and raise you one!'

Cork captain, Mary O'Connor, after her side's victory over Dublin in the 2009 All-Ireland final

Hughes' Shop – Grand Central For Big Day Tickets

PJ Cunningham

Hughes' Shop opposite Croke Park on the Hogan Stand side of the stadium served for decades as the trading centre of the most precious commodity on the GAA stock exchange – All-Ireland tickets.

In the build-up to hurling and football finals as supporters of counties desperately sought to get their hands on a 'Hogan', a 'Cusack', a 'Nally' or at worst a terrace ticket, people rang around the four provinces looking to call in favours.

There was often the quid pro quo arrangement of swopping All-Ireland hurling tickets for someone else's football pair in any given year. That was all very fine if you had time and if you trusted the post to deliver in such a frenetic week.

Often the news that your source had just got his hands on "a pair" came via the landline late Friday night or during the day Saturday or worse still Saturday night or early Sunday morning.

In cases where people could not meet up, they often left envelopes to be collected at hotels on the way into Dublin, or in the city centre itself.

While such venues accounted for some of the business, Hughes' Shop was the epicentre of brisk trading from Friday right up to minutes before the 3.30 throw-in on the Sunday afternoon.

The little ice-cream, sweet and grocery shop was manned by the Hughes sisters, whose father hailed from Tullamore, Co Offaly, before setting up business in the capital. For decades this premises was the unofficial All-Ireland ticket centre and in time his daughters were the GAA handmaids who fans turned to in their hour of need.

The three ladies Bridgie, Maisie and Imelda were the sweetest of human beings, always dressed up in shop coats and always smiling as customers entered and left their iconic premises.

Neither Bridgie nor Maisie ever married and ran the business from the beginning before being joined by Imelda after her husband had died.

The shop opposite Croke Park has many happy memories for many people… it was their final port of call to get in to the theatre of football and hurling dreams across the road.

The build-up to Leinster and All-Ireland finals were the busiest times as they kept pace with selling 3d and 6d wafer ice-creams for supporters, who more often than not would also enquire if tickets had been left in their name for collection.

At those times, you'd be amused when spotting locals residents enter the premises. Obviously they hadn't a clue about who was playing, but they were caught up in the frenzy… and all they were doing was their daily shopping, looking for a slice of cooked ham or a batch loaf.

In those decades, times were tough for some of those Dublin folk and the sisters had a reputation for being generous, even if the hard-pressed customer had no money to buy their groceries on a given day, they were never sent away empty-handed.

Looking back, you'd wonder how they managed to cope with the hundreds of tickets exchanging hands on All-Ireland days. I know of one city centre hotel where some smart boys used to hang around and wait for their moment to pounce.

A friend of mine actually witnessed a prominent judge dropping off a pair of tickets to be collected by a 'Mr Murphy'. Within 10 minutes, an unlikely looking fella presented himself as the aforementioned 'Mr Murphy'. Without any interrogation to prove his bona fides, the impersonator got his hands on those tickets when they were selling like gold dust.

That sort of try-on wouldn't work with the Hughes sisters. They had great antennae and would spot a chancer a mile off. It helped that they remembered faces and also that they could read faces. You'd want to be up very early indeed to pull the wool over their eyes.

I used their free service extensively as a Dublin resident who could get his hands on tickets for an Offaly fan base which at one time in the eighties seemed to be in Croke Park every other Sunday either for Leinster or All-Ireland finals.

I never once was let down by them; never once heard of them making a mistake, never once got anything but the friendliest, almost personal, service.

Yes, they may have been little women in stature but they were giants of the GAA and thousands of GAA fans owe them a debt for carrying out a sacred duty which was so vital at the time.

PJ Cunningham is a native of Clara, Co Offaly and is the compiler and editor of this book. A journalist and author, he is married to Rosemary and they have five grown up children.

Cycle Warriors
(c. 1970)

Eileen Casey

Helmets down like visors, flashing spokes
quicken heartbeats. Drab convent school
uniforms are hitched above bare knees,
hair back-combed until sparks fly.

The Kinnitty Hurling Team cycle into Birr Stadium;
pulses soar high as the goalposts. Hurley sticks
strapped to carriers are swords or spears –
instruments of war on the pitch.

Outside the changing rooms, bicycle steeds
tether in a row of glinting steel. Coloured
scarves banner handles, binding favours,
love tokens from besotted teen-age girls.

After the match, players leave the field,
mud splattered, steaming. Those luckiest
amongst us are carried off on the crossbars,
pleated skirts riding up – high as modesty dares.

The rest look on, dust rising in a cloud of regret.
Our warriors cycle towards the town,
hungry for chips and greasy kisses.

*Eileen Casey lives in Dublin where she is a creative writing tutor.
She has had numerous creative works of his own published in
periodicals and books*

Grace – Before And After

Ned Cuggy

It would be after the Leinster Final and they'd win but not too well,
And you'd meet with Grace in McTernan's and ask,
"Have they a hope in hell?"
And he'd fix you with a wounded look
and he wouldn't shout but roar,
"They'll beat the pick of Munster,
they won't give 'em a friggin score."

And yet, in the papers on Monday morning,
you'd see a quote from Grace:
"Our boys were bad, 'tis very sad, they couldn't last the pace.
They'll never win the All-Ireland – still, we won't despair,
We'll feed 'em up, we'll train 'em well and maybe they'll be fair."

Some worries other than hurling would be the order of your day,
It could be crows among the barley or the remnants of the hay,
Then you'd meet with Grace in Langton's and say,
"Paddy, what do you think?"
"They'll beat the pick of Ireland, don't be worrying, have a drink."

And yet, in the papers on Monday morning,
you'd see a quote from Grace:
"Our pick is small, will we have fifteen at all? This we'll have to face.
Still the lads are up there training and they'll try their living best,
And come the day, you can never say, maybe, they'll pass the test."

Then on the day, they'd hold the sway and play like men inspired
And their fame would grow by the fireside's glow,
passed from man to boy to child.
And you'd meet with Grace in Barry's and say, "Paddy, they were good."
"They'd beat the pick of Europe, shure I told you that they would."

And in the papers on Monday morning,
you'd see a quote from Grace:
"Our boys were fast, I knew they'd last.
They were first in every race.

I knew they'd win the All-Ireland – ah, our pick is very strong.
Shure I was saying it in the papers that they'd win it all along."

Paddy Grace won All-Ireland medals in 1939 and 1947 and, for over 30 years, was the GAA Co. Secretary in Kilkenny. He was a huge hurling man, ahead of his time, known to care deeply about player welfare which sometimes included providing a nervous player with a drop o' the craythur! In 1957, Kilkenny, having won only one All-Ireland in the previous 16 years, the legendary P. de Grás introduced coaching, in the form of Fr. Tommy Maher, thereby revolutionising Kilkenny hurling.

Paddy suffered for his passion, once spending the final 10 minutes of a match in the Croke Park dressing-room because he couldn't bear to watch. He was Tommy Walsh's grandfather and, not alone did he pass on to him his hurling talent but also, his exuberance and love of the game.

This poem, 'Grace Before And After', written by Ned Cuggy in 1986, captures Paddy's irrepressible personality full flight!

Portlairge Abú

(Air – 'Sean South of Garryowen')

'Twas on a bright October morn'
We left our native town
On the second trip to Dublin,
To win that hurling crown.
There were men from the Glen
And from every street,
And some from Grange Park too,

Where e're they came,
They all looked the same,
In the famous white and blue.
Our hearts were throbbing with delight
As we left the Dublin train.
We were there in Nineteen-fifty-seven
And here we were again.
The weather had changed,
'Twas all arranged.
Our spirits rose anew,
Sure, God must love old Waterford,
Sure, his Mother wore the blue.

The ball thrown in, the game began,
Our hearts commenced to dance,
As ash met ash and man met man,
There was nothing left to chance.
Like a mighty wave
That swell and raves,
On a wintry Tramore Strand,
Our men swept to Kilkenny's goal
'Till the umpire raised his hand.

On goal we had young Eddy Power,
A mighty 'Power' was he,
Whilst Harney, Barron and Austin Flynn
Went on a hurling spree.
Martin Óg from Mount Sion
Held a grand half-line,
Mick Lacy by his side;
And a bird all alone, from old Erin's Own,
Jackie Condon our hurling pride.

There was Seamus Power and Philly Grimes
Of the greatest Munster stuff,
With Walsh and Flan and that Cheasty man,
The King of Ballyduff.
With Guinan the great,
Always lying in wait,
With Cunningham well inside,
And one of the best, the man from the West;
John Kiely of Abbeyside.

When the final whistle blew
We rained our flags on high;
And there amid the joy and cheers
I saw an old man cry.
I watched him stand,
With cap in hand,
His eyes were raised to Heaven,
He wiped his tears
And gave three cheers
"Amen to fifty-seven."

Through sickness some had missed the game,
Others could not raise the fare!
God help them all, 'tis well we know
They were all in spirit there.
And how their poor hearts leapt will joy
And that wonder Michael O'Hehir

Said: "The day is done,
The Deise have won,
Agus slán agaibh go leir."

So, we raise a toast to a gallant team
To trainer John Keane too.
Since forty-eight, it's been his dream
To see our heroes through.
We'll make one boast
And raise a toast
To the finest of them all
To the people of Portlairge
Who rallied to the call.

There is no doubt my dream is out
And never more I'll dream.
But I'll lie awake and stock I'll take
Of our great hurling team.
Let Clohossy take Frank Walsh's hand,
The spleen is there no more.
So now tonight when all is quiet
The Suir will kiss the Nore.
Dw (The Dreamer)

The Green Above The Red

Thomas Davis, Young Irelander

The "Green above the Red" colours so valued by Dr Croke and Colonel Blake were undoubtedly selected in response to the Young Irelander Thomas Davis' poem:

Full often when our fathers saw the Red above the Green,
They rose in rude but fierce array, with sabre, pike and scian,
And over many a noble town, and many a field of dead,
They proudly set the Irish Green above the English Red.

But in the end throughout the land, the shameful sight was seen-
The English Red in triumph high above the Irish Green;
But well they died in breach and field, who, as their spirits fled,
Still saw the Green maintain its place above the English Red.

And they who saw, in after times, the Red above the Green
Were withered as the grass that dies beneath a forest screen;
Yet often by this healthy hope their sinking hearts were fed,
That, in some day to come, the Green should flutter o'er the Red.

Sure 'twas for this Lord Edward died, and Wolfe Tone sunk serene-
Because they could not bear to leave the Red above the Green;
And 'twas for this that Owen fought, and Sarsfield nobly bled-
Because their eyes were hot to see the Green above the Red.

So when the strife began again, our darling Irish Green
Was down upon the earth, while high the English Red was seen;
Yet still we held our fearless course, for something in us said,
'Before the strife is o'er you'll see the Green above the Red.'

And 'tis for this we think and toil, and knowledge strive to glean,
That we may pull the English Red below the Irish Green,

And leave our sons sweet Liberty, and smiling plenty spread
Above the land once dark with blood-the Green above the Red!

The jealous English tyrant now has banned the Irish Green,
And forced us to conceal it like a something foul and mean;
But yet, by Heavens! he'll sooner raise his victims from the dead
Than force our hearts to leave the Green, and cotton to the Red!

We'll trust ourselves, for God is good, and blesses those who lean
On their brave hearts and not upon an earthly king or queen;
And, freely as we lift our hands, we vow our blood to shed
Once and for evermore to raise the Green above the Red.

Win! Win! Win!

Sean Hallinan

Win! Win! Win!
Dance of the cogs
On the dressing room floor
Assistant coach holding shut
the door…

All eyes on the jersey bag…
Who will dash out in glory?
Or walk behind to lag
In the fading din…
Dying echoes of…
WIN! WIN! WIN!

Coach pleading… "Lads…
Today is the pinnacle of many weeks…
Spirits…press-ups…laps
Bone creaks…
In hail, rail and piercing wind
The message to send…
Pain is the price of gain"
WIN! WIN! WIN!

The final team talk…
"We know they are good
Take no hostages…
Get stuck in, as ye should…
Spray the ball about…
Play the wings…
Express yourselves…
Enjoy the whole thing…but
WIN! WIN! WIN!"Minds…

Drift to dreams...
Lovers...
Girlfriends...
Flowers...
Well taken scores...daisy-cutter goals...
"COME ON...COME ON...

Fire in the belly...
Be proud to wear the jersey...
Don't think of defeat...
It's a sin"
WIN! WIN! WIN!

"They're coming...they're coming"
The fans expectant shout...
As the team's stream out...
To huddle again...
Amid the awful din...come on ref. ...begin!
Come on Lads...
WIN! WIN! WIN!

Up For The Match

Moira Gallagher

Your county has qualified for the final.
Everyone wants to be in Croke Park for the match.
How can one get hold of a ticket?
Plots and plans begin to hatch.

First port of call, the local GAA Club.
They wonder how many members will go.
"Tickets are scarce, we can't promise,
Members must get the first chance, you know.

After that it depends if there are any to spare.
Of course, we will keep you in mind."
By then you know that the chances are slim
That a ticket from the club you will find

Now it's time to spread the net a bit further afield.
In your own county, the time do not waste.
Every last ticket will already be snapped up
By the hungry pirates as for booty they chased.

Take a look at the counties not in the final.
There must be plenty of contacts spread around.
Hasty phone calls to ask a wee favour.
"Happen to know where a spare ticket might be found?"

Then all you can do is wait and pray
That somewhere out there lurks the prize.
Don't want to be the only one left in the county
Watching on television, tears of disappointment in your eyes.

My poor husband, for the final last time was unlucky.
To cheer him, shopping next Monday I went.

Brightening up our fireside with a lovely new rug
Purchased with the money that in Croke Park he'd have spent.

Did that help? Oh no, afraid I have to admit
The rug just reminds him of that fateful day.
And if he had been there to cheer on his team
Sam Maguire might have travelled up this way.

*Moira Gallagher is a native of Creeslough, Co. Donegal but lives in
Lifford. Married with three children, she is a retired teacher whose
main hobby is creative writing.*

Caoineadh ar Ashling Ní Mhurchú

Máire Ní Chonchúir

Solas na síochána ortsa a Ashling,
a mhúinteoir spreagiúil, cliste, caoin;
a cheoltóir chumasach, a dhearbhaigh oidhreacht na nGael,
banlaoch a ghlac an camán le fonn.

Do shealbhaigh spiorad an cheoil tú Ashling,
do'd threorú trí cheobharáin chianta,
ag nochtadh truamhéala 's dóchas ár muintíre,
an veidhín ag géilleadh do chumhachta, do cheoil.

B'uafásach brúidiúil, fíochmhar, fealltach d'imeacht uainn,
beocht do bheatha, múchta, sciobtha
gan taise, gan trua, gan choinne,
ar bhruach na canálach órga,
tráthnóna aoibhinn Eanáir.

Go gcodlaí go sámh tú Ashling,
i do chreafóg dhúchasach chlúthar;
do cheol ag líonadh na bhFlaitheas,
le draíocht 's sonas suan.

A Ticket For Tom

Brendan O'Connor

I'm appealing to you Dessie,
Here is my request,
I know it won't be easy,
But I'm sure you'll do your best.
Now great is my dilemma,
It's my young son Tom you see,
A dedicated Meath supporter,
From the tender age of three.

Yes – he's been a regular to Croke Park,
Since that Summer three years ago,
In fact the only games he missed,
Were the two against Mayo.
We've been to games all over Ireland,
To Cork, Galway and Derry,
We even went down to Limerick,
For a league play-off with Kerry.

We go to every game in Navan,
In the wind and rain and cold,
But when it comes to All-Ireland tickets,
That counts for nothing – so we're told.
Now he celebrates his seventh birthday,
The very day before the game,
And if I can't get him that special present,
It will be a crying shame.
You're now my last hope Dessie,
'Cos down here they just can't be had,
So a ticket please for my son Tom,
And another for his Dad.
(September 1999)

Song Of The Hurler

Gerry McLaughlin

I am the smack of a sliotar on a green field of May
When the beating heart of a hurler knows
That his aim is true, and his love is near
And his hurl is a wand of Heaven under an Irish sky.

I am the smash of the ash for the blue and gold
Of those bounding boys of Sliabh na mBan
The giants of Tipperary who bent the knee to no man
I am the cool clean strike of Eddie Keher

For the black and amber and the Rose of Mooncoin
I am the granite in the 'guth' of the great Joe Connolly
When the West awoke in 1980 and the moon danced on Claddagh
And the world was only as wide as a woman in maroon.

I am the voice of Joe McDonagh who sang the song of songs
The greatest anthem of the dispossessed
I am the smiling face of Anthony Daly
when the Banner scraped the sky
And looked the stars in the eye and told Biddy Earley... goodbye!

I am the roar of the crowd when Christy Ring was carried shoulder high
By those giants of Wexford who held a hero in their hands.
I am Nicky Rackard, the most brilliant of those brawny boys of Wexford
I am Mick Mackey, a gladiator in Limerick green who went through
defences like a German tank on tour.

I am the darting D J Carey, black magic wrists, veins of ice
A shimmering Shakespeare of ash-sorcery of summer
I am Terence 'Sambo' McNaughton – the eternal warrior of the Glens
Who was never afraid to go in where timber tests the soul.

I am every man who followed Cuchulainn
And played the game of the Gael-the game of the gods
With flashing scimitars of ash on sweltering Sundays in Thurles Town
Home of the great Jimmy Doyle who died with very little

Apart from a photograph of his hero Christy Ring next to his heart
I am every hurler who won a county championship.
For the pride of his village and the glint in the eye of his girl
I am the follower of the great Matt Hughes our own local hurling hero

I am Gerry McLaughlin who held a hurl for almost 30 years
And played in six different counties - sometimes under strange names
When I was young and thought I was grand
And will never forget 1984 when we hurled like heroes

And won THAT centenary county title
for our tiny town on the Banks of the Erne
And we walked like kings in our own townlands
And we sang rebel songs deep into the dawn.
For the song of the hurler is forever strong and forever young.

*Gerry McLaughlin's book of poetry entitled 'The Breed Of Me' was
launched earlier this year to critical acclaim.*

Ode To Devenish

Michael Joseph Burns

Come on all you Gaelic football fans
Attention to me pay
Tis about the County Final
A few words I wish to say.

With thirty stalwart players, Fermanagh's cream and pride
And Roslea went down gallantly to a victorious Devenish side.
T'was the second Sunday of September, in the year of '63
And every car, van and lorry headed for Lisnaskea
The weather was not so pleasant and the rain came tumbling down
But it didn't stop the Melvin men from taking home the crown.

Now a final is an important game, as footballers know
And against last year's champions, it was not an easy go
Devenish were the outsiders as well they wished to be
For Roslea were red hot favourites according to the B.B.C.

Now the football it was excellent, and deserved the many cheers
And as we reached the half-way stage,
our boys were three points in arrears
But our lads soon scented victory, and they did not delay

But swept right on like champions, led by the Reverend P.J.
Now to lose a final is very hard, as I need hardly say
And it must have been disappointing on these lads of dear Roslea
For these boys were oft' victorious and were known near and far.

Let's start with the brilliant Carty who was gallant beneath the bar
With O'Shea, Loughlin and Feely, many a forward paid the price
When it went to sound defending, they were like Lavery,
Murphy and Rice

Now our half-back line was very sound, with
Flanagan, Treacy and McGurran

And in that memorable second half, they beat off each attack in turn
And in the centre Tommy Gallagher with Michael Treacy there
They were the cause of several headaches for the gallant Roslea pair.

On the forty we had our Ulster star, who is now well known to all
flanked by Loughlin and Benny Carty, they got plenty of the ball
The goal getter Father Lonergan with Gerry Treacy and McCauley too
They were the stars of North West Fermanagh,
these fifteen men in Blue.

The presentation of the trophy was a most memorable feat
While Saint Mary's Band supplied the music,
with an ancient Gaelic beat
While John James' speech and tribute would fill your heart with pride
Sure we were glad to have him captain our victorious Devenish side.

What lies ahead of this fifteen is hard to say
For they could keep on winning for many a long day
We wish them luck in future games and behind them we will cheer
And let's hope they take home the Senior League
in this most memorable year.

PJ Cunningham

PJ Cunningham is a former club senior footballer with Clara Co. Offaly and was a member of the Wicklow senior football management team for three years within the last decade.

A former Deputy Editor of the Sunday Tribune and Evening Herald, he was also Sports Editor of the Irish Independent and has been a columnist with various publications in Ireland, the UK and New York for a number of years.

He is the author of six books, two of which – 'About That Goal (The Story of Seamus Darby)' and 'The Long Acre' – were shortlisted for the Book Of The Year awards in their own categories in 2019 and 2014 respectively.

Together with Dr Joe Kearney, PJ has compiled and edited three collections of books on rural life – 'Around The Farm Gate'; 'Then There Was Light' and 'From The Candy Store To The Galtymore'.